Historical Perspectives on
Business Enterprise Series

COURTS AND COMMERCE

Gender, Law, and the Market Economy
in Colonial New York

DEBORAH A. ROSEN

OHIO STATE UNIVERSITY PRESS / COLUMBUS

Maps of Dutchess County and the Colony of New York were drawn by
Otto Brouwer, University of Wisconsin Cartographic Laboratory.

Figures 3.1, 3.2, and A.11 appeared previously in slightly different form in
Deborah A. Rosen, "Courts and Commerce in Colonial New York," *American
Journal of Legal History* 36 (1992): 139–63.

Rosen, Deborah A., 1955–
    Courts and commerce : gender, law, and the market economy in
Colonial New York / Deborah A. Rosen.
        p.   cm. — (Historical perspectives on business enterprise
series)
    Includes bibliographical references and index.
    ISBN 0-8142-0736-7 (cloth : alk. paper). — ISBN 0-8142-0737-5
(pbk. : alk. paper)
        1. Capitalism—New York (State)—History.   2. New York (State)—
Economic conditions.   3. Sexual division of labor—New York
(State)—History.   4. Women—Legal status, laws, etc.—New York
(State)—History.   5. Debtor and creditor—New York (State)—
History.   I. Title.   II. Series.
HC107.N7R67   1997
330.9747′02—dc21   97-10411
                                                                CIP

Text and jacket design by Nighthawk Design.
Type set in Bembo by Keystone Typesetting, Inc., Orwigsburg, Pennsylvania.
Printed by McNaughton & Gunn, Inc., Saline, Michigan.

The paper used in this publication meets the minimum requirements of the American
National Standard for Information Sciences—Permanence of Paper for Printed Library
Materials. ANSI Z39.48–1992.

9   8   7   6   5   4   3   2   1

For
William E. Rosen and Diana B. Rosen

And for
Susan R. Stein

Contents

Illustrations

Figures

Maps

Tables

Acknowledgments

I am grateful to all my friends and colleagues who read various parts of my manuscript and provided useful advice. My dissertation work, which appears here in chapters 3 and 4, gained tremendously from the close guidance of Alden T. Vaughan and from the insightful suggestions of William E. Nelson and Richard L. Bushman. As I developed my thesis further after graduate school, other scholars provided useful comments when I presented parts of the book at the Conference on New York State History, the Legal History Colloquium at the New York University Law School, the Yale Law School Legal History Forum, the Feminist Research Group of the Lehigh Valley, the Southeast American Society for Eighteenth-Century Studies, the American Society for Legal History, and the Law and Society Association.

After I finished the rough manuscript of the book, Alden T. Vaughan, Richard L. Bushman, Stuart Bruchey, and Michael Robertson generously agreed to read the manuscript, and they provided useful suggestions for improvement. I would particularly like to thank them for their time and their thoughtfulness. In the most recent stages of producing this book I also benefited greatly from the contributions of the editors and staff at Ohio State University Press and the recommendations of their readers for revisions to the final manuscript.

Archivists at the Hall of Records in New York City and the New York State Library and Archives in Albany, especially Bruce Abrams, Joseph Van Nostrand, and James Folts, provided knowledgeable, helpful, and courteous assistance as I conducted my research. I also appreciate the help of staff members at the Adriance Memorial Library, the Columbia University Law Library, the Dutchess County Clerk's Office, the Museum of the City of New York, the New-York Historical Society, the New York Public Library, the Orange County Clerk's Office, the Richmond County Clerk's Office, and the Westchester County Clerk's Office.

Finally, I am grateful to Lafayette College for awarding me a Junior Faculty Leave in the spring semester of 1994 to give me time to complete a full draft of my manuscript, and I appreciate the financial support for my project provided by a grant from the Lafayette College Academic Research Committee, an Alice Hanson Jones Fellowship, a Littleton-Griswold Research Grant, and a John E. Rovensky Fellowship in Business and Economic History.

Abbreviations

ACCGS Min	Albany County Court of General Sessions of the Peace Minutes
CC Min	Chancery Court Minutes
Col Laws NY	Colonial Laws of New York from the Year 1664 to the Revolution
DC Tax Lists	Dutchess County Tax Lists
DCCCP Min	Dutchess County Court of Common Pleas Minutes
DCCGS Min	Dutchess County Court of General Sessions of the Peace Minutes
Doc Rel	Documents Relative to the Colonial History of the State of New York
Doc Hist	The Documentary History of the State of New York
H&B Min	Hamlin and Baker, Minutes of the Supreme Court of Judicature in *Supreme Court of Judicature of the Province of New York,* vol. 2
Jour Leg Coun	Journal of the Legislative Council of the Colony of New-York, 1691–1775
Jour Gen Ass	Journal of the Votes and Proceedings of the General Assembly of the Colony of New York, 1691–1765
MC Min	New York City Mayor's Court Minutes
Min Exec Coun	Minutes of the Executive Council of the Province of New York
Min Com Coun	Minutes of the Common Council of the City of New York
NY Col Ms	New York Colonial Manuscripts
NYC Tax Lists	New York City Tax Lists
NYCGQS Min	New York (City) Court of General Quarter Sessions of the Peace Minutes

OCCCP Min   Orange County Court of Common Pleas Minutes

RCCCP Min   Richmond County Court of Common Pleas Minutes

SC Min   Supreme Court of Judicature Minutes

WCCCP Min   Westchester County Court of Common Pleas Minutes

Introduction

Historians who have written about the emergence of a market economy, the declining role of women in the economy, and the role of law in economic development have portrayed an unrealistically abrupt change from the eighteenth to the nineteenth century. This study shows that a market economy based on arm's length relationships did not suddenly emerge in the nineteenth century but existed throughout the eighteenth century; that women became peripheralized from the economy well before industrialization sent their husbands off to factories; and that law shaped economic development a century or more before judges began to redefine the substance of the law to protect manufacturers and railway owners against expensive lawsuits by injured employees, neighbors, and consumers.

Scholars' focus on the nineteenth century has paralleled a recent romanticization of the colonial period as a golden age for communal values. In 1970 Michael Zuckerman, Kenneth Lockridge, Philip J. Greven, and John Demos published books on colonial New England portraying their close, corporate communities dominated by a "moral economy."[1] Since then, many other historians have described an idealized—and prolonged—precommercial America, a simpler America in which families and communities worked together.[2] The view of the colonial period as a golden age for communal values is based on the assumption that colonists, especially rural colonists, were not materialistic, entrepreneurial, profit oriented, or litigious but, rather, chose to produce at subsistence levels and for home consumption, to forgo purchases of consumer goods, and to be cooperative and self-sufficient within families and close community circles. People in the community, who were bound by networks of personal, reciprocal ties, exchanged "gifts," not "commodities." Historians taking this view have tended to portray the colonial period in a positive light as a time when society was healthier because of the absence of individualism and capitalism. Close, interdependent communities were good because they appealed to and reinforced people's better instincts (i.e., they acted in the more human, communal interest rather than in their own private, selfish interests) and because members could feel secure in the protective warmth of the community.

The notion that individual families in colonial America were entirely self-sufficient has been soundly overturned by scholars who have described the presence of many consumer goods in preindustrial New England and Chesapeake households, found indicators of the importance accorded private landownership, and shown evidence of surplus production of agricultural goods.[3] Furthermore, the commercial values of Anglo-American merchants are well established.[4] Substantial scholarship still assumes, however, that outside the merchants' world colonists maintained "traditional" communal relationships. Although it is acknowledged that communities were not individually self-sufficient, it is still maintained that they remained tightly connected through interdependence. The interdependence model assumes that relationships within the community were personal and nonmarket in nature. That interdependence itself has been romanticized.

Thus Christopher Clark describes a communally oriented economy characterized by customary, reciprocal modes of local exchanges in western Massachusetts extending decades into the nineteenth century. Michael Merrill has identified a household mode of production, in which exchanges between farmers were gifts rather than market commodities, extending into the mid-nineteenth century. Steven Hahn writes about upcountry Georgia yeomen relying primarily on noncommercial exchanges until late in the nineteenth century. Allan Kulikoff describes eighteenth-century yeomen farmers who maintained noncommercial, informal exchange relationships within the local community, even as some of them became involved in worldwide commodities markets; only with the Revolutionary War did a bourgeois revolution begin. James Henretta also assumes a noncommercialized colonial economy, which began to change and break down only owing to the new opportunities opened up by the Revolutionary War and the ratification of the Constitution.[5]

Other scholars have at the same time acknowledged that commercialism spread and still maintained that interdependence and communalism thrived. For example, Stephen Innes describes the development of "moral capitalism" in Puritan New England: commercial success through the Calvinist work ethic without sacrificing social solidarity or devotion to God. Similarly, Michael Bellesiles has identified what he calls "communal capitalism" in early Vermont. Christine Heyrman describes commercial development in two Massachusetts seaport towns even while traditional beliefs and relationships survived. Jack Greene has vigorously and persuasively argued that although early Massachusetts and Connecticut were communal in orientation, the New England model does not apply to the Chesapeake, the Lower South, or the Middle Colonies, which experienced a higher degree of commercial orientation from the beginning. Greene is, however, less convincing when he portrays that commercialism as the mere "pursuit of happiness," which did not undermine community but, rather, actually made the colonies south of New England more cohesive and more communal over time.[6] These four historians have made a significant contribution to the accurate portrayal of colonial economic lives, but they have denied the logical social implications of commercialism, materialism, and individualism. As is shown in this book, the expanding economy of the colonial period had more of an impact on social and economic relationships than these four authors acknowledge.

The idealized image of a communal colonial society remains in, even dominates, current historiography. The presumption also influences the historiography in fields outside economic and social history and even shapes historiography on the revolutionary, early national, and antebellum periods. For example, scholars of legal history have picked up the golden age model and, in their analysis of law, have idealized the colonial period by portraying it as communal and precommercial. The authors of two of the most important books in the field of early American legal history, Morton J. Horwitz and William E. Nelson, have both asserted that a precommercial consciousness opposed to market values still dominated rural America throughout the first half of the nineteenth century, and consequently they presumed an eighteenth-century legal system that was anticommercial, anticompetitive, jury dominated, and more concerned with overall fairness than with strict contractual terms.[7] Thus legal scholars who have written about early American history have typically adhered to the common conception of an idealized colonial community.

Another example is the field of political history, where the assumption of an anticommercial colonial world is most obviously evident in scholarship describing the ideals of the American Revolution. Bernard Bailyn, Gordon Wood, J. G. A. Pocock, and Robert Shallhope have led the way in claiming that the dominant ideological strain in revolutionary America was a kind of communitarian idealism that was most concerned about maintaining virtue, that is, the disinterested commitment to the common good, independent of private, selfish interests.[8] The argument that the market revolution occurred only after the Revolution is an essential foundation for such historians' portrayal of a transition from republicanism to liberalism in the postrevolutionary era.

Similar examples could be drawn from other fields of history and from scholarship focusing on the seventeenth, eighteenth, and nineteenth centuries. In short, despite the work of historians who have identified elements of a commercial society in the colonial period, there remains a pervading presumption of a family-like, interdependent, colonial society that shunned commercialism, individualism, and materialism. It is difficult not to find such portrayals of the communal colonial world—as contrasted with the nineteenth-century world wrought by industrialization—very appealing, even comforting. Whatever one thinks of the desirability or morality of individualism and capitalism, however, the historical record shows clearly that in the eighteenth century colonists did not shun commercial and market values or consistently treat either neighbors or strangers as family. Large numbers of them borrowed money, purchased goods, sued one another, and could expect to be held to the strict terms of their financial arrangements. Yet this reality is usually not reflected in historical literature. Edwin Perkins, Richard Hofstadter, Louis Hartz, and others have long explicitly argued that (as Carl Degler phrased it) capitalism arrived in America on the first ships, yet the precommercial, communal model of colonial America survives.[9]

This book shows that the transition to capitalism was a lengthy process that began well before the Revolution; it did not just occur suddenly in the mid-nineteenth century. My research addresses not only the question of the degree of market participation but also the question of the nature of economic exchanges. Most significantly, my study challenges the assumption that economic relationships in the eighteenth century were primarily a form of family-like, reciprocal, noncommercial local exchange. In colonial New York at least, relationships between people—between strangers, between neighbors, and between family members—were affected by expanding commercialization; they were not isolated from economic change.

My work complements the writings of many of the scholars cited above in describing the expansion of a market economy in eighteenth-century New York but takes a different approach to studying colonial commercial development in a number of ways. First, while scholars studying mercantile practice have focused on urban areas and historians analyzing the transition to capitalism have tended to focus exclusively on rural areas, I analyze both urban and rural regions, compare patterns in the two regions, and examine their interaction. Second, this study is the first to use debt litigation as an indicator of distanced, market relations; indeed, this book is unique among economic histories in the extent to which it examines the important role of law in colonial economic development. Third, this volume integrates the history of both women and men, describing how gender affected one's experiences in the expanding market economy of the eighteenth century.

Commercial Development in Rural and Urban Areas

Economic historians who have examined the emergence of a market economy or, more broadly, of a capitalist economy, have focused their studies on nonurban areas, asking when rural Americans became market oriented. In answering that question, many scholars have concentrated on the precapitalist nature of colonial America, assessing evidence of a market orientation among farmers only in the nineteenth (or sometimes in the late eighteenth) century.[10] The transition to capitalism is often portrayed as the loss of rural people to commercialism. In fact, rural people are often portrayed as heroically, but futilely, resisting the market economy.[11]

The loss of farmers is lamented more deeply in the scholarly literature than any comparable loss of urban dwellers because of the perception of rural areas as somehow purer than cities. Such dichotomization of the urban and the rural is not new. Many generations have reassured themselves that the past is not entirely gone by imagining that it still exists in some protected part of the contemporary society, usually a rural part of society. For example, as Raymond Williams has pointed out, people have often created images of the city and the country that implicitly preserve the positive attributes of the old society in the country while branding the city with the negative characteristics of the new ideas, whether those new ideas or new threats were money and law (sixteenth and seventeenth centuries), wealth and luxury (eighteenth century), the mob and the masses (late eighteenth and nineteenth centuries), or mobility and isolation (nineteenth and twentieth centuries).[12] Scholars dichotomize urban and rural areas not only in their own time but also in the past: while acknowledging the existence of crasser relationships in the urban past, they often see healthier attributes preserved for the future in protected rural areas. Thus in viewing the colonial American world, some scholars have particularly idealized rural communities as warm, close, supportive, stable, and "human." Americans' special affinity for the rural past, the protectiveness that we feel for pure farming communities, may explain why historians have focused so exclusively on rural areas when debating the rise of commercial and capitalist values.

This book studies the economic relationships among urban dwellers as well as rural people. Even if traditional economic relationships in the seventeenth century had been to a large extent limited to one's close, tight-knit community and had been bolstered by personal relationships, trust, and mutual dependence, by the early eighteenth century New

Yorkers bought increasing quantities of consumer goods and the economy expanded, leading them to develop more businesslike relationships
with people in their own communities and to begin to extend their
economic relations outside the local community.

Although in the late seventeenth century there was a wide gap between
people in urban and rural areas in the range of consumer goods they
owned and in the extent to which they extended loans and incurred debts
backed by written instruments, by the end of the colonial period urban
and rural patterns of consumption and debt had significantly converged in
New York. By the mid-eighteenth century, for example, a majority of
both urban and rural people owned such basic household items as tables,
chairs, and mirrors, and a sharply increasing percentage of them also
owned such luxuries as teaware, china, table forks and knives, and watches
and clocks. Ownership of such items came about only through participation in a colony-wide and international market, through connections
between urban and rural areas and between merchants and farmers. Because the structure for economic integration was in place, and a large
number of people were participating in market relationships made possible by that integration, by the mid-eighteenth century, this book places
the emergence of New York's market economy in the colonial period.

Debt Litigation and the Market Economy

In addition to assessing the question of exactly when a commercial economy emerged in America, economic historians have asked a second basic
question as part of the transition debate: What caused, or what permitted,
the expansion of the market economy? Most historians who have examined the rise of capitalism have focused just on proving that a change in
orientation or in practice occurred at a particular time, though a few of
them have attempted to provide social, economic, and technological explanations for the shift, such as change in mentality, increased ability to
produce surplus, or easier access to markets through improved transportation. While such factors may have contributed to that shift, one essential
factor has gone almost entirely unrecognized by economic historians: law.
Occasionally an early American economic history text refers to labor law
or land law, but references to commercial law or the court system are
extremely rare.[13]

Colonial economic historians' neglect of the role of the legal system in
economic development is largely due to the fact that legal historians have
tended to assume that an active relationship between the courts and the

economy emerged only in the nineteenth century. As noted above, most legal historians have until very recently implicitly or explicitly assumed a communally oriented and economically neutral colonial legal system. They have idealized the legal system as they have idealized colonial society: legal historians have long maintained that the legal system became tainted with instrumentalist, procommercial content only in the nineteenth century. Just in the past decade has that view been challenged, most notably by Bruce Mann, and the newer view has yet to have its full impact either within or outside the field of legal history experts.[14] Yet clearly the legal system played an essential role in the expansion of market relationships in colonial America.

Impersonal market relationships between people from different communities could not depend on trust and mutual dependence because the traders did not know each other well personally or have regular, personal contact with each other. Increased purchases therefore required an outside enforcer of debt relationships: the legal system. In New York during the first half of the eighteenth century, reliance on the legal system allowed urban and rural men from a wide range of occupational and wealth groups to engage in market relations. As society became more contractualized in the eighteenth century, the courts increasingly held people to their agreements. More specifically, this book shows how economic relationships were more likely to be outlined in writing, and courts were less likely to impose fairness by adding conditions to agreements, increasingly likely to enforce the explicit terms of agreements, and more likely to rule against monopoly and in favor of freer competition. As the legal system became more rationalized and formal, debt collection became more predictable. My study describes the most important legal development of the period: the decline in jury trial. This change reduced the role of unpredictable decision makers (jurors) in the legal system. Debt collection could consequently be governed by consistent and impersonal legal principles. The primary remaining nonlegal variant was wealth, which worked to the advantage of the most commercialized colonists: because litigation was expensive, merchants and other wealthy litigators enjoyed greater clout in forcing favorable negotiated settlements. Overall, through the decline of jury trial, New York's legal system became more supportive of commercial relationships.

Because the legal system was the essential enforcer of contracts, it was the supportive and protective connector that enabled different communities of men to become economically integrated: merchants with craftsmen, merchants with farmers, wealthy men and poor ones, urban people with rural dwellers. Because it was the legal system that provided the foundation for economic integration, this book concludes that law was one of the most important factors that permitted New Yorkers to become engaged in market relationships. The legal system was essential for the expansion of the economy in the eighteenth century.

Furthermore, the extent to which people used legal process to enforce their economic arrangements is a good indicator of the degree to which they viewed those arrangements as impersonal, market exchanges. That is, the rate of debt litigation provides an excellent measure of market involvement. It is in fact a much better indicator of market relations than is the use of cash—a marker commonly used by those who have concluded that rural America was not market oriented until the nineteenth century. This volume shows how a debt litigation model is much more useful than is a cash transaction model for assessing the nature of economic relationships.

More specifically, the book describes the rise of debt in colonial New York as evidenced in probate inventories and court records. Although some New Yorkers paid for their purchases with cash, commodities, or financial instruments, most buyers relied on credit to finance their purchases. Attitudes toward debt were mixed in the society, but thousands of creditors went to court to force payment of money owed. The high debt litigation rate revealed in the legal records shows that eighteenth-century economic relationships were arm's length business arrangements, not familial or communal in nature. Furthermore, participation in litigation by a wide range of New Yorkers shows widespread involvement in the market. Not only wealthy merchants but also farmers, craftsmen, and other men of average or even of modest wealth participated in debt litigation, reflecting their engagement in impersonal, distanced economic relationships.

Women and Men in the Commercializing Economy

This book examines both men and women in the rising capitalist economy. There is a need for analysis of economic history that takes both men's and women's experiences seriously. Women's economic and legal experiences cannot be discussed in isolation from broader economic and legal developments, and economic history and legal history scholarship that focuses exclusively on men so leaves out an important part of the story. Women in early America were affected by the same developments that had an impact on men's lives, but the experiences of women did not parallel those of men during this period. Both women's and men's experiences need to be examined.

Few publications relating to the transition to capitalism include any discussion of women's experiences. Christopher Clark and Allan Kulikoff are the rare exceptions, and both only touch on the subject of women.[15] Most notably absent from scholarship on early American economic history is analysis of the process by which women were marginalized from the core of economic relations as the economy and the legal system became more contractualized and formalized. Social historians have written about women's contributions to the household economy and their informal bartering with neighbors during the colonial period, legal historians have written about women's lack of property rights, and students of the nineteenth century have described the exclusion of women from most economic opportunities outside the home in the industrial era. But nobody has yet adequately studied the increasing exclusion of women from economic opportunities in the developing commercial world of the eighteenth century or explained the connection between that exclusion and women's legal position. Like the rest of this book, the sections relating to women focus on the differences between rural and urban regions and on the role of law in shaping economic relationships.

This study contrasts urban and rural women, examining their different roles and experiences in the market economy. Laurel Thatcher Ulrich's recent books and Alice Morse Earle's, Alice Clark's, and Mary Sumner Benson's earlier books on the colonial period have described women's functions in the early American household, and Nancy Woloch, Glenna Matthews, and Mary Ryan, among others, have incorporated such descriptions into their general surveys of women's history. Less has been written about women's economic activities outside the home. The most notable exceptions are the scholarship of Ulrich, who has studied women's economic exchanges within the community, Mary Beth Norton, whose recent book explores gendered aspects of power relationships between 1620 and 1670, Julie Matthaei, whose book provides a Marxist analysis of the whole course of American women's history, and Patricia Cleary, who has studied female shopkeepers.[16] This book devotes only brief attention to topics already covered in those studies (such as women's household work, women shopkeepers, and women's and men's political and religious authority) and emphasizes instead characteristics that distinguish the urban from the rural experience for eighteenth-century women, a subject that has not previously been analyzed.

Married rural women found a productive niche in the developing market economy of eighteenth-century New York. Most notably, they became significant producers of butter and cheese, but they also made fabric, cider, and other products. The households of married urban women,

however, were far less likely to include the livestock or equipment necessary for female production, so they were less likely to participate in the
market economy. The situation was reversed for single and widowed
women, however. Such women were more likely to be cared for by a family member in the countryside than in the city, and there were more
opportunities for independent women to sell "women's work," such as
laundering and sewing, in urban areas. Consequently, more widows
earned wages from their labor or payment for their goods in the city than
in rural counties. The income that urban women earned from such activities, however, typically allowed them no more than a mere subsistence.
One result was an increase in female urban poverty. More broadly, in the
eighteenth century women's relative degree of economic opportunity
declined compared to men's, and therefore their overall power and status
relative to men also declined.

This monograph also examines the role of law in shaping women's
economic experiences in the market. Other scholars have written about
women's lack of legal ownership of economic resources. In particular,
there is a substantial body of scholarship describing women's inheritance
rights and property rights in early America, most notably books and
articles by Toby Ditz, David Narrett, Marylynn Salmon, Lisa Wilson,
Linda Biemer, and Joan R. Gunderson and Gwen Victor Gampel on the
colonial period, several essays in Ronald Hoffman and Peter Albert's
collection on women in the revolutionary period, and a survey of inheritance law throughout American history by Carole Shammas, Marylynn
Salmon, and Michel Dahlin.[17] Outside the subject of women and property, little has been written about women and the law in colonial America
that relates to women's roles in the economy. Only one other scholar
has written about colonial women and the litigated economy: Cornelia
Hughes Dayton includes a chapter on women and debt litigation in her
superb recent book on women in civil, criminal, and divorce actions in
New Haven County between 1639 and 1789.[18] The present book complements the work of all those historians by connecting law with economic experience—by describing the impact of limited property rights
and contract rights on the economic lives of urban and rural women and
by providing a broader economic context for understanding women's
experiences in the legal system.

The extent to which common law limitations on women were actually
enforced was questioned by Richard Morris and Mary Beard, but this
study concludes that those two authors overstated the extent to which
equity courts tempered the impact of harsh common law rules regarding coverture.[19] In fact, the rules of law were genuinely restrictive for

women, not merely prescriptive. That is, formal limitations on women's legal rights were real constraints on women's economic options. To some extent, Morris's and Beard's arguments are part of the common idealization of the colonial period as a golden age for women. Just as the colonial community has been romanticized as free of corrupting commercial values and the colonial legal system has been portrayed as economically neutral and supportive of communal values, so the position of women in the colonial economy and society has been idealized by some scholars.

Even today some historians continue to portray the colonial period as a better environment for women than any post-revolutionary time. Many of those who do so have focused their study on colonial women who were the rare exceptions and then implicitly extrapolated their evidence to suggest that the extraordinary situations actually reflected most women's experiences. Other historians, seeming eager to blame gender inequalities on capitalism, industrialization, and domesticity, have simply presumed that in the colonial world that (they assume) came before these developments women and men must have lived together as equals. This idealized view does not accurately describe colonial life.

Another dubious position is the essentialist view taken by some scholars, who ignore the external constraints on women and assert that their distance from the worlds of the courtroom and the marketplace was a matter of bold and admirable choice. I reject essentialist arguments that women "naturally" rejected the competitive capitalist economy and the adversarial legal system. Instead it is shown clearly here that the constraints on women's economic opportunities came primarily through law. The law of coverture severely limited what married women could do independently, and the rules of inheritance had the effect of depressing widows' financial resources and standard of living, leaving them with little to invest in the expanding economy. All women were thus handicapped in the economy by their position under law.

As this book challenges the accepted timeline for a shift to a market economy and the underlying assumptions of scholars who have contrasted the economic world of the nineteenth and eighteenth centuries, it also asserts that historians need to reexamine assumptions about women's relationship to the public economy in the colonial period as contrasted with the nineteenth century. I explore what the scholarship of Mary Beth Norton, Linda Kerber, Suzanne Lebsock, Nancy Cott, Jeanne Boydston, Gerda Lerner, Nancy Grey Osterud, Joan Jensen, and Barbara Welter relating to women in revolutionary, early national, and antebellum America suggests about the lives and the position of colonial American women.[20]

New York

The geographic focus of this study of an emerging market economy is the colony of New York. New York was divided into ten counties: New York County (i.e., New York City, or what we now call Manhattan), Richmond County (Staten Island), three Long Island counties (Kings, Queens, and Suffolk), and five Hudson River counties (Westchester, Orange, Dutchess, Ulster, and Albany). See the accompanying map. This book focuses primarily, though not exclusively, on the biggest urban center, New York County, and a representative rural area, Dutchess County, which covered the 38 miles between Westchester County and Albany County and extended 26 miles from the Hudson River east to New York's boundary with Connecticut.[21] Dutchess County was chosen because it had the widest range of colonial records available: tax assessment lists covering most of the period from 1717 to the end of the colonial period, account books, minutes of the early Court of Common Pleas, and pleadings and other court documents from eighteenth-century cases.

Colonial New York has long received less scholarly attention than Massachusetts and Virginia. Indeed, historians have generally slighted the Middle Colonies, focusing their studies on New England and the South instead. Yet, as Frederick Jackson Turner and Woodrow Wilson observed a century ago, and as Milton Klein and Patricia Bonomi have noted more recently, the mid-Atlantic region was both significant and characteristic in the nation's early history.[22]

Klein proposes a number of explanations for colonial historians' neglect of New York and the other Middle Colonies. Among the reasons he lists are that the Middle Colonies are difficult to define geographically; the early contributions of the Middle Colonies cannot match the political liberties, common law system, and Puritan concept of divine providence that early English settlers brought with them to Massachusetts and Virginia; and the revolutionary and early national political heritage of Massachusetts and Virginia is perceived to be much nobler than that of New York. Perhaps the most significant reason is that both New England and the South were more comfortably homogeneous and nonurban in comparison with the Middle Colonies, and New England in particular seemed to fit the idealized image of a rural, family oriented, communal society, whereas the Middle Colonies were more commercially advanced.[23]

Economic historians of colonial America have tended to focus primarily on New England and the Chesapeake, giving much less attention to the Middle Colonies. Wayne Bodle's 1994 review of scholarship on

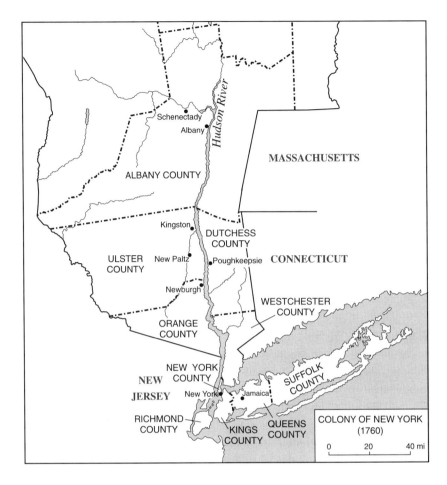

that region concludes that "[t]he economic history of the Middle Colonies remains in much the same tentative state" as it did in the late 1970s. To this date, for example, there have been no published studies of household goods and standard of living in colonial New York, though such studies abound for other colonies to the north and south.[24] Cornelia Hughes Dayton's 1993 review of colonial legal history notes that legal scholarship has overwhelmingly focused on New England, and little has yet been published about legal development in the Middle Colonies.[25] There is, therefore, a need for further discussion of economic and legal development in New York and the other Middle Colonies. This book is intended to make a contribution to that discussion. New York's experience is neither entirely representative nor entirely unique, but it is surely an important part of the story of colonial America.

This study of colonial New York is divided into three parts. Part I describes the emergence of a market economy in the colony, part II focuses on the economic and legal experiences of men, and part III focuses on the experiences of women. In part I, chapter 1 examines the rise in consumer purchases and the increased polarization of wealth in eighteenth-century New York, while chapter 2 details the increased use of cash and circulating financial instruments, evaluates the rise of debt, and examines debt collection practices.

The next two chapters constitute part II. Chapter 3 describes how New York's legal system supported the growing economy by providing an increasingly effective and predictable process for collecting debts and strictly enforcing contractual arrangements and how more commercialized groups adapted more quickly to the legal changes than did less commercialized groups. Chapter 4 describes the spread of market relationships evidenced by the increased volume and rate of litigation and more widespread participation in litigation in both urban and rural courts of eighteenth-century New York.

Chapters 5 and 6 illustrate how women as a group became more peripheralized from the core of New York's economy at the same time as more men were increasingly participating in expanding market relationships. Chapter 5 describes urban and rural women's shared low rate of participation in litigation and contrasts rural and urban women's economic roles outside the home, while chapter 6 examines the reasons for women's low rate of participation in litigation and independent market activities, focusing on the role of law and limited financial resources. Finally, chapter 7 concludes by looking ahead to reflect on issues relating to the market economy, law, and gender in the era of the American Revolution and the early national period.

Economic History, Legal History, and Women's History

While there have been opposing voices, an idealized view of colonial community, economic relations, legal system, and gender relations continues to prevail among a large proportion of historians of seventeenth-, eighteenth-, and nineteenth-century America. Although a number of economic historians have described commercial developments of the colonial period, a few legal historians have pointed out ways in which law and economic development were interconnected in that period, and some scholars of women's history have taken a realistic view of colonial gender relationships, that literature often fails to cross historical fields and consequently has had inadequate impact on the dominant larger view of the colonial period.

Studies of economic history, legal history, and women's history have, in isolation from one another, mutually reinforced a common image of a communal colonial society. Such an image may help give the colonial period a distinctive identity in American history, thus providing a different model of Americanness, making it clear that the story of colonial America is not just about the coming of the American Revolution, and offering a clear point of contrast for descriptions of the nineteenth-century impact of industrialization on economic, legal, and gender relations. But the image is not accurate.

The purpose of this book is to describe the expansion of the market economy, the relationship between the legal system and the economy, and the position of women in the economy of one colony, New York, so as to strongly undermine the myths and idealization of colonial America in a way that crosses boundaries and integrates three fields of history. The study explicitly cross-applies findings in economic history, legal history, and the history of gender so as to avoid the continued isolation of any one of the three fields from the other two. Such isolation has often resulted in misunderstandings and false assumptions. I cast aside the restrictions of narrow subfields and show how the interaction of economic history, legal history, and gender history can enrich our understanding of historical processes.

PART I

The Market Economy

CHAPTER 1

The Consumer Revolution
in Colonial New York

Until recently, the rise of consumerism in the eighteenth century received little scholarly attention. Though some historians are now beginning to examine the style of life in early America, many of those who study the economy of the nineteenth century continue to describe an unrealistically abrupt shift to capitalism and tend to underestimate colonists' involvement in the consumer goods market.[1] They seem to assume that market values emerged only in the nineteenth century. More appropriately, however, the date for the rise of capitalism, a consumer mentality, a market economy, and an entrepreneurial spirit should be pushed back into the eighteenth century and even into the seventeenth century. It seems likely that, as Edwin Perkins, Richard Hofstadter, Louis Hartz, and other scholars have maintained, the European colonists were inclined from the beginning of settlement to seek market involvement in order to enhance their financial condition and standard of living, but lack of markets, poor transportation, and difficulties developing a successful commodity product for export hampered economic development and left frontier settlers largely dependent on self-sufficient household production and barter.[2]

By the mid-eighteenth century, New York had developed some moderately successful export products. At that time New York's most successful staple good was flour. Farmers on Long Island and along the Hudson River grew wheat as well as other grains, such as maize, oats, rye, and barley. Mid-eighteenth-century travelers through the colony, such as Peter Kalm and Andrew Burnaby, observed that New Yorkers along the

Hudson River sent down to New York City for export not only wheat and flour but also peas, lumber, and staves. They also noted other export products: pork, pig iron, and whale oil and bone.[3] In addition, New Yorkers received English payments and credits for building ships, shipping goods, and provisioning British troops. Though the value of New York's imports and credits rose more rapidly than the value of its exports during the century, creating an imbalance of trade and a scarcity of specie, the income gained from sale of these goods and services provided some basis for purchase of imported goods.[4]

Although many necessities continued to be produced in the home in the eighteenth century, colonists living in developed areas in New York and in other northern colonies were also linked to markets and able to trade goods and cash for a wide variety of imported basic and luxury items. Consumption patterns in colonial New York have not previously been studied. This analysis of surviving account books, probate inventories, and mortgage books demonstrates that the economic behavior of eighteenth-century New Yorkers was not as starkly different from that of their nineteenth-century counterparts as it is usually portrayed. This study further shows that urban and rural patterns of consumption of household goods converged significantly during the last century of the colonial period.

The Consumer Revolution in New York

Over the course of the colonial period, urban and rural New Yorkers purchased an increasing number of consumer goods (particularly luxury goods) and an increased amount of agricultural equipment, craft tools, and transportation vehicles. In the 1690s, purchases and sales of products in the colony took place at markets held weekly at designated places in each county.[5] In New York City the number of market days was increased during the early eighteenth century; by 1731 there were six market days each week, and there were four different market locations.[6] People also bought goods from shopkeepers, from itinerant peddlers, and occasionally at public auctions.[7] Swedish traveler Peter Kalm observed in the late 1740s that there was at least one store in every large village.[8]

By the 1750s, every issue of New York newspapers such as the *New-York Mercury* contained many advertisements for imported goods. For example, on one page alone on June 4, 1753, six different merchants advertised the availability at their stores of "A choice assortment of European and India Goods." Other merchants gave more detail about the items they had for sale: on the same page of the *New-York Mercury,* Corne & Van Dam listed over 50 different products recently imported from London, Ebenezer Grant described the recently imported books he had for sale, Philip Livingston mentioned over 20 kinds of items for sale, and Dirck Brinckerhoff advertised over 50 recently imported products.[9] The value of imports into New York more than doubled between 1715 and 1740 and then grew even more dramatically between 1740 and 1775.[10] Carole Shammas has calculated that by 1768–72, the average American colonist spent 30.5% of his or her budget on imports from outside the colony of residence.[11]

Court documents from 22 Dutchess County cases in which shop-keepers sued customers to collect payments list the items purchased from the stores. Table 1.1 shows the items purchased that were the basis of these 22 rural debts.[12] As one can see, most of the goods were imported from England, not locally produced. The most commonly purchased item (bought by 21 of the 22 debtors) was fabric. Materials used in making clothes, such as needles, thread, thimbles, and buttons, were also common purchases in the period. This suggests an early trend away from women's making fabric in the home, though a continuation of their making clothes from imported fabric. The other main category of goods purchased was food items, especially sugar, tea, and rum.

The items listed in these accounts are consistent with the kinds of goods enumerated in probate inventories of eighteenth-century shop-keepers. The inventory of William Teller (1701), for example, highlights a variety of fabrics (linen, cotton, silk, calico, and damask) and also lists buttons, ribbons, hatbands, stockings, gloves, knives, nails, hinges, locks and bolts, shoemaker's awls, fishhooks, weights, brushes, combs, curtain rings, copper tobacco boxes, books, psalmbooks, pepper, allspice, sugar, nutmeg, and cloves. Evert Byvanck's inventory (1773) lists fabric, ribbons, lace, thread, buttons, handkerchiefs, stockings, caps, shoes, testaments, paper, combs, brushes, knives, scissors, buckles, pins, wool cards, candlewicks, tallow, beeswax, indigo, cups, bowls, pots, boxes, nutmeg, chocolate, ginger, allspice, and coffee.[13]

Peter Kalm was particularly struck by the consumption of tea in New York and the other Middle Colonies. Older colonists told him that 30 or 40 years before the time of his visit, tea was unknown to them, but by 1749 colonists had tea every morning with breakfast and another cup in the middle of the afternoon. In fact, he noted, tea was "so common at present that there is hardly a farmer's wife or a poor woman who does not drink tea in the morning." Even chocolate, which had been unknown in the childhoods of the older colonists, had become a popular

Table 1.1
Goods Purchased in 22 Dutchess County Suits

Goods	No. of Customers	Goods	No. of Customers
Salt	6	Hat/cap	10
Tea	6	Garters	1
Sugar	13	Shoebuckles	2
Pepper	8	Kneebuckles	1
Ginger	1	Rug	2
Allspice	1	Blanket	2
Rice	2	Skins	4
Molasses	4	Bottle	1
Liquor	1	Pewter	1
Rum	10	Plate	1
Beer	1	Bason	1
Cider	3	Teapot	2
Punch	2	Knives	2
Chocolate	1	Compass	3
Indigo	1	Comb	1
Fabric/cloth	21	Snuff	2
Buttons	10	Pipe	1
Thread	6	Beeswax	1
Needles	5	Gun	2
Thimble	2	Powder	2
Paper pins	6	Shot	5
Paper	7	Lead	4
Scissors	1	Brimstone	1
Tape	1	Chisel	2
Wood cards	2	Ax	1
Stockings	2	Awl	2
Handkerchief	4	Nails/brads	7

Sources: See n. 12.

accompaniment to breakfast in rural areas.[14] Another indication of the extent to which at least some New Yorkers were purchasing goods well beyond necessaries was Edward Haddon's notice in a 1753 newspaper putting up a reward of 40 shillings for the return of a large green parrot that had recently been stolen from his house.[15]

By the 1740s, rural people, like urban dwellers, had acquired luxuries. During a trip up the Hudson River, the Scottish doctor Alexander Hamilton had occasion to stop in a farming area just south of Poughkeepsie to obtain water. He went to a small log cottage occupied by a couple in their thirties and seven young children. The children, he observed, "seemed quite wild and rustick." Yet when he and his traveling companion entered the modest house, they found severall superfluous things which showed an inclination to finery in these poor people, such as a looking glass with a painted frame, half a dozen pewter spoons and as many plates, old and wore out but bright and clean, a set of stone tea dishes, and a tea pot. These, Mr. [Milne] said, were superfluous and too splendid for such a cottage, and therefor they ought to be sold to buy wool to make yarn; that a little water in a wooden pail might serve for a looking glass, and wooden plates and spoons would be as good for use and, when clean, would be almost as ornamental. As for the tea equipage it was quite unnecessary.[16]

When Hamilton reached Albany, he noticed that in their houses they "affect pictures much, particularly scripture history, with which they adorn their rooms. They set out their cabinets and bouffetts much with china."[17]

This anecdotal evidence of luxuries is substantiated by an analysis of hundreds of probate inventories, which listed personal property owned by New Yorkers at the time of their deaths and therefore provide some indication of the extent of ownership of goods among the living. Studies based on inventories are limited in some ways: the inventories do not include real estate, the estates of people with property are more likely to be inventoried than those of people without property, inventories give no indication of possessions recently given to relatives, and comparisons over time are difficult because the proportion of inventories by wealthy or poor decedents might vary in practice from decade to decade.[18] New York's inventories have not previously been analyzed, however, and despite the limitations, they do provide some useful information not available from other sources.

In 523 of the 600 inventories, the county of residence was indicated: 139 of the decedents resided in New York City or Albany, and 384 resided in more rural counties.[19] The data were organized in five periods covering the years 1680–99, 1700–19, 1720–39, 1740–59, and 1760–75.[20] New York decedents in the last period owned a wider range of consumer goods than did decedents in the earliest period. Table 1.2 shows the increase in the percentage of decedents owning selected items and illustrates the difference between urban and rural ownership of consumer goods.[21] Four luxuries and five more common consumer goods were analyzed. The increased ownership of imported luxury goods is particularly notable. About 2% of decedents in the first period owned table forks and knives, but by the last period 40% owned them. Only 2% of decedents in the first period owned teaware, but by the last period 34% owned teaware. Twelve percent of decedents dying between 1680 and

Table 1.2

Percentage of New York Inventories Listing Selected Consumer Goods in
Two Periods

	All Decedents		Rural Decedents		Urban Decedents	
	1680–99	1760–75	1680–99	1760–75	1680–99	1760–75
Teaware	2	34	0	29	3	43
Forks/knives	0	40	0	41	3	39
China	10	27	3	16	10	36
Watch/Clock	12	27	0	20	13	39
Pictures	23	29	0	10	42	46
Tables	64	81	48	71	87	82
Chairs	66	83	58	76	87	86
Candles	52	61	42	45	55	71
Looking glasses	63	71	45	53	77	79

Source: Colonial New York Probate Inventories.

1699 and 27% of those dying between 1760 and 1775 owned a watch or
clock. Ten percent of decedents in the first period and 27% by the last
period owned china. The percentage of New Yorkers owning more common goods, like tables and chairs, also grew somewhat between 1680 and
1775, though less dramatically than luxury goods.[22] Throughout the period, urban dwellers were more likely to own consumer goods than were
rural dwellers. As expected, wealthy decedents were more likely than
poor decedents to own luxuries. For example, in the earliest period only
decedents from the top third by wealth owned teaware (7%). By the latest
period, 55% of the top third, 30% of the middle third, and 14% of the
bottom third owned teaware.

Ownership patterns between 1699 and 1760 varied. For example,
ownership of teaware in urban areas jumped between the second period
(1700–19) and the third period (1720–39), but in rural areas it increased
most significantly between the fourth period (1740–59) and the fifth
period (1760–75). Ownership of watches and clocks in rural and urban
areas advanced gradually and steadily rather than in one sudden burst.
Although the overall pattern of ownership of tables and chairs was up-
ward, it was not a steady increase at all; rather, the pattern was irregular,
with small declines evidenced in rural or urban areas in some periods.

Another way to assess patterns of ownership of consumer goods is to
create an index of luxuries and an index of amenities.[23] To determine an
overall score for luxury goods, the presence or absence of the following 4
items was coded 1 or 0, added up, and then averaged for each time period:
watches or clocks, table forks and knives, teaware, and china. For the

index of amenities, the presence or absence of the following 19 items was coded 1 or 0, added up, and then averaged for each time period: wigs, looking glasses, candles or candlesticks, watches or clocks, pictures, Bibles or other religious books, secular books, household linens, quilts, chairs, tables, table forks and knives, imported foods, teaware, earthenware dishes, pewter dishes, china, gold objects, and silver objects. The higher the amenities score, the broader the range of consumer goods owned by the decedent.

Both scores were lower in rural than in urban counties, but since they increased more in the former than the latter, the gap between rural and urban became smaller as the colonial period progressed. The luxuries score went from .03 (out of a possible 4.00) in rural areas in the early period to 1.06 in the last period (a 3,433% increase) and in urban areas from .29 to 1.57 (a 441% increase).[24] The overall rise in consumer goods was less dramatic than the rise for luxuries. In rural areas the amenities score rose from 4.7 (out of a possible 19) in the period from 1680 to 1699 to 6.59 in the period from 1760 to 1775 (a 40% increase), and in urban areas it rose from 8.97 to 9.39 (only a 5% increase).[25]

What did these purchased household goods mean for colonial people's lives? First, the widespread purchase of fabrics, as is evident from court records and shop inventories, relieved women to some extent from spinning and weaving duties. Continued purchases of buttons, thread, ribbon, and lace, along with the fabric, however, indicate that women were still making clothes at home. Second, a number of the purchased goods, such as beds, sheets, blankets, and quilts, made everyday living more comfortable. There was even a small rise in leisure goods, such as books and musical instruments. The availability of imported food items allowed the colonists to make and enjoy a wider variety of foods. Pepper, salt, ginger, nutmeg, and allspice added new flavor to colonial dishes, while sugar, molasses, and chocolate provided luxurious sweeteners. Third, imported tea and teaware became the basis for more elaborate and ritualized social visits. China, forks and knives, tablecloths, napkins, and larger numbers of pewter serving vessels, chairs, and candles permitted colonists to entertain dinner guests in more elaborate style, and perhaps also to display their family's social status.

New Yorkers bought not only items for personal consumption but also tools and equipment to allow them to produce for the market at the same time as they were also increasingly buying goods in the market. Rural dwellers dying at the end of the colonial period were more likely than decedents of the late seventeenth century not only to have purchased consumer goods but also to have invested in most forms of craft tools,

Table 1.3
Percentage of Rural Inventories Listing Craft Tools,
Agricultural Equipment, or Transportation Vehicles

	1680–99	1760–75
Spinning wheel	32	55
Loom	3	22
Candle molds	0	21
Dairying equipment	24	60
Shoemaker tools	3	10
Carpenter tools	26	35
Blacksmith tools	6	0
Cooper tools	0	4
Plow	53	63
Harrow	12	31
Cart or wagon	47	42
Sled or sleigh	0	35
Boat	13	22

Source: Colonial New York Probate Inventories.

agricultural equipment, and transportation vehicles. The increased percentage of decedents whose estates included such items is shown in
table 1.3.

The increased percentage of rural households with spinning wheels,
looms, candle molds, and dairying equipment is particularly notable: it
reflects rural women's increasing contribution to household and market
production, which is discussed in chapter 5. Ownership of the items in
table 1.3 was, however, less common in the city. In the latest period, only
7% of urban decedents owned spinning wheels, 4% owned looms, 21%
had candle molds, 10% had dairying equipment, none had shoemaker
tools or blacksmith tools, 18% had carpenter tools of some kind, and 4%
had cooper's tools. Seven percent had plows, 7% had harrows, 4% had a
boat, 7% a sled or sleigh, and 14% a cart or wagon. The different levels of
ownership of tools and equipment in urban and rural areas reflects the
greater specialization of labor in cities. As is discussed in chapter 5, the
different levels also indicate a disparity between urban and rural women's
home production of goods for the market.

The general pattern of increased consumption was not confined to the
colony of New York. Studies of inventories from New England and the
Chesapeake show similar increases over time. Lois Green Carr and Lorena
Walsh, who based their amenities scores on 12 inventory items, found
that in the colonial Chesapeake the average score in the seventeenth
century was 2, but by the 1770s the average score had risen to 5, a 150%

increase. Gloria Main calculated amenities scores for different regions and different wealth groups in New England in three periods, 1638–1729, 1730–49, and 1750–74. The amenities score increases for her different groups ranged from 45% to 207%.[26]

Some scholars have evaluated not only what kinds of personal property people owned but also the total value of that property. Such studies have found that the mean value of consumer goods as a percentage of the mean total estate value did not increase significantly in rural Pennsylvania, New England, or the Chesapeake during the period when people of those regions were dying owning a wider range of goods.[27] Those findings do not necessarily mean that people did not spend more on consumer goods, however. The decline in prices of many goods and the easier availability of cheaper substitutes for previously expensive goods, which enabled people to buy more with less money, do not completely explain the steady proportion of wealth spent on consumer goods. First of all, those studies measured value of consumer goods as a percentage of total aggregate wealth, so as the total amount of wealth increased, the actual value of consumer goods would also have increased. Second, inventories, which record only property owned at death, do not reflect all accumulated expenditures over time (i.e., for replacement goods), and consumers in the seventeenth and eighteenth centuries apparently were buying more disposable, less durable goods. Therefore, although the proportion of total wealth that was invested at the time of death in consumer goods may have remained steady, people may very well have been spending more over the course of their lifetimes on consumer goods. In any case, whether or not New Yorkers in the eighteenth century were buying equally expensive and durable goods as in the seventeenth century, they were buying more goods (and, as is discussed in the next chapter, accumulating more debt).

Why was there an increase in the purchase of goods, especially luxury consumer goods, in the eighteenth century? Persuasive explanations have been presented by Lois Green Carr and Lorena Walsh and by Cary Carson. From their study of the colonial Chesapeake, Carr and Walsh found a number of reasons that might apply also to New York: (1) wider and more consistent availability of consumer goods as the population density and number of stores increased in formerly remote areas, (2) active efforts by merchants to promote purchases (displaying goods attractively, advertising in local newspapers, allowing customers to buy on credit), (3) decreased prices resulting from lower manufacturing and transportation costs, and (4) shifts in cultural attitudes, marked by increased concern with gentility and fashion.[28] Cary Carson argues that the acquisition of consumer goods was part of a new system of social communication that became necessary when large numbers of people began moving beyond their local villages, either as travelers or as colonial settlers. The traditional markers of reputation and status in their own communities were inadequate in a wider geographic setting. For migrants and those with whom they came in contact, the ownership of certain goods, combined with demonstrated skills in the prescribed social use of those goods, served as internationally recognized status signifiers.[29]

Visitors to the area commented negatively on the consumption of luxuries and the profit orientation of many New Yorkers. Peter Kalm found that "many people can never be contented with their possessions, though they be ever so large. They will always be desirous of getting more, and of enjoying the pleasure which arises from a change. Their extraordinary liberty and their luxury often lead them to unrestrained acts of selfish and arbitrary nature." Kalm found the people of Albany to be particularly money oriented: "The avarice, selfishness and immeasurable level of money of the inhabitants of Albany are very well known throughout all North America," he wrote. In Albany, he had to pay for everything: "If I wanted their assistance, I was obliged to pay them very well for it, and when I wanted to purchase anything or be helped in some case or other, I could at once see what kind of blood ran in their veins, for they either fixed exorbitant prices for their services or were very reluctant to assist me."[30]

The more widespread ownership of luxury goods in the 1730s, 1740s, and 1750s was also commented upon negatively in New York newspapers. For example, an essay published in the *New-York Weekly Journal* in 1736 admonished people for seeking ownership of unnecessary material goods. People should do what they can to protect themselves from hunger, thirst, and cold and should not buy goods beyond those necessary to such ends, the writer asserted; they should not indulge in conspicuous consumption: "A Cottage may keep a Man as warm as a Palace; and there is no absolute Necessity of covering our Bodies with Silk. Is there no quenching of our Thirst, but in Chrystal? No cutting of our Bread, unless the Knife has an Agat Handle? We may wash as clean in an Earthen Vessel as in a Silver, and see as well by a Candle in a Pewter-socket, as in a Plate."[31] In 1735, an essay in the *New-York Weekly Journal* asserted that it is a crime to spend beyond one's means, but it is even wrong to spend what one has on luxuries. The author wrote, "It is our Wisdom to banish [Objects of Luxury] from our Thoughts, and to be as sparing in the Use of them as the Circumstances of the Age and Country we live in will permit." He asked:

> Has Nature fixed no Limits to our Desires, and are there no super-
> fluities that contribute neither to the Necessaries nor Decencies of
> Life? And is it not becoming every wise and good Man to break
> himself of all Inclinations to Things of this Sort, and to hold them in
> Disesteem and Contempt? For the smallest Degree of Indulgence of
> them, even tho only in Compliance with the Fashions of the World,
> and the Tyranny of Custom, is of dangerous Experiment, in Regard
> of the ill Habits which by that means may be contracted, and the
> early Transition there is from one Degree of Voluptuousness to
> another, and greater.

"The Perfection of Wisdom," he continued, "has ever been esteemed to
consist in the moderating of our Desires." An important lesson could be
learned, he said, from the experience of the ancient Greeks and Romans,
who were strongest, most successful, and happiest when they held "false
Pleasures, and immoderate Riches" in contempt. He expressed admira-
tion for those ancients, for whom "Luxury at Tables, and Expence in
Apparel were Things looked on as criminal, or at least unbecoming Persons of Worth and Distinction." And he reminded readers that as the
Greeks and Romans became less moderate, admitting first luxury, then
avarice, followed necessarily by corruption, bribery, fraud, violence, and
wars, their society was destroyed and they became easy prey for tyrants.[32]

Although these eighteenth-century commentators focus on what they
perceive to be an indulgence in luxuries, it is important to keep in mind
that much of what eighteenth-century New Yorkers were buying were
not in fact luxuries. They bought not only items for personal consumption but also tools and equipment to allow them to produce for the
market.

Polarization of Wealth

Thus both anecdotal evidence from newspapers and travelers' accounts
and quantitative evidence from probate inventories show that as the eighteenth century progressed, New Yorkers bought more goods. Even the
most modest men and women participated to some extent in the consumer revolution. Although consumer purchasing was clearly widespread,
however, it was also variable: commercial development enabled some
people to buy more than others could. The resulting disparity is apparent
to us when we study tax assessment records, which indicate a definite
polarization of wealth in both urban and rural counties of eighteenth-
century New York.

Table 1.4
Distribution of Taxable Wealth, New York City, 1734

	Top 1/10	Top 1/3	Middle 1/3	Bottom 1/3
% of Wealth owned	44	74	18	8
Average tax assessment	£109	£55	£14	£6
Range of assessments	£55–675	£20–675	£10–20	£5–10

Source: New York City Tax Lists.

Table 1.5
Residence and Average Assessment of New York City
Taxpayers, 1734

Ward	% of Taxpayers (*N* = 1497)	% of Taxable Wealth
Dock	15	20
East	23	32
Montgomerie	12	7
North	16	10
Out (Bowry)	5	4
Out (Harlem)	3	2
South	14	15
West	12	11

Source: New York City Tax Lists.

Table 1.6
Distribution of Taxable Wealth, Dutchess County, 1735

	Top 1/10	Top 1/3	Middle 1/3	Bottom 1/3
% of Wealth owned	34	67	24	9
Average tax assessment	£39	£23	£8	£3
Range of assessments	£25–130	£12–130	£5–12	£2–5

Source: Dutchess County Tax Lists.

Table 1.7
Distribution of Taxable Wealth, Dutchess County, 1754

	Top 1/10	Top 1/3	Middle 1/3	Bottom 1/3
% of wealth owned	43	76	17	4
Average tax assessment	£21	£12	£3	£1
Range of assessments	£12–210	£4–210	£1–4	£1

Source: Dutchess County Tax Lists.

Table 1.8

Residence and Average Assessment of Dutchess County Taxpayers, 1754

| Precinct | Taxpayers | | Average Assessment |
	%	N	(£)
Crum Elbow	20.7	451	4
Beekman	19.4	424	3½
Southern	16.4	358	2
Rhinebeck	16.2	353	8
Rombout	15.6	340	7½
Poughkeepsie	7.6	166	7
Northeast	4.1	89	4
Total	100.0	2,181	

Source: Dutchess County Tax Lists.

Table 1.4 shows disparity of wealth some forty years before the Revolution. In New York City, not only was wealth unequally divided among households, it also was unevenly divided among the seven wards: some neighborhoods were wealthier than others. Table 1.5 shows the distribution of population and wealth in the wards in 1734 as calculated from the tax lists of that year.[33] Unfortunately, since no tax lists are extant for colonial New York City after 1735, the distribution of wealth of later periods cannot be determined from tax records.

The historiographical assumption seems to be that although there may have been a wealth hierarchy in urban areas, wealth did not become significantly polarized in rural areas of the Middle Colonies until the era of the American Revolution.[34] The Dutchess County assessments make it clear, however, that in eighteenth-century New York stratification of wealth was not solely an urban phenomenon. For Dutchess County, unlike for New York City, there are tax records from both the 1730s and the 1750s, so one can study change over time. In Dutchess County, there were a total of 2,100 taxpayers listed on the 1754 tax list and 428 on the 1735 list. As shown in Tables 1.6 and 1.7, the top third of taxpayers in 1754 owned 76% of the taxable wealth, while the bottom third owned only 4%; in 1735, the top third owned 67% and the bottom third 9%. In comparison, in 1734 the top third of city dwellers owned 74% of the wealth and the bottom third owned 8%. Thus the degree of stratification among taxpayers in rural Dutchess County was not substantially different from that in urban areas, even as early as the mid-1730s.[35]

As in urban New York City, in rural Dutchess County wealth was not evenly distributed among neighborhoods; some precincts were wealthier than others.[36] Table 1.8 shows the distribution of Dutchess County tax-payers by precinct in 1754. It should be noted that these calculations apply to taxpayers only. The 2,100 taxpayers in the county constituted only 15% of the total population of 14,148 (in 1756) and 68% of the white males over the age of 16 (3,076). Many of the younger men, for example, be-tween the ages of 16 and 21, were still financially dependent on fathers, so the number of independent single people or heads of families presumably was actually lower than 3,076 and therefore the percentage of them repre-sented on the tax list was actually higher than 68%. There were, neverthe-less, some financially independent men who were too poor to be included among taxpayers, few women were listed, and of course slaves and ser-vants also were not included in the taxpayer population. If all residents of the county were included in the calculations of degree of stratification, the disparity between the top and the bottom wealth categories would have been even greater than the numbers provided in the charts.[37]

Conclusion

This chapter shows that many New Yorkers were involved in a consumer goods market in the eighteenth century. Urban merchants and craftsmen increasingly used the profits of their businesses to fill their homes with consumer goods; meanwhile, farmers' sale of grains and other agricultural products allowed rural people, too, to buy a range of goods available in the market economy. Both urban and rural people increasingly purchased such luxuries as teaware, table forks and knives, china, and watches and clocks. A majority of urban and rural probate inventories listed ownership of tables, chairs, looking glasses, and other basic household items by the mid-eighteenth century. The index of amenities and the index of luxuries jumped between 1680–99 and 1760–75 in both urban and rural regions. Overall, the urban–rural gap in consumption patterns of household goods narrowed significantly between 1680 and 1775. At the same time, how-ever, rural people, who continued to engage in a wider range of agricul-tural and craft activities than individual city dwellers did, owned a wider range of tools and equipment throughout the period studied.

Although most people who participated in the market were primarily buying basic household goods and tools and equipment necessary for their work, contemporaries who were concerned about increased con-sumerism focused their criticism on the increased consumption of lux-uries. Interestingly, those critics were more concerned with the presence of a few luxury goods in modest homes than they were about the more significant detrimental impact of the expansion of the market: the increased polarization of wealth and more notable presence of a poor class. Even as early as the 1730s, the top third of taxpayers in New York City owned three-quarters of the taxable wealth. At that time the top third of taxpayers in rural Dutchess County owned two-thirds of the taxable wealth, and within two decades they owned three-quarters of the wealth. The polarization of wealth was not just an urban phenomenon; there was a significant polarization even in rural areas of colonial New York.

The eighteenth-century surge in consumer demand for goods and tools occurred at a time when there was also increased demand for land as families grew.[38] Yet the ability to pay for those goods, tools, and land did not always keep pace with desire. The next chapter describes how urban and rural New Yorkers increasingly borrowed money to pay for their purchases. As will be seen, with regard to debt as with regard to consumer purchases, the eighteenth century witnessed a substantial convergence of urban and rural patterns.

CHAPTER 2

The Rise of Debt

Early in the colonial period, New Yorkers, especially rural New Yorkers, exchanged commodities for consumer goods and tools. As the eighteenth century progressed, they became increasingly likely to pay for their purchases using cash, the medium that allowed for the easiest exchanges, or, alternatively, using financial instruments. Most significantly, New Yorkers increasingly relied on credit to finance their purchases of goods, tools, and land. Despite the importance of private credit in the economy of the northern colonies, however, scholars have written little about it.

McCusker and Menard's 1985 review of the status of scholarship on colonial American economic history noted how little is known about private finance in that period. Since then, Edwin Perkins has published his excellent study of public finance and financial services in early America. In addition, some aspects of private rural credit have been touched on by Richard L. Bushman, John L. Brooke, and Mary M. Schweitzer, though there is as yet no full study of the subject. Thomas M. Doerflinger and Julian Gwyn have written about business credit, Wilbur C. Plummer has examined consumer credit in Philadelphia, Bruce H. Mann has studied the legal side of book debt in colonial Connecticut, Peter Coleman has surveyed colonial statutes relating to debt, and Alice Hanson Jones and Jackson Turner Main have analyzed financial assets in probate inventories, but none of those books and articles focuses on the extent of debt, the forms of debt, or the nature of debt collection before the American Revolution.[1] Although the following analysis of those subjects focuses on New York, it is likely that the other northern colonies experienced similar patterns.

This chapter begins with a short description of the increased use of cash and financial instruments and then addresses the existing gap in scholarship by examining the rise of rural and urban debt and attitudes toward debt and debt collection in colonial New York. The use of cash as a form of payment increased, and the use of agricultural goods and labor correspondingly decreased, in both urban and rural areas over the course of the eighteenth century; the use of cash continued, though, to be more common within the city than in agricultural counties. In other ways, however, the city and the countryside became more alike: although at the end of the seventeenth century urban and rural areas differed in the extent to which they extended loans and incurred debts backed by written instruments, by the end of the colonial period urban and rural patterns had converged significantly.

Increased Use of Cash and Financial Instruments

New Yorkers'—especially rural New Yorkers'—use of such commodities as wheat, pork, and beef as mediums of exchange in the seventeenth and early eighteenth centuries is evident in Dutchess County court pleadings claiming noncash payments owed for rent or for goods sold. In the 1720s, for example, widow Catherina Brett claimed that Jacob Musir owed her 32 schepels of good merchantable winter wheat for the rent of a farm where he lived.[2] While the use of alternative forms of payment was common in the colonial period, however, the use of cash and equivalents of cash increased in urban and rural New York as the Revolution approached. A comparison of five account books illustrates the increased use of cash at the local level, particularly in urban areas (see figs. 2.1–2.6). Three of the account books are from Dutchess County, those of storekeeper Francis Filkin (1734–46), miller Hendrick Denker, and storekeeper Hendrick Schenk (1764–84). One of the account books is from Suffolk County, that of blacksmith Henry Smith (1750–92). The fifth book is that of New York City merchant (shoeseller) Charles Nicoll (1759–65).[3] The graphs below show the distribution of forms of payment used by a rough sampling of customers of each of the five.[4] All percentages are of the total value of credits applied to those customers' accounts. The earliest account book (Filkin's) shows the lowest percentage of credits in cash (5%) and the highest use of agricultural goods (33%) and labor (48%) as forms of payment. Rural account books from later periods show a rise in the use of cash and a corresponding decline in the use of wheat, rye, flour, eggs, butter, livestock, meat, and other agricultural goods. For example, storekeeper Hendrick Schenk received 39% of his payments in

cash, 18% in agricultural goods, and 18% in work.[5] The storekeepers and
the blacksmith, whose customers came from a broad range of rural people, were less likely to receive cash for their goods and services than was
the miller, who was more likely to grind large amounts of grain for
wealthier, more cash-oriented, clients. The account book showing the
highest percentage of cash credits belonged to the New York City merchant Charles Nicoll, who only rarely received agricultural goods or
work in exchange for the shoes he sold; instead, he received 80% of his
payments in cash, 11% in leather and skins (shown as "agricultural goods"
in the pie graph below), and 9% in sundries (i.e., imported or manufactured goods).[6]

Although payment in cash became more popular in the eighteenth
century, the government provided an alternative medium of exchange for
people when it raised money for governmental expenses (especially military ventures) by issuing bills of credit. Because the bills of credit were
made legal tender, they could serve as a form of money, passing from hand
to hand in payment of private commercial transactions, as long as they were
outstanding.[7] The first paper money (£13,000 worth) was issued in 1709,
followed by additional issuances in 1711 (£10,000), 1714 (£27,680),
1715 (£6,000), 1717 (£16,607), 1723 (£2,140), 1724 (£6,630), 1734
(£12,000), 1737 (£48,350), and 1746–47 (£81,000).[8] By the end of
1747, out of a total of £225,425 in bills of credit issued since 1709,
£189,601 were still in circulation.[9] During the French and Indian War,
New York issued another £535,000 in paper money.[10] The bills of credit
issued by the government significantly increased the amount of "money"
in circulation in colonial New York.

Individual commercial people also used private financial instruments,
such as bills of exchange and promissory notes, as mediums of exchange.
A promissory note is a promise by A to pay B a certain sum of money; a
bill of exchange is a written order from A to B, directing B to pay C a
certain sum of money. Both instruments could be transferred to other
parties, functioning like money. The private bills and notes of individual
merchants circulated in the domestic economy of America. Such negotiability of financial instruments reflects the high level of commercial
development in colonial New York.

The Duke's Laws of 1665 permitted assignment of written instruments
that were formally executed, with witnesses and a seal. A statute of 1684
extended the provision to allow the assignment not only of debts due on
bonds but also of any "note in writting." Herbert Johnson believes that
because the economy of 1684 did not require assignment of notes, the law
of that year was not taken advantage of and was forgotten about, but when

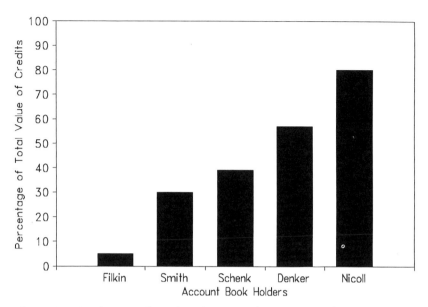

Figure 2.1 Credits in Cash, Colonial New York Account Books

Sources: Francis Filkin, *Account Book of a Country Store Keeper in the 18th Century at Poughkeepsie* (1734–46); Hendrick Schenk Account Book, Ledger B, 1764–84, New York Public Library, Rare Books and Manuscripts Room, New York; Hendrick Denker Account Book, 1750–65, New-York Historical Society; Henry Smith Ledger, 1750–92, New-York Historical Society; and Charles Nicoll Ledger, 1759–65, New-York Historical Society.

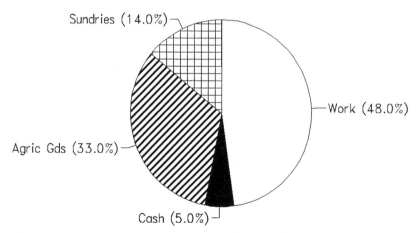

Figure 2.2 Forms of Payment to Francis Filkin, Storekeeper, Dutchess, 1730s

Source: Francis Filkin, *Account Book of a Country Store Keeper in the 18th Century at Poughkeepsie* (1734–1746).

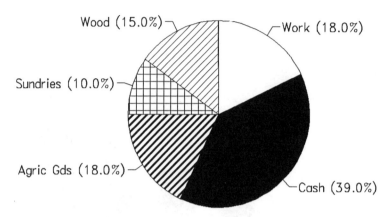

Figure 2.3 Forms of Payment to Hendrick Schenk, Storekeeper, Dutchess, 1760s

Source: Hendrick Schenk Account Book, Ledger B, 1764–84.

the English Promissory Note Act of 1704 formally made promissory notes assignable under English law, the New York economy had grown sufficiently to take advantage of its provisions. Morton Horwitz, though, maintains that the English statute did not automatically apply in America and expresses the view that probably neither a New York law of 1767 (vetoed by the Crown) nor one of 1773 made notes negotiable. He acknowledges, however, that, whatever the official law was, in practice promissory notes were frequently assigned in eighteenth-century New York.[11]

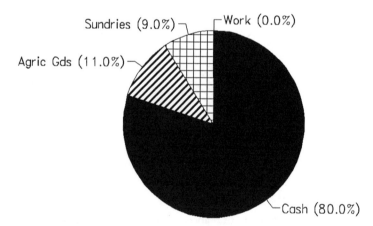

Figure 2.4 Forms of Payment to Charles Nicoll, Merchant, New York, 1760s

Source: Charles Nicoll Ledger, 1759–65.

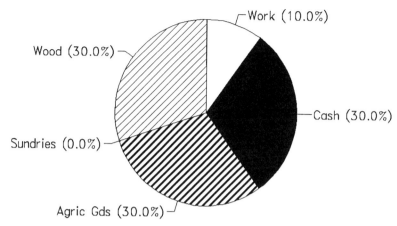

Figure 2.5 Forms of Payment to Henry Smith, Blacksmith, Suffolk, 1750s

Source: Henry Smith Ledger, 1750–92.

The transferability of notes to third parties in practice is indicated, for example, by an advertisement placed in a New York newspaper by Moses Levy, who had lost his pocketbook containing several promissory notes. The ad stated that the finder could not gain from keeping the notes since Levy had already given notice to stop payment—suggesting that in the absence of such notice the notes might have been honored and payment made to a stranger. Levy offered a reward for the return of the pocketbook and notes, with "no questions asked."[12] Other evidence comes from a lawsuit by an assignee of a promissory note against the original drawer of

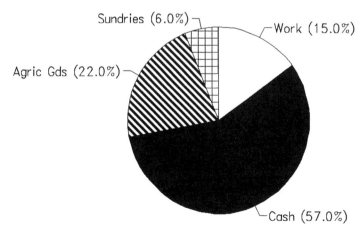

Figure 2.6 Forms of Payment to Hendrick Denker, Miller, Dutchess, 1750s

Source: Hendrick Denker Account Book, 1750–65.

the note for payment in the late 1730s. In the note, William Richardson
had promised to pay "William Cosby or order" the sum of £8 on demand. The fact that the original promissory note was payable to Cosby *or
order* indicates that at this time IOUs were *expected* to serve as a circulating
medium. Cosby endorsed the note, ordering the £8 to be paid to James
Mills instead. When Richardson failed to pay the amount owed, Mills
brought his lawsuit.[13] In a later period, a letter from Francis Baird to William Alexander complained that Alexander had not paid off a "note"—it
may actually have been a bill of exchange—that Baird had used to pay a
debt owed to James Abeel. Baird wrote, "I hope your Lordship will
endeavour to answer that demand immediately for it is impossible for me
to get Money any other way to discharge it. Besides am afraid shall not be
able to pass your Other Notes to my Creditors by reason of your back-
wardness in discharging the former and then what shall I do."[14] The
assignability of bills of exchange is further evident from the numerous
references in merchants' and lawyers' letterbooks to the use of such bills to
pay debts owed to English merchants.[15]

The Rise of Debt

Although at times currency was supplemented by the trading of commodities, bills of credit, or circulating bills of exchange or private notes, as
the economy expanded New Yorkers also did much of their business on
credit.[16] Credit relationships could be informal. Often, though, they were
formalized in written agreements, not just based on oral promises or book
debt. In the eighteenth century, such documents appeared increasingly in
probate inventories and court records. The most formal method for for-
malizing debts was the bond, though some lenders had their borrowers
sign less formal promissory notes. In Dutchess County court cases from
the 1750s for which we have court documents, for example, almost half
were based on a bond, one-fifth were based on a written note, and about
one-third were based on oral statements such as promises to pay for
"goods, wares, or merchandise" purchased.[17]

Bonds and notes were attractive for commercial people because the
obligations of the parties were easily proved if a misunderstanding should
arise. Conditional penal bonds, which doubled the amount owed in the
event of failure to pay, were used not only to ensure payment of debts but
also to ensure the performance of other acts by the promisor. A bail bond
is an example: the accused signed a bond obligating him to forfeit a
substantial amount of money if he did not appear for the trial. When a

creditor went into court to collect money owed on a bond, the debtor could argue in defense only that the document had been altered, that the signature was not his own, or that he had performed the conditions required by the terms of the bond; the terms of any agreement underlying the bond were often irrelevant to the case. If the debtor in a bail bond failed to appear in court for trial, the underlying merits of the original charges against him would not matter; he would still owe on the bond if he did not appear as required. Because bonds and promissory notes provided better support for money owed, therefore, New York creditors often used them to back up their loans.

As Edwin Perkins has pointed out, since there were no banks, the colonial credit system was highly decentralized and atomized.[18] In New York, however, the system was also very extensive. Virginia Harrington has estimated that perhaps one-half to three-quarters of a typical New York merchant's business was conducted on credit, and if the merchant engaged primarily in overseas trading, then essentially all his business would be based on credit.[19] For merchants, financing purchases helped increase sales. As Perkins has pointed out, "Suppliers of inventories routinely offered financial services in conjunction with their merchandising functions since granting lenient credit terms was a critical factor in promoting sales." Competition among merchants forced them to offer their customers better terms—including the opportunity to buy on credit—in order to attract more customers. The increased availability of paper currency discussed above, which eased the periodic inadequate supply of specie, presumably reassured merchants selling on credit that they had an improved chance of being repaid. Credit was an essential sales device for shopkeepers too; it was practically impossible for them to sell goods to retail customers without extending credit to most buyers.[20] Craftsmen also usually purchased their equipment and raw materials and sold their products on a credit basis.[21] The expansion of credit is itself therefore clear evidence of more active markets for goods and services. The urban chain of credit extended from London merchants to New York City merchants to craftsmen to consumers.

Outside the city, the chain of credit extended to country shopkeepers and farmers, who also relied on credit arrangements to facilitate sales. In many cases farmers' debts arose from the purchase of consumer goods and tools. The extent of the debts owed by farmers to rural shopkeepers is indicated by a letter to the *New-York Weekly Journal* in 1739. The anonymous letter writer proposed that no country storekeeper be permitted to serve as a judge, clerk, or register in the courts, or in any of a number of other official positions, because of the power they held over their customers, local farmers "who for the most Part are their Debtors, and must as Jury's determine all Causes, and on Elections Vote as the mighty Man will."[22] It should not be assumed that those farmers were merely buying luxury consumer goods; many were borrowing money to buy livestock and equipment necessary to establish or expand their farms. Lewis Dubois is an example. In October 1753, Teunis VanBunschoten and Court VanVoorhees sued Dubois to collect £166 9s. 3d. owed for cows, sheep, horses, farmers' implements and utensils, slaves, and other (unspecified) items.[23]

But farmers went into debt for other reasons as well. St. John de Crèvecoeur, who noted the high rural debt level, attributed it to two factors: not only the many tempting English goods sold in country stores but also the costs of clearing (or draining) land and setting up farms.[24] Common purposes for which farmers borrowed money were also listed by the author of a 1737 newspaper essay on the subject of paper money and usury. He described the impact of high interest rates on "an industrious honest Farmer" who had borrowed money "for the Reasons of Mis-Crops, the building a comfortable House, or the buying a Piece of Land to enlarge his Farm, which is often the Case."[25] That is, many farmers incurred debt to pay for land, which was becoming increasingly expensive after 1745.[26] In order to obtain farms not only for themselves but also for their sons, rural men often had to go into debt.

As the economy expanded in the first half of the eighteenth century, both the total amount of outstanding credit in New York and the proportion of the male population involved in formal credit-debt relationships increased in both urban and rural areas. Contemporaries commented on the rise of debt. For example, in 1734, "John Farmer" of Long Island observed in the *New-York Weekly Journal* that New Yorkers' debts had "swell'd . . . to a prodigious Bulk and Size."[27] In 1754 another writer, to the *New-York Mercury,* lamented New Yorkers' "continuing to import such large Quantities of European Goods, from England and Holland, which drains us not only of all our Specie, but evidently involves us more in Debt, and if so obstinately persisted in, will be the utter Ruin of a City, which hitherto has (through the Providence of God) supported in Credit much beyond any in North-America."[28] St. John de Crèvecoeur later observed of rural New York that "[t]he number of debts which one part of the country owes to the other would greatly astonish you."[29]

The widespread nature and increasing amount of debt are evident from references to debt and credit in wills and probate records. Men from the whole range of occupations and geographic residences provided in their wills that before any distributions were to be made to their beneficiaries,

Table 2.1
Debts Owed to Rural and Urban Decedents, 1680–1775

	% of Inventories Showing Debts Owed to Decedent		Ratio: Credit Extended / Personal Wealth	
	Rural	Urban	Rural	Urban
1680–99	10	36	.02	1.09
1700–19	32	44	.13	.68
1720–39	59	65	.50	1.26
1740–59	54	71	.70	.80
1760–75	60	62	1.53	1.16

Source: New York Probate Inventories.

their debts must be paid off.[30] Inventories of estates include among decedents' assets lists of the debts owed to them in the form of bonds, notes, or book debts (though they usually did not list debts owed by the decedent). Analysis of 600 probate records from colonial New York shows that between 1680 and 1775 an increasing percentage of people died as creditors.[31] Twenty-six percent of estates inventoried between 1680 and 1699 included debts owed to the estate (i.e., credit extended by the decedent). The percentage increased to 40% between 1700 and 1719; 59% between 1720 and 1739; 56% between 1740 and 1759; and 58% between 1760 and 1775.[32] The proportion of people's estates held as financial assets, especially loans, increased over this time span. Among the inventories studied, the ratio of total known credit extended to total other personal wealth increased from .46 between 1680 and 1699 to .71, .56, and .68 during the three succeeding twenty-year periods and then increased to 1.42 between 1760 and 1775.[33]

As shown in table 2.1, the percentage of rural decedents holding any credit instruments was substantially (26 percentage points) below that for urban decedents at the beginning of the period, the gap decreased in the middle period from 1700 to 1760 (to between 7 and 17 percentage points), and by the final period approximately equal percentages of urban and rural decedents held credit instruments. Even though rural dwellers were likely to hold a larger portion of their total wealth in real property than urban dwellers were, the ratio between known credit extended and other personal wealth (excluding credit extended) for rural decedents lagged significantly behind that of urban decedents in all periods up to 1740.

The average total value of credits held by a New York decedent by the end of the colonial period was £305. To the extent that the decedents studied reflected the colonial population, the average debt per family would also have been approximately £305. In practice, decedents not inventoried were probably poorer than those who were inventoried, so the average amount of credit extended per family throughout the colonial New York population—as well as the average amount of debt owed per family—would have been somewhat lower than £305, though how much lower is difficult to estimate.[34]

Large loans were often secured by land, especially in rural areas. The government itself extended credit through its loan offices. No loan office records for Dutchess County survive from the colonial period, but Jean Peyer studied the Queens County Loan Office records. She found that from 1756 to 1760 that office gave out 23 loans ranging from £25 to £100 at 5% interest. Most borrowers were yeoman farmers, and their land provided the security for the loans.[35]

More significant sources of large loans were New York's private mortgage lenders. Mortgage books are available for two of the seven precincts of Dutchess County: Crum Elbow Precinct and Rombout Precinct. (See the map of Dutchess County.) Analysis of those records shows patterns of mortgage lending between 1754 and 1770, when there were 231 mortgages recorded for Crum Elbow Precinct and 88 in Rombout Precinct.[36] The average amount secured by the mortgages in Crum Elbow was £290 and in Rombout the average was £321. Loans were secured by an average of 194 acres in Crum Elbow and 164 acres in Rombout. The mortgage records do not state what the money was being borrowed for. Most likely it was being used to purchase or improve land.[37]

Seventy-eight percent of Crum Elbow borrowers and 59% of Rombout borrowers were farmers, and 13% and 36%, respectively, were craftsmen (most of whom also worked as farmers). Although probate inventories show debts owed to farmers, the mortgage records show few farmer mortgagees. Farmers were only 8% and 19% of lenders, respectively, in the two precincts, and craftsmen were 3% and 12% of lenders. While merchants made up only 4% of borrowers in Crum Elbow and 0% in Rombout, however, they were 50% and 37%, respectively, of lenders in the two precincts.

Although none of the mortgagors (the borrowers) was a widow, widows did a significant amount of mortgage-based lending in Dutchess County. Widows acting on their own (not counting those acting with male coexecutors) constituted 16% of mortgagees in Crum Elbow Precinct and about 9% in Rombout Precinct between 1754 and 1770; their loans averaged £222 in value. Of the 37 loans made by widows in the two

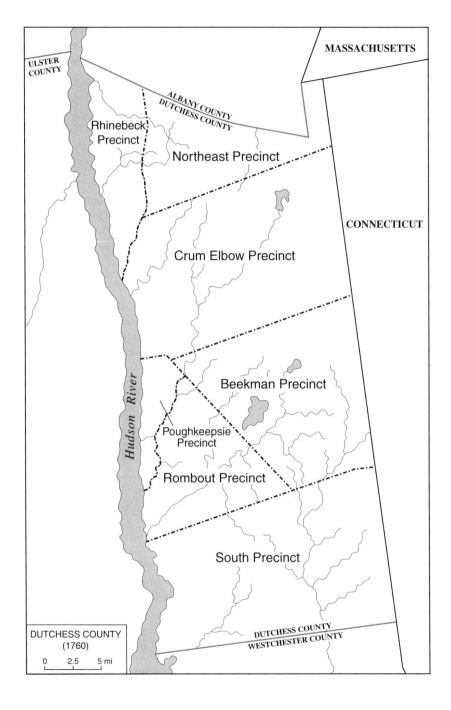

ULSTER
COUNTY

MASSACHUSETTS

ALBANY COUNTY
DUTCHESS COUNTY

Rhinebeck
Precinct

Northeast Precinct

CONNECTICUT

Crum Elbow Precinct

Hudson River

Beekman Precinct

Poughkeepsie
Precinct

Rombout Precinct

South Precinct

DUTCHESS COUNTY
(1760)

0   2.5   5 mi

DUTCHESS COUNTY
WESTCHESTER COUNTY

precincts, 29 were made by widows of New York City merchants or lawyers. The biggest lender, in terms of the total value of mortgage loans extended, was Ann Chambers, widow of New York City attorney John Chambers; she lent out a total of £1,631 covered by 7 mortgages in Crum Elbow Precinct. Mary Walton and Mary Walton, Jr., together or individually, made a total of 11 loans adding up to £1,548 and secured by mortgages on 1,068 acres of land in Crum Elbow. Helena McPhaedris extended 6 loans totaling £1,282 and secured by mortgages on 1,969 acres in Crum Elbow. All three of these women may have lent additional funds in other Dutchess County precincts; the mortgage records are not available to find out for sure. New York City women who each made one loan in Crum Elbow or Rombout Precinct include Ann Elizabeth Schuyler (whose loan of £1,000 was covered by a mortgage on 438 acres in Crum Elbow), Jane Knox (£100 on 75 acres in Crum Elbow), Mary Willson (£360 on 60 acres in Rombout), Magdalena Cook (£202 on 238 acres in Rombout), and Ann Waddell (£225 on 200 acres in Rombout).

The most notable widow from a rural county who lent money in Crum Elbow or Rombout Precinct was Mary Elmendorph, widow of Petrus Edmundus Elmendorph, of Kingston in Ulster County, who made 5 loans in Rombout totaling £1,297 between 1761 and 1770; the mortgage documents referred to Mary Elmendorph as a "merchant." Sarah Morris, widow of attorney and political leader Lewis Morris of Morrisania, lent £300 on 95 acres in Crum Elbow. The two other female rural lenders, each of whom made one loan in the period before 1770, were both from Dutchess County: Catharyna Brett (£208 on 204 acres in Rombout) and Eve Traver (£50 on 117 acres in Crum Elbow).[38] Thus widows provided a significant amount of capital to Dutchess County farmers.

Widows lent money to urban borrowers as well. Sarah Arnold is an example of a widow who both carried forward her deceased husband's debts and lent additional money on her own. When her husband, Henry, died in 1764, he left her a number of bonds. When she died four years later, her inventory listed 19 such bonds still outstanding. In addition, however, there were 7 new bonds representing money lent by Sarah Arnold after her husband's death. One of those loans was to two women, Margaret Ross and Margaret Parks, in the amount of £150. Altogether, Sarah Arnold lent £677 between 1765 and 1768, and she carried forward £2,600 of her husband's bonds—with interest.[39] Another example of a wealthy widow lending money was William Livingston's mother, who lent money at interest to such merchants as Isaac Willet—and William made sure the interest was in fact paid by threatening to force full payment on the bonds otherwise.[40] As is discussed in chapter 5, the vast majority of widows were not in any position to lend out large sums of money. But those who inherited large amounts of cash from their husbands were able to invest that capital profitably. Wealthy colonial widows' loans in New York were consistent with the longer term pattern of preindustrial European and American societies. In his excellent synthesis of the historical literature on women and credit, William Chester Jordan describes how wealthy widows in medieval and early modern Europe invested inherited money in mortgages and municipal bonds. Cornelia Hughes Dayton and Lisa Wilson also found that widows were an important source of loans in early New Haven County and Philadelphia, respectively.[41]

Debt Collection

During the colonial period, the debtor-creditor relationship caused substantial stress and hardship for people who borrowed beyond their means or who suffered unexpected financial losses. As has already been remarked, some people condemned those who bought luxuries they could not afford. As discussed in this section, however, many others were sympathetic toward and tolerant of struggling debtors, and they urged forbearance in the face of nonpayment and pressed for bankruptcy legislation. Nevertheless, some debtors ended up languishing in jail when their creditors insisted on—and the courts delivered—strict enforcement of financial agreements despite the debtors' inability to pay. Consequently, some debtors came to fear their creditors, and their debts became a source of substantial anxiety.

Late in the colonial period, for example, the family of widow Mary Cooper participated in the market economy on Long Island. Although they raised a variety of crops (wheat, corn, potatoes, pumpkins, and hay) and livestock (sheep, hogs, horses, ducks, turkeys, and bees), they also habitually purchased such items as sugar, molasses, tea, salt, indigo, cotton, linen, flannel, thread, wool cards, scissors, and nails from shopkeepers and engaged the services of carpenters, shoemakers, dressmakers, masons, coopers, and other craftsmen. In her diary, Cooper expressed her anxiety about the debts her husband had incurred in return for those purchases. "A fine clear morning with a cold north wind," her entry began one day late in August. "My hearte is burnt with anger and discontent, want of every nessesary thing in life and in constant feare of gapeing creditors consums my streth and wasts my days. The horrer of these things with the continuel cross of my famaly, like to so many horse leeches, prays upon my vitals, and if the Lord does not prevent will bring me to the house appointed for all liveing."

Earlier in the month she had commented, "I feele much distrest, fearing I shall here from some of my credtors." Two years later, she was still worried about money. "Justice Townend is here, writen adertisemants to make a vandue. O Lord, support this famaly in this sene of darkness. O thou didst multiply the widdo's oyl that she might pay her debts, have mercy on us and help us and let not our eys fail O Lord, while we are waiteing on thee for helpe." There is no later mention in Mary Cooper's diary of a vendue (an auction) taking place, though entries two months later suggest that she gave additional security for the debts: "Mr Smi[th] sent word that he will take the security," she wrote one day. Then two weeks later she added, "About 8 or nine a'clock this morning Tom Smith come here and brought a morgage deed and relees, which he with an unhearde of impudence required me to sign all [   ]. I complied with [   ]."[42]

Cooper's reference to God's multiplying the widow's oil was based on the biblical story of the woman who went to the prophet Elisha to find a way to avoid selling her sons into bondage to pay her debts. Elisha told her to borrow vessels and fill them with oil. Miraculously, the little oil that she had filled all the vessels, and she was able to sell the oil to pay her debt.[43] This story was repeated in sermons by ministers in the colonial period to ease people's anguish about their poverty and their debts. For example, in 1715 Boston minister Samuel Moodey published "The Debtors Monitor Directory & Comforter: Or The Way to get & keep out of Debt, In Three Sermons." There were a number of lessons to be drawn from the story of the oil, he said. The first lesson was that it was a "sad and lamentable thing to be deeply in Debt," so one should try to avoid debt by shunning bad company and idleness, living a frugal life, and not spending in advance of anticipated gains. Nevertheless, he noted, even good pious people sometimes ended up in debt, as victims of unanticipated calamities or imprudent management of their finances. In any case, though, all debts did have to be repaid. God can help people out of debt even if they owe more than they are worth, but debtors have to follow God's direction in helping themselves. He said, "If we [thus] believe and trust in God, He will enable us to Answer, both the Demands of our Creditors, and the Necessities of our Families: We shall have wherewith to Live Honestly, and Comfortably." Finally, he admonished creditors that they should act compassionately toward their debtors, and he reminded everyone that they should feel pity and charity toward debtors and try to help them.[44]

A later eighteenth-century pamphlet, entitled "Debtor and Creditor: or A Discourse On the following Words, Have Patience with me, and I will pay thee all," stated that trade depended upon repayment of debts, and creditors were absolutely entitled to punctual repayment, but that creditors should nevertheless be patient with honest, prudent debtors when they had to delay payment because of unforeseen accidents.[45] Even a popular merchants' guide (published in London but read by colonial merchants) advised forbearance. "If it happens, that Debtors omit paying what they owe at the Times agreed on, the Creditors should not oppress them with an extravagant Interest." In the end, the author wrote, making it tougher on debtors could just push them to financial failure. Such failure might result in the creditor never collecting the debt, and, besides, the creditor would be left feeling guilty for helping to cause his debtor's misfortune.[46] A letter to the *New-York Weekly Journal* in 1734 repeated the advice (supposedly) given by a man on Long Island to his son in the city: "Fear not to ask any Man for that which rightly belongs to you: If he is able and unwilling, then, and not till then, make use of the Law to Compell him. If willing, but unable, forbear, lest you suffer not only in your Purse but also in your Character."[47] Thus the attitude of the rural man (who must have been born before 1700, to have an adult son by 1734) was to refrain from going to court unless a debtor willfully refused to pay money owed.

Many creditors did show forbearance, though not always out of compassion and sympathy. Rigidity in insisting on punctual repayment of debts and exact performance of obligations could result in the end of a profitable trading relationship. So merchants exhibited some degree of flexibility and toleration within their own community. For example, in 1751 Schenectady merchant John Sanders was extremely dissatisfied with the performance of business partners Samuel Stork and Alexander Champion, his English source for manufactured goods. He wrote to the two partners, listing all the things wrong with the most recent shipment: they sent nails that were too large and too sharp instead of the small, flat-point nails he had requested, they sent men's gloves that were too small for any of his adult male customers rather than the women's gloves he had asked for, they sent him the wrong kind of cloth, and they sent additional items that he had not requested. But rather than terminating the trading relationship or taking them to court, he firmly asked them to "Ratifie" the situation: "Wherefore must Desire you," he wrote, "that you ordr Better Care may be Taken as has now been done & that you Send me what I wrote for in the memorandums & Not fine Chints for Blew Calico & 20d Nales for 24d Nales, As has been done now And then you will Verry much oblidge me." Later letters to the same London merchants indicate that Sanders's trading relationship with them did continue.[48] Sanders complained to another London merchant, James Bonbonous, that Bonbonous had overcharged him for some scythes. He had to press his claim several times over several years, but he continued to order more goods from Bonbonous during that period.[49] Sanders made repeated requests to John Wendell that Wendell pay £356 owed to the estate of Sanders's deceased brother. Robert Sanders died in May 1765, yet John Sanders (as executor of the estate) was still requesting payment in 1768. His letters explain that he had "Orgent Occasion for the money" because it was needed to support his brother's five "fatherless and motherless Children," yet he apparently did not sue for the money.[50] Sanders complained to other trading partners that they sent him the wrong item, sent him unmerchantable goods, or overcharged him. He firmly demanded rectification but continued his trading relationships with those merchants.[51]

It may very well have been easier for creditors to be lenient with debtors from within their own community—where relationships were somewhat more personalized and supported by reputation—than with debtors from outside their community. Among creditors and debtors in Dutchess County, late payments were routinely tolerated. Creditors made extensive informal efforts to collect money before commencing legal action, delaying lawsuits for an average of one and a half to two years after the bond or note came due.[52] Merchants constituted a community based on occupation, and certainly we see evidence that merchants tolerated less-than-perfect performance from each other in order to allow trading relationships to continue.

When there was less potential for regular and continuing commercial relationships, however, there was less reason to tolerate late payment. Sometimes widows of merchants experienced the sudden cooling of trade relationships after their husbands died. The fact that trading partners presumably anticipated no continuing business relationship with the widow may explain their lower tolerance for late payment of the deceased man's debt than they probably would have shown to him during his lifetime. For example, in 1755 New York attorney William Livingston wrote to Elizabeth Beaven reminding her that "Mr Van Zandt" had given her time to pay her deceased husband's debt to Van Zandt, but that Van Zandt now wanted to sue her for the money. Livingston once again asked her to pay up speedily so that he would not have to bring an action against her.[53] Because creditors often demanded payment of overdue debts only when the debtor died, in practice the real burden of household debt often fell on widows, many of whom had difficulty paying their deceased husbands' debts.[54] While the original debtor was alive, though, creditors often tolerated delays in repayment in order to maintain a profitable trading relationship.

Creditors often made public demands for payment of debts due before they commenced any legal action. Those requests usually appeared in the newspaper. For example, upon the death of a creditor, the executor typically placed an announcement in the newspaper requesting all debtors of the estate to pay their debts as soon as possible. Some ads left implicit the threat of a lawsuit for nonpayment, saying that debts should be paid soon to "prevent further Trouble and Charge." Other ads, such as that posted in the *New-York Mercury* by Petrus Rutgers's executor in 1754, were more direct: if debtors did not pay, "they may expect to be prosecuted by a due course of law, without further Notice," the executor declared. Jeremiah Lattouch and Frind Lucas were similarly explicit when they called for people to pay their debts to the recently terminated Lattouch-Lucas partnership: those who did not pay the debts would be sued without any further notice.[55]

People placed newspaper advertisements not only for repayment upon the death or departure of the creditor. Such ads were also posted in more ordinary, nontransitional situations. For example, in 1749 a shoemaker placed an advertisement in the newspaper addressed to "the Person who calls himself a Gentleman of the City of New York." The gentleman had placed an order for a specially designed pair of shoes (one larger than the other) but had never come to pick them up and pay for them. The shoemaker asked the unnamed gentleman to pay for the shoes. Since neither the shoemaker nor the gentleman's name is stated, one cannot check the court minute books to determine whether this request was followed by a lawsuit, although the notice's last line implicitly threatens the gentleman by begging him to pick up the shoes and pay for them "lest I expose him more publickly." Another creditor, Frederick Becker, also placed a newspaper advertisement to request repayment of debts before resorting to the courts. He explained that he needed to collect debts owed to him because he himself was being pressed by his own creditors for repayment of debts he owed them. Any of his debtors who did not pay up by a named date, he concluded his notice, "may expect to meet with what Trouble the Law shall direct in Cases of this Kind." John Zenger published requests that subscribers pay their arrearages for the newspaper. If they did not pay up speedily, he stated, he "shall leave off sending; and seek my Money another way," that is, presumably, pursue legal action.[56]

Imprisonment for Debt

Even though some lenders did show forbearance, diarist Mary Cooper's anxiety about her family's own creditors was natural, particularly considering that debtors could end up in prison. It was the usual practice to jail defendants in civil actions until they put up bail. Anyone who was sued for a debt and was unable to provide bail or satisfy the plaintiff's claims might remain in jail until the case was resolved or the debt paid. Scholars of the nineteenth century assume that pretrial imprisonment was fictitious,[57] but in colonial New York it was genuinely the practice. Imprisonment was intended not only to ensure defendants' appearances in court but also to pressure defendants into paying their debts as quickly as possible before any form of adjudication.

If a court entered judgment against a defendant who could not pay the sums owed, he or she could be arrested again and imprisoned until the debt was paid. Significant numbers of imprisoned debtors early in the eighteenth century are suggested by the New York City Common Council's ordering the building of a prison for debtors on the top floor of the new City Hall in 1704.[58] Those who could not put up bail or pay debts might be imprisoned for quite some time. Records refer to a number of such debtors, including merchants Isaac Lattouch and Henry Lane (who, it is suggested by attorney William Livingston's letters, were imprisoned for over fourteen months in 1754 and did not "stand any Chance of being delivered from their Confinement save only by breaking Jail"), Francis Goelet (who, Livingston said, "has Mortgaged his Interest in the Snuff works long before he broke, and he is now worth nothing"), John Coe (who petitioned for his release from jail after being imprisoned for sixteen months in 1691 and 1692 pursuant to a judgment against him that had been reversed by the New York Assembly), David Provoost (who at the time of his 1711 petition had been in jail for fourteen months because he was unable to pay a judgment of £4,000 owed to Abraham DePeyster), William Trusdell (who was detained for nine weeks in 1734 after being arrested for nonpayment of a debt), printer John Peter Zenger (who spent over eight months in jail awaiting trial), Hendrick Oudenarde (who spent twenty months in jail for nonpayment of a debt in 1766), Joseph Gale (who claimed in 1756 that he had already spent at least four years in an Ulster County jail because he was unable to pay his debts), widow Sarah McCulleum (who claimed in 1765 that she had been a prisoner in jail for more than four years on a debt case), and Elizabeth Sydenham (who spent eight months in jail after being arrested when she tried to take possession of "her" farm, which her estranged husband had leased to another man).[59]

Although few of the imprisoned debtors were women, many of the men who were imprisoned left behind wives and children. It must have been difficult for wives to support themselves and their families during the long imprisonments of income-producing members of the family. As Oudenarde pointed out in "Seven Letters to the Honourable Daniel Horsmanden, Esq; Concerning the unnecessary and cruel Imprisonment of Hendrick Oudenarde, Late Merchant in the City of New-York," which he published in an attempt to gain public support to pressure Horsmanden to allow his release, as long as he sat in jail he was unable to pay his debt because he could not carry on his business and he was hindered in his own debt collection because "debtors think less of their creditors whilst they are in confinement."

There was considerable sentiment in colonial America against imprisonment for debt, especially for honest people who were innocent victims of circumstance. A 1754 pamphlet expressed the opinion that it is wrong "to judge a Man's Principles or Conduct, to be Good or Bad, meerly from his Success and Prosperity, or his Misfortunes and Adversity." Yet, the author pointed out, that is exactly what one is doing when one imprisons insolvent debtors. Nonpayment of a debt is not always the fault of the debtor; anyone might risk money and then lose it through misfortune. Why call someone a rogue or a villain, the writer asked, if he was just unlucky? He noted that "in some special Cases, a Man may break his Promise and Contract, and yet be an honest Man." Such a man should be treated differently from someone who makes a promise with the intent of breaking it, or who makes a promise and makes little effort to perform it. As he put it, one should distinguish between the "Sons of Belial" and the "Sons of Misfortune," that is, one should treat the unfortunate honest man differently from the villain. Credit was essential to the economy, the writer pointed out:

> Trade, we know, is supported by Credit; and Credit is to Trade, what the Blood is to the Body: If Credit fails, Trade stagnates; if the Blood don't circulate, the Body dies. The Circulation in Trade is kept up, by Men's duly performing their Contracts, Agreements, and Promises: But when a Man in Trade breaks his Agreements, Contracts, and Promises, so that there can be no well grounded Dependence upon him, he is soon discovered, hunted down, undone, and perhaps cast into Prison: Punctuality is therefore the Life of Trade.

Fear of prison leads financially shaky tradesmen desperately to borrow money at usurious rates and to sell goods at 10 to 20% loss, which makes their financial situation even worse. If an honest debtor could be protected by a law of bankruptcy, he would not have to sink quite so low, which would result in his retaining more funds with which to repay creditors. The best solution for the society as a whole, the pamphleteer observed, was to provide a way for partial payment of debts where full payment was impossible. If a man did not have enough money to pay all his debts, the law should allow him to give his creditors each a fair proportion of their debts and then move on to engage in other business. Imprisoning a debtor only makes him less able to repay his creditors and leaves him useless to society and unable to support his wife and children. And having no provision for partial payment of debts means in practice that an unmerciful creditor will end up collecting the full debt while a more compassionate creditor might get nothing. A bankruptcy law, the pamphleteer concluded, would ensure that payments would be equal and fair.[60] In fact, in the seventeenth and eighteenth centuries the New York Assembly did pass legislation that made lengthy prison stays less likely; though not all such statutes were enacted primarily for that purpose, some were insolvency statutes that released debtors from prison and discharged their debts under certain narrow circumstances. Imprisonment for debt, however, was not entirely abolished in New York until 1831.[61]

As will be seen in the next chapter, the bottom line was that in eighteenth-century New York large numbers of lenders did demand payment of debts, even though lawsuits could force those debtors to suffer the severe consequences of lengthy imprisonment. Although a few voices called for creditors to treat their debtors gently, in practice thousands of debtors were taken to court—and many of those to prison as well—when they were unable to repay their debts. This fact more than any other indicates the extent of self-interested behavior in colonial New York. The mutually supportive and tolerant economic relationships normally attributed to a communal society do not lead to lawsuits. Only more distanced and impersonal business relationships typical of a market economy lead to debt litigation.

Conclusion

During the eighteenth century New Yorkers increased their load of debt in order to raise money to buy consumer goods, tools, livestock, equipment, and land. Although some of them paid for their purchases with cash, commodities, or financial instruments, most buyers relied on credit to finance their purchases, and lending of money was widespread. New

Yorkers borrowed money backed by bonds, by mortgages, or simply by entries in book accounts. By the mid-eighteenth century, over half of both urban and rural probate inventories included debts owed to the estate, and by the end of the colonial period both urban and rural inventories included a higher total value of financial instruments than of other personal property. Lenders included not only merchants and gentlemen but also craftsmen, farmers, and widows. Attitudes toward debtors were mixed, with some contemporaries criticizing those who purchased goods, especially luxuries, on credit and insisting on prompt repayment regardless of circumstances while others acknowledged the importance of credit in the economy and urged tolerance of financially strapped debtors.

In any case, credit-debt relationships were not self-enforcing. They required either complete trust and sharing of interests (as one finds within a family) or else an outside enforcer. The extension of credit relationships beyond the local community—which was a necessary prerequisite to the consumer revolution in eighteenth-century New York—was possible only because of the existence, and adaptation, of an effective outside enforcer: the legal system. As will be shown, creditors used the legal system to force repayment of thousands of debts. The resulting elevated litigation rate evidenced in the legal records indicates clearly that eighteenth-century debt relationships were arm's length business arrangements, not familial or communal in nature.

PART II

Exchange Relationships among Men: Law and Early Capitalism

CHAPTER 3

Changes in the Legal System

Law is always shaped to some extent by economic factors, and economic development is always affected by its legal context. Contrary to the implications of some legal historians, this was nothing new in the nineteenth century.[1] In fact, the American legal system underwent steady change in response to the demands of the economy well before the alleged modernization in the nineteenth century.

Legal adaptations of the eighteenth century have received little attention by historians, perhaps because the changes were more procedural than substantive, because debt cases, the dominant form of action in the eighteenth century, are considered less notable than personal injury actions, or simply because of an assumption that there was no early connection between commercial and legal elites. In fact, though, in New York at least, eighteenth-century law and legal practice adapted to and served the colonies' commercial needs in ways that are just as significant as the nineteenth-century developments that have received so much more attention. The consequence of the inherent differences between a commercial and an industrial elite plus the differences in their legal situations—the nineteenth-century elite's having little opportunity to predetermine the relevant law through contracts and their being more likely to be defendants rather than plaintiffs—was that the two elites placed different demands on the law and the legal system. In both centuries the law was shaped to serve the interests of the economy, but in different ways.

Law played an essential role in economic development in eighteenth-century New York. The formalization of the legal system in this period allowed for more predictable and rational enforcement of contracts in court. Legally enforceable contracts, including promises to deliver goods and services and promises to repay money borrowed, bolstered the credit-based market economy. Contracts made it possible to buy goods, tools, and land; contracts made borrowing money possible. This chapter describes the increased contractualization of economic relationships, increased legal support for competition, and increased formalization of the legal system in colonial New York.

The Communal Model of Legal Process

The Horwitz-Nelson portrayal of the colonial legal system parallels the view of communalist social and economic historians. Following that model, a precommercial society had to have an anticommercial legal system that promoted community unity, for example, a legal system that did not encourage economic competition or enforce contracts that failed to provide an equal or fair exchange. In the Horwitz-Nelson model, both competition and high-risk/high-profit speculative contracts were seen as embodying anticommunal values and therefore had to be avoided in the colonial period. The law and legal system worked to preserve neighborly relationships rather than encouraging or supporting distanced, contractualized, business relationships. According to their model, only in the nineteenth century were contracts interpreted according to the expressed wills of the parties, and only in the nineteenth century, marked in particular by the *Charles River Bridge* case of 1837, did the courts encourage free competition.[2]

Bruce Mann's excellent book on colonial Connecticut has vigorously challenged the Horwitz-Nelson model.[3] This study complements Mann's book by studying more closely the meaning of legal change for the economy and for economic relationships and opportunities. As will be seen, there are a number of legal similarities between New England and the Middle Colonies, though also some differences.

In New York, as in Connecticut, the court records show that in practice the legal system often deviated from the pattern described by Horwitz and Nelson. The earlier use of negotiable financial instruments than Horwitz claimed was already mentioned in chapter 2. As noted there, negotiability indicates a more highly commercialized colonial economy than the Horwitz-Nelson model portrays.[4] Three other examples in areas not emphasized by Mann relate to courts' support for free competition, strict interpretation of contractual terms, and support of a contractualized conception of colonial relationships.

First, legal historians have maintained that colonial courts consistently protected monopolies and freedom from competition. Horwitz, for example, asserted that law and the courts were anticompetitive until the second quarter of the nineteenth century.[5] Actually, however, at times eighteenth-century courts reinforced and promoted competition. The best example is the New York Supreme Court's action in response to a challenge to Albany's monopoly of the fur trade. In 1723 Johannis Myndertse was charged with violating a local ordinance against trading with the Indians in Schenectady. The Common Council of Albany had passed the ordinance to block outsiders' competition with fur merchants of that city. Myndertse, who was being held in jail pending payment of his fine, took the matter to the Supreme Court on a writ of habeas corpus and also brought an action for trespass and false imprisonment against the aldermen of Albany. In 1726 the Supreme Court of the province ruled in Myndertse's favor.[6] The case effectively destroyed Albany's monopoly of the fur trade and opened up the trade to free competition. Legal historians have always assumed that the *Charles River Bridge* case of 1837 was the major turning point in a shift toward judicial support for competition.[7] But *Myndertse v. Aldermen of Albany,* a judicial action overturning a legislatively created monopoly and promoting a kind of democratic capitalism, predated that famous case by more than a century.

Second, the Horwitz-Nelson model assumes that colonial courts did not enforce the strict terms of contracts; they maintain that courts were more concerned with assuring an objectively reasonable exchange than with enforcing the will of the parties as expressed in their contract. Yet cases from colonial New York relating to the sale of slaves suggest that courts would enforce the agreements as they stood rather than presuming any promises about the health or status of the slaves. The court did not step in to rectify the arrangement when a buyer bought as a slave someone who turned out to be infirm, or who turned out to be a free person rather than a slave. The court would, it seems, enforce only promises that had actually been made as part of the contract.[8]

A third example of deviation from the communal model of the legal system is the courts' involvement in relationships that in a "precommercial" world would not be expected to call for judicial resolution. In colonial New York, even disputes within churches were seen as contractual matters warranting adjudication in the courts, as evidenced by a 1724 action by a dismissed minister, Louis Rou, against the Consistory of the French Church. The court determined that the relationship between a minister and his congregation was more analogous to a commercial agreement than to a family situation and that therefore the matter could come before the courts as any other business contract would. Thus the court explicitly rejected a more informal, communal model of relationships and dispute resolution.[9]

These examples of deviations from the Horwitz–Nelson model illustrate the inaccuracy of their portrayal of the colonial world. Study of the overall patterns of legal decision making provide even more powerful evidence of a legal system that supported and encouraged commercial growth in colonial New York.

Formalization of Law

The resolution of disputes became more rationalistic and formalistic in colonial New York as the society became more commercialized. The pattern that is evident in New York mirrors Bruce Mann's description of Connecticut, though in explaining the shift from an informal to a formal legal system in eighteenth-century Connecticut Mann devotes more attention to the increased technicality of pleading and the correlated emergence of professionalized lawyers than this analysis does, and he describes a shift from decisions by juries to decisions by judges whereas this study found a more significant shift from decisions by juries to out-of-court settlement.[10]

In New York the most important development in legal practice during the colonial period was the dramatic decrease in the percentage of cases resolved by jury trial. A rational legal system—in the Weberian sense—is one in which disputes are settled in accordance with fixed rules, unaffected by arbitrariness, subjectivity, or considerations of politics, ethics, or larger social fairness. Juries have a tendency to express those "irrational" characteristics, so their presence in the legal process undermines rationality of decision making.[11] A decline in the proportion of cases resolved by jury trial, therefore, reflects increased rationalization of the legal system. Communalist legal historians portray juries as central to the colonial legal system. Jurors express the collective voice of the community in legal disputes and ensure that the communal interest is given priority over private individual interests. Both Horwitz and Nelson describe a shift in the power and influence of juries occurring only in the nineteenth century.[12] This study shows, however, that the use of juries declined well before the American Revolution.

Figure 3.1 shows the declining rate of jury trial (as a proportion of all civil cases) in the New York City Mayor's Court and the Dutchess County Court of Common Pleas between the 1690s and the 1750s.[13] The graph uses a five-year moving average, which makes the overall pattern clearer and smoother by dealing with the data in five-year blocks: a pri-

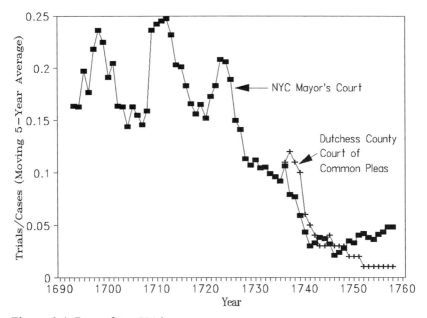

Figure 3.1 Rate of Jury Trial

Sources: MC Min and DCCCP Min.

mary year plus the two preceding years and the two following years. Each dot on the graph represents the ratio of the average number of trials for a five-year period to the average number of cases for that period. Figure 3.2 shows that the jury trial rate also fell as compared with population.[14] The number of trials as a proportion of all lawsuits initiated provides interesting information about the activity of judges in court, whereas the number of trials per capita provides insights on the larger question of the dispute resolution role of courts in the society.[15] Figure 3.1 shows that in the Mayor's Court the rate of jury trial rose in the 1690s (peaking in 1698), dipped and then recovered in the 1700s (up to a peak for the entire period, in 1712), fell in the later 1710s, rose briefly from 1721 to 1724, and then began a steady, significant decline. Specifically, for the five years around the peak in 1712 (1710–14) there was an annual average of 89 cases and 22 trials, whereas for the five years around the lowest point in 1746 there was an annual average of 133 cases and only 3 trials. By 1750 the jury trial rate was one-sixth of what it had been in 1700 (and less than one-seventh of what it had been in the peak year 1712).[16]

The Dutchess County Court of Common Pleas, though established in 1716, was slow to mature into a regularly working court; few cases came to

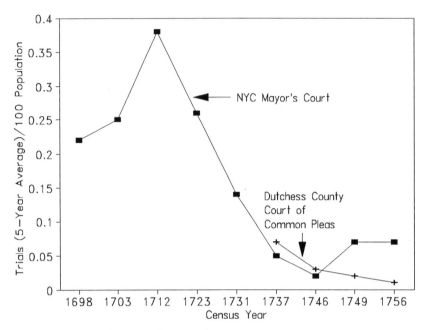

Figure 3.2 Rate of Jury Trial in Population

Sources: MC Min and DCCCP Min.

the court before the 1730s, and none reached jury trial before 1734. Figures 3.1 and 3.2 reveal that the jury trial rate in Dutchess County paralleled that in New York City: it started at a later date but exhibited a pattern very similar to that of the city.[17] For the five years around the trial rate peak in 1737, there was an annual average of 21 cases and 2.5 trials; by 1752 there was an annual average of 214 cases but still only 2.5 trials. By the time the rural Courts of Common Pleas were established, the Mayor's Court had already dealt with and resolved certain issues, providing precedents that could be used to settle cases in other courts. In this sense, urban areas led rural areas in the evolution of the legal system, contrary to the assumptions of Richard Morris and others who have concluded that the American legal system and law were shaped primarily by the nonurban frontier.[18] The engine of legal change was commercialization, not frontier life.

No line graph comparable to the above figures can be drawn for the Supreme Court or the justices of the peace because we do not have a continuous run of minutes for either: the minute books of the Supreme Court have many gaps, and we do not have available justice of the peace minute books from throughout the colonial period. We do know, however, that the ratio of number of trials to number of cases in the Supreme Court in the 1750s was approximately one-fifth of what it was in the 1690s; that trial rate declined from .369 in the earlier period to .077 in the later period. Specifically, between 1694 and 1696 there was an annual average of 28 cases and 9 trials, whereas between 1754 and 1756 there was an annual average of 342 cases and 15 trials.[19] The rate of jury trial in cases before the justices of the peace was apparently similar to that in the Supreme Court: in cases that came before Dutchess County Justice of the Peace Roswell Hopkins in 1764 and 1765, for example, the jury trial rate was .076—an annual average rate of 157 cases and 12 jury trials.[20] Overall, then, in the period from 1690 to 1760 we can see a decline in the rate of jury trial in all three of the major courts under study: the New York City Mayor's Court, the Dutchess County Court of Common Pleas, and the Supreme Court.

Litigants avoided jury trial in a number of ways: by resorting to jury control devices (such as motions for a new trial and demurrers to evidence), by appealing cases to judges on higher courts, and most of all by using bonds to formalize their commercial agreements.[21] Cases based upon a written instrument such as a note or bond were conducive to default and out-of-court settlement, rather than jury trial, because the document itself both provided proof of the debt and established the amount of recovery; there was typically no need for a jury to make such determinations.[22] Therefore, the overall pattern was a shift from jury trial to resolution by default or out-of-court settlement.

As a percentage of cases shown as resolved in the minute books, defaults ("judgments for want of a plea") increased in the Supreme Court from 13% in the 1690s to 67% in the 1750s, while the proportion of cases going to trial decreased from 52% to 9%. In the Mayor's Court the percentage of defaults increased from 44% to 69% as the proportion of trials declined from 25% to 12%.[23] The majority of cases commenced in court, however, were not actually resolved there at all. By the 1750s 51% of Supreme Court cases and 69% of Mayor's Court cases were settled out of court.[24] A study of one lawyer's Supreme Court cases provides evidence as to how cases were resolved out of court: the majority were worked out between the parties with a full payment, partial payment, provision of additional security, or some other agreement.[25]

In the vast majority of cases, therefore, creditors were able to collect their debts—and without having to go through a whole jury trial process. A decline in full litigation does not mean that law itself is playing a smaller role, nor that the courts have lost influence. Rather, it means that the courts are supplying clear standards for interpreting contracts and are enforcing them predictably.[26] That is, law became more important in the eighteenth century, not less important.

Lawsuits are not just a means of collecting money. They can also be a way of using a public forum to reinforce or restate community values, especially during periods of change.[27] Those who have been disadvantaged by changes would be those most likely to challenge them in ways that bring them into court, by lashing out verbally, physically, or legally against those who represent change. And the resulting lawsuits would be the ones most likely to be resolved by jury trial.

In general, non-debt-related cases were more likely to be contested—to go to trial—than were debt-related cases. One can see this most clearly in the minutes of the Richmond County Court of Common Pleas. The extant minute books of Richmond County do not cover every year of the period being studied, but they do offer one unusual benefit: from the first term in 1726 to the first term in 1747, they indicate at the time of initiation of the case what kind of action it was (a practice not followed by the clerks of other courts). Consequently, one can determine which actions dominated the court's docket and which were most likely to be resolved by jury trial. During the 21½ years for which the information is available in Richmond County, only 14% of all cases were actions to recover for injuries sustained—including assault, defamation, trespass, trover, replevin, detinue, and ejectment—but 93% of all trials were in that category. To state it the other way, 86% of the Richmond County cases were actions to collect money owed, but those debt-related cases constituted only 7% of jury trials.[28] Clinton Francis's statistical study of litigation in England between 1740 and 1840 also found that noncontract actions were resolved by jury trial significantly more often than were contract actions. For example, actions in trespass went to trial 5.25 times more often than actions on bonds, and actions in assault went to trial 7.5% more often.[29]

In noncommercial disputes, monetary compensation was often considered inadequate, and therefore it was more difficult to settle neutrally out of court; because honor and prestige were often at stake in those cases, the disputants were less likely to be satisfied by a quick, private payment of money. Where honor was at stake, the adversary had to be publicly labeled as having been wrong. The jury trial served the essential function of providing a dozen people from the community who could pronounce with authority who was right and who was wrong and therefore allocate honor appropriately in such cases.[30] The jury, in short, could express the consensus of the community on difficult issues.

An example of a lawsuit in which the jury was called upon to establish a community norm is *Thomas Byersly v. Thomas George and Lydia George.* Lydia George acted to prevent her neighbor's use of a new technology; more broadly, she tried to retain older economic values. Lydia and her husband Thomas lived next door to Thomas Byersly in the South Ward of New York City. In 1714 Byersly complained that Lydia George had maliciously thrown stones and other objects into the pump in his well, which stopped up the pump and deprived Byersly of the use of the well. The Georges alleged in response that Byersly had recently replaced the rope and bucket in his well with a pump, and that since then he had drawn such large quantities of water for bathing and washing that there was not enough water for the Georges' necessary uses. In fact, the little water that remained had become "dirty, nauseous, foul and useless." Therefore, they said, Lydia George had been acting lawfully when she threw stones into Byersly's pump to prevent the same thing happening again. Byersly responded to the Georges' allegations by saying that he had not drawn inordinately from the well and that an adequate quantity of clean water remained for the use of the Georges. The case appeared in court on July 13, 1714, and trial was held a month later. The jury sided with the defendants, agreeing with their justification of the alleged action. Byersly collected nothing in the lawsuit, and he had to pay the defendants £2 17s. 9d. for costs. The case shows a balancing of interests by the jury: Lydia George's action was found to be a justifiable response even though perhaps technically it was no defense. This case is particularly interesting because the jury applied a traditional, antidevelopmental view of property rights. Advanced technology is not allowed if it interferes with previously existing uses, here the use of water.[31]

Such jury rulings, however, had the potential to inhibit economic advances. Given the disadvantages that women faced in the new, commercialized economy, one could argue that it would have been to their advantage for lawsuits to continue to be resolved by juries like the one that decided *Byersly v. George.* But this view gave way as the eighteenth century advanced, and juries became increasingly willing to support the values and the property interests of commercial people, while at the same time commercial people found ways of avoiding juries in situations that might prompt community resistance.

The most commercialized people in New York society had the most to gain from a shift in the legal system away from resolution by juries because of (1) the ability of wealthier litigants to use their wealth to force settlement of their cases without juries, (2) merchants' more frequent use of written instruments to formalize economic relationships, (3) craftsmen's and farmers' dominance of juries and greater likelihood of a favorable verdict,[32] and (4) merchants' interest in not allowing their money and their economic relationships to stagnate.

Thus one sees different legal behavior by commercialized and non-commercialized people in the early eighteenth century. Examination of litigant pairs reveals that in New York City merchants were less likely to push their cases to trial than craftsmen were, in rural areas merchant-plaintiffs were also less likely to go to trial than farmers were, and in both urban and rural areas women were more likely to have their cases resolved by trial than men were. That is, craftsmen, farmers, and women valued the more traditional judicial function and retained the older form of practice after merchants shifted their legal behavior.[33] One also sees, though, a converging of behavior by different occupational groups of men by the end of the colonial period as more men, including craftsmen and farmers, found ways of taking advantage of commercial opportunities as more of them became more like merchants; as artisans and other groups became more commercialized, their patterns of litigation shifted to become more like the patterns of the merchants. Women, who could not take advantage of commercial opportunities the way men could, were increasingly disadvantaged in the legal system.

The high cost of litigation was an especially significant factor favoring wealthier and commercialized people in particular, and men in general, in court. The maintenance of an increasingly expensive court system—a system in which the defendant had to choose between default or forced settlement on the one hand and a long, drawn-out procedure on the other—inhibited poor litigants from carrying their cases through to jury trial. In this way the system favored wealthier litigants, such as merchants, who enjoyed enhanced negotiating leverage because they could afford high attorneys' fees and court costs. The increased costs of the full litigation process gave them more bargaining power to force favorable settlements. Figures 3.3 and 3.4 show the total costs for cases resolved in the Supreme Court in the 1750s at different stages of the legal process.[34]

The costs of litigation affected various occupational groups differently. The average annual income of an established merchant in New York City was over £900, while shopkeepers earned approximately half that amount. In contrast, the average craftsman in the colonial period earned an income of 5s. per day, or £60 per year. This income barely covered living expenses for a moderately sized family. Meanwhile, the average laborer earned only 3s. a day (£35 a year), and the average mariner earned 2s. a day (£25 a year), which just covered the living expenses

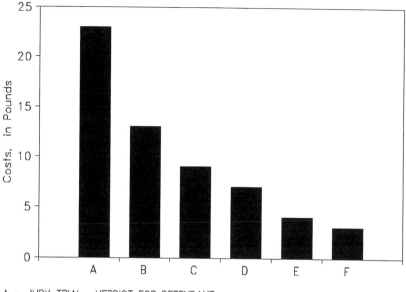

A = JURY TRIAL, VERDICT FOR DEFENDANT

B = NONPROSS AFTER PLEADING

C = DISCONTINUANCE BEFORE PLEADING

D = SETTLEMENT AFTER ALL PLEADING

E = SETTLEMENT AFTER DECLARATION

F = SETTLEMENT AFTER CAPIAS

In settled cases, each party pays own costs; in other cases, loser pays all costs.

Figure 3.3 Plaintiffs' Litigation Costs, Supreme Court, 1750s

Sources: William Smith, Jr., "A Scheme for Drawing out Bills of Costs in the Supream Court of New York Digested into Tables," William Smith Papers, vol. 9, New York Public Library, Rare Books and Manuscripts Room, New York; William Livingston, "The Lawyers Fee for the Supreme Court," and "A Regulation for the Taxation of Costs in the Supreame Court," in Livingston's "Lawyer's Book of Precedents," 412–14 and 448–59; William Livingston's "Cost Book," New York Public Library.

of a single man.[35] Thus the income of most groups in New York City left little reserve to cover the costs of initiating or defending a lawsuit.

In a typical lawsuit resolved by jury trial in the New York Supreme Court in the 1750s, the plaintiff would have to pay for over fifty feeable services and the typical bill would total about £15, and even if the lawsuit were resolved or terminated before trial, the plaintiff's legal and court fees would typically range from £4 to £7. If the plaintiff won the case, all or part of his costs might be paid for by the defendant, but if he lost the case

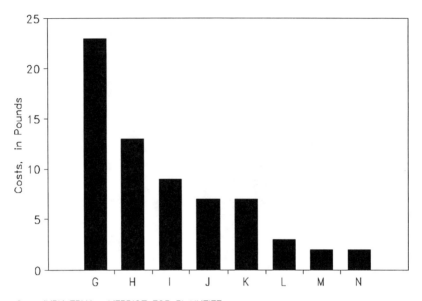

G = JURY TRIAL, VERDICT FOR PLAINTIFF
H = DEFAULT, WITH INQUISITION
I = DEFAULT, CONFESSION OF DAMAGES   In settled cases, each party pays
J = DEFAULT, DAMAGES FIXED   own costs; in other cases, loser
K = CONFESSION OF JUDGMENT   pays all costs.
L = SETTLEMENT AFTER ALL PLEADING
M = SETTLEMENT AFTER DECLARATION
N = SETTLEMENT AFTER CAPIAS

Figure 3.4 Defendants' Litigation Costs, Supreme Court, 1750s

Sources: See figure 3.3.

he would normally have to pay the defendant's costs on top of his own. Some paupers received the benefit of free legal services, although this was not common. In 1761 the issue arose as to whether someone who loses a case to a pauper has to pay the pauper's attorney, as he would pay the fees of the attorney of someone who was not a pauper. The fact that there was no precedent for deciding this issue as late as the 1760s suggests that paupers were not often in court—or at least that they rarely or never won.[36] The fact that people lived in colonial New York who were too poor to purchase adequate food, clothing, and firewood indicates a considerable population had difficulty gaining access to the courtroom.

To this extent, then—and, further, to the extent that all people in a lower class were expected to behave deferentially toward people in au-

Table 3.1
1754 Tax Assessments of All Litigants
and Trial Litigants, Dutchess County,
1721–1755 (£)

	All	Trial
Plaintiffs	19	12
Defendants	5	8
Difference	14	4

Source: Dutchess County Tax Lists.

thority and toward others who were their superiors—the legal system was less accessible to all poor people. Thus, class affected the availability of legal remedies, and litigation was a lighter financial drain for wealthy people than for poor people.

This meant not only that it was easier for wealthier people to take on the expenses of litigation but also that their ability to pay for lengthy court proceedings consequently afforded them extra leverage during those proceedings. Settlement was naturally often on the terms determined by the stronger party. Since the usual rule was for the loser in the case to pay all the costs (court costs, witness expenses, attorneys' fees), and since the plaintiff usually won, in practice litigation was usually quite inexpensive for those who initiated lawsuits. The loser-pays-all-costs rule encouraged creditors to use the courts to collect debts.[37] The real impact of high litigation rates fell primarily on defendants. This invisible legal process explains in part the fact that different wealth and occupational groups fared differently in the courtroom, with wealthier people, especially merchants, more likely to win in court than were other groups and more likely to be able to force out-of-court settlement.

We can see the impact of disparity in wealth, for example, by comparing the tax assessments of all litigants and trial litigants in the Dutchess County Court of Common Pleas in 1754–55. Such a comparison reveals a significant difference marking the pairs that went to trial. As shown in table 3.1, plaintiffs and defendants who continued their cases to trial were closer in wealth than were other plaintiff-defendant pairs. Note that it was not the wealth of a particular litigant in the Dutchess County Court of Common Pleas that influenced whether that litigant went to trial. Rather, it was the relative wealth of the plaintiff and the defendant in each case that shaped the legal proceedings. This provides some evidence that greater disparity of wealth meant stronger clout in forcing settlement out of court.[38]

The decline of jury trial and the rise of out-of-court settlement and default were beneficial to, and condoned by, commercial people. With these changes, the legal system took on a very modern character. The patterns that were established in colonial New York continued in the legal system of the new state after the Revolution and for more than two hundred years thereafter.

Conclusion

The shift away from jury trial in eighteenth-century New York represented a move toward a more "rational" legal system, the kind of system that is best suited to a rational, impersonal market economy. Pure market relations focus exclusively on the commodity exchange itself, not on the human aspects of interaction. Therefore, the ideal system for resolution of commercial disputes is one that similarly ignores the personal in favor of abstract principles. It is essential to a commercial economy that contracts be strictly enforced and that the law be predictable and calculable.[39] By making credit arrangements more predictably enforceable, the decline of jury trial created a legal system that was better suited than the traditional system was to supporting and fostering a commercial, consumer economy and therefore gave a boost to the colonial New York economy. The availability of the court system to New Yorkers allowed them to feel confident about extending their commercial relationships beyond their local community. By providing an enforcement mechanism for credit arrangements, the courts in general and debt litigation in particular allowed the economy to continue to function and grow despite the continuing shortage of currency.

During the early years of the colony, exchanges of goods and services took place among friends, neighbors, and family. Shocks to the economic system occurring outside the community had little effect on that community. Trust between borrower and lender was reinforced by local community ties and mutual dependence. Because the economy of the early colonial period functioned successfully on this basis, judicial intervention was needed only in unusual cases. As New Yorkers bought more goods and the economy expanded, more men did business with strangers and more men were tied into the larger provincial, intercolonial, and international economies. Individual borrowers and lenders throughout New York were vulnerable to the potentially devastating effects of economic shock waves originating in distant colonies or distant countries. The geographic range of credit, debt, and trust expanded. Personal ties within the neighborhood no longer sufficed to bolster trust. The courts were needed to fill this role. Without a court system to ensure creditors that their debts would be collected—and collected without requiring lengthy jury trials— New Yorkers would have been reluctant to sell goods or provide services on credit and the economy would have been stifled. The next chapter shows that, with recourse to the law available, the trading relationships could expand. With the backing of the courts, men from widely disparate geographic and occupational communities could conduct business with one another. The trust could continue under protected conditions.

CHAPTER 4

The Spread of Market Relationships

The issue of the timing of the transition to capitalism is largely a relative question. Historians have come up with conflicting answers partly because they have examined different geographic areas (which may have changed at different times) but also because of differences in definition and focus. Some have studied the rise of a market economy; others have insisted that one must address primarily the rise of wage labor. Some have focused on ways in which an area has become more capitalistic, while others have focused on ways in which an area has retained older economic forms; they may be describing the same place, just concentrating on different aspects of an economy in transition, an economy that evidences both new and old elements at the same time. Surely the transition was a process instead of an overnight event; one cannot clearly and definitively label one time and place in which precapitalism became capitalism.[1]

This book does not point to any sudden emergence of capitalism. Rather, it describes a process that extends throughout the course of the seventeenth and eighteenth centuries and later continues into the nineteenth century. Certainly the early, and still partial, spread of market relationships that is evidenced by the legal and economic records discussed in this volume did not mean that colonial New York was fully "capitalist." In particular, there is no indication that there existed the kind of wage labor society that would fit a Marxist model of capitalism. Furthermore, participation in markets did not necessarily mean that colonial New Yorkers were entirely market driven or market dependent; farmers produced for their own consumption as well. As I show, however, New York's colonial economy cannot accurately be labeled precapitalist or communal in nature. By the mid-eighteenth century market relationships were widespread in New York, and the process of expanding to a fully capitalist economy had begun.

One measure of the degree of participation in impersonal market relationships associated with a credit-based consumer economy in colonial New York was the extent of the society's participation in litigation, and an indicator of the extent of economic integration was the degree to which participation in litigation was widespread throughout that society. The analysis of legal records in this chapter reveals that a wide range of groups of men—varied by wealth, occupation, and ethnicity—became increasingly involved in the market economy in the eighteenth century.

Indicators of a Market Economy

Scholars trying to identify when America became capitalist, or when it developed a market economy, have pointed to a variety of indicators of economic development. Perhaps the most common marker of market orientation in recent scholarship has been the cash transaction. Christopher Clark observes that "[a] debt paid off in cash implies abstraction—a social distance between buyer and seller—because the form of payment can be turned to any use." The fact that eighteenth- and early nineteenth-century Americans tended to pay local debts with goods or services rather than cash, he says, demonstrates that those local exchanges were less commercial in nature than were long-distance exchanges between strangers.[2] Thomas Wermuth similarly maintains that Ulster County, New York, farmers' avoidance of cash in their transactions "may reveal attempts to resist developing commercial relations."[3]

Certainly one can understand why cash is most suitable for one-time exchanges between strangers whereas people who live in the same community and who engage in regular exchanges might find payment in goods and services acceptable and convenient. The form of payment, however, does not actually tell us how commercial or how neighborly the relationship was. It does not, for example, tell us how insistently the creditor demanded immediate repayment or how tolerant he was of delays. In short, the form of payment itself does not indicate how friendly or personal the economic relationship was; it does not tell us whether it was a market-type relationship. Thus, although, as shown earlier, there was an increase in the use of cash in New York over the course of the eighteenth century, the use of cash alone is inadequate, possibly even useless, as a marker of a capitalist or market mentality. There are better indicators of the capitalist nature of the economy.

Winifred Rothenberg's excellent study of rural Massachusetts between 1750 and 1850 lists other correlates of a market economy. She found a break point between 1785 and 1800 in the expansion of commodity markets, a capital market, and labor markets. The expansion of commodity markets is indicated by farmers' records of marketing trips that show both the proliferation of market towns and the concentration of central marketplaces and by account books and price indexes that show the synchronous movement of rural and urban prices, the convergence of farm prices, and the price elasticity of the slaughter weight of hogs. Furthermore, the development of a capital market during that period is evident from probate inventories and administrators' and executors' accounts that show an increased frequency of free-floating interest charges on debts, enhanced negotiability of credit instruments, an increased proportion of decedents' estates held as financial instruments, and widened and thickened credit networks. Finally, the development of labor markets is demonstrated by account books that show the convergence of wage rates for hired farm labor, and tax valuations indicate increased agricultural productivity.[4]

The factors examined by Rothenberg are persuasive as indicators of the presence of commodities, capital, and labor markets. Clearly the economy of 1800 described by Rothenberg was more advanced than the economy of the first half of the eighteenth century. Most notably, wage labor was far more limited early in the century than it was by 1800. The development of commodities markets and a capital market were, however, processes that had already begun by 1750.

Rothenberg's study of commodity markets relies most heavily on prices recorded in farm account books. Unfortunately, as she herself notes, farm price data from before 1750 are too scarce to allow for a study of such markets comparable to hers for most of the colonial period.[5] Somewhat more information is available, however, regarding the development of a capital market before 1750. Two of Rothenberg's criteria for a capital market were discussed in chapter 2. As described there, credit instruments—bills of exchange and promissory notes—were negotiable or assignable and circulated in the colonial New York economy. Furthermore, the proportion of New York estates invested in financial assets (cash, notes, bonds, mortgages, and book accounts) increased during the eighteenth century. These two factors suggest the beginnings of a capital market in the colonial period.[6]

A third indicator is interest charges in economic transactions. The rise of debt described in chapter 2 suggests a thickening of credit networks; frequent interest charges on those debts further reinforce the point that a capital market was developing. That interest was charged in at least 38% of the debts underlying Dutchess County cases in 1754–55 for which court documents survive indicates the debts were regarded as business, rather than personal, debts, since charging interest indicates that extending credit is regarded as an investment rather than an extension of aid to a neighbor. Probate inventories also reveal application of interest to loans. For example, according to the inventory of the widow Sarah Arnold (1768) interest was being charged on every one of the nineteen loans she initiated or carried forward from the time her husband died in 1764.[7] Account books, too, indicate New Yorkers' awareness of the benefits of interest. In his account book in the 1740s, for example, Francis Filkin meticulously lists the profits to be gained from lending out £1,000 for a month at 5%, 6%, 7%, or 8% interest, mentions paying a creditor "out of an interst bond," and refers to a quantity of wheat that was "to be Given again next year with intrs."[8]

One also sees frequent references to money at interest in colonial New York wills. Often, money from a man's estate was put out at interest in order to provide an annual annuity for his widow. For example, in 1736 Theophilus Elsworth, mason of New York City, left his wife Hester the interest on his estate during her widowhood; in 1772 Martin Hoffman of Dutchess County and New York City stipulated (in accordance with an antenuptial contract) that his executors were to put £5,000 at interest in order to provide his wife Alida with £300 a year during her widowhood; in his 1771 will New York City merchant Gabriel Ludlow instructed executors to set aside enough capital to supply his widow with an annual income of £250 and his sister Sarah an income of £15; and in his 1773 will New York City physician James Magra provided that £1,000 was to be put at interest for his wife Elizabeth during her life. Quite frequently, wills refer to money being set aside at interest in order to provide continuing funds for the education and maintenance of minor children. See, for example, the wills of leather dresser John Smith (probated 1762), lawyer Anthony Rutgers (1760), merchant Thomas Noble (no date of probate), cartman John Smith (1765), all of New York City; and see also the wills of Thomas Dwight (probated 1758) and Henry Cuyler (1777). Men also set aside money at interest for other relatives, such as married daughters (e.g., Joseph Reade, who instructed executors to put his legacy to his daughter Sarah at interest for her during her life and then to give it to her children), grandchildren (e.g., Robert Watts had £1,000 put at interest for his grandson Robert until he turned 21), or parents (e.g., Lawrence Reade left the interest on £800 to his mother for life).[9]

In the mid-eighteenth century, high interest rates were considered a problem by some. In 1734 "John Farmer" of Long Island claimed that high rates were causing a lack of cash. He wrote in the *New-York Weekly Journal:* "our Condition at present is such, that our Cash is got into the Hands of Usurers, who make very great Advantages of poor Peoples Necessities, by Reason of . . . the great Interest they are suffered to take." If interest rates were lower, he was convinced, money would circulate better. Therefore, he recommended that the New York Assembly pass legislation keeping interest rates low.[10] Two months later a New York City tradesman entered the debate, reiterating some of "John Farmer" 's "observations." Most of the "griping Userers we have in this Province," he wrote, would "rather put their Money out upon Interest than pay the poor Trades-Man for his Labour." He pointed out that "[t]he Merchant suffers by this greatly; for the poor Man can not pay till he has wherewith. The poor Trades Man suffers more, for often he is obliged to give extravagant Interest for a Sum to pay away either to preserve his Credit, or to avoid a Goal." The remedy, he agreed with "John Farmer," was to encourage the assembly to pass a law prohibiting extravagant interest, which would "force them to trade, and consequently encrease the running Cash of the Province."[11] The assembly did reduce interest rates from 8% to 7% in 1737, though this did not solve the problem.[12]

Rothenberg noted an increased incidence of interest charges as a capital market developed in Massachusetts. Before the Massachusetts transition decade, the 1780s, interest was charged in only 5% of sample probate accounts, whereas interest was charged on 20% of accounts from 1781 to 1800, 33% from 1800 to 1810, and 37% from 1810 to 1838.[13] Rothenberg does not specify what percentage of Massachusetts court documents referred to interest being charged or whether she would expect the percentage to follow the probate record numbers. The charging of interest in over one-third of debts underlying Dutchess County court cases does, however, seem to suggest the early development of a capital market. Rothenberg's second indicator of interest being regarded as the price of money, however, was fluctuation in interest rates as the market changed. The Dutchess County court records typically indicate only that "lawful interest" was charged, which suggests that the rate was not changing with the market. Interest rates in New York were set by law at 6% in 1717, 8% in 1719, and 7% in 1737.[14] Cathy Matson has found that during times of war, interest rates in colonial New York did rise as high as 9%, clearly reacting to a market in money, but such variations cannot be found in the court records for a mere two-year period in the 1750s. Unfortunately the kind of supporting court documents that might mention interest are not sufficiently available for the years prior to the 1750s to make thorough analysis of stable or fluctuating interest rates possible through court records.[15]

The negotiability of financial instruments and their increasing presence in probate inventories and the common charging of interest hint at the beginnings of a capital market in colonial New York. Studying commodities markets is more difficult. In the absence of sufficient farm account books, one has to rely on alternative sources to study the extent of colonists' involvement in commodities markets. Thus far, the only alternative measurable source used by historians has been probate inventories, which provide good evidence of the extent to which colonists purchased goods in the market. As shown in chapter 1, probate inventories of colonial New York reveal that both urban and rural dwellers possessed a wide range of consumer goods in their homes.

The few rural account books that are available are a potential source of information about New Yorkers' market orientation. For example, one account book illustrates rural New Yorkers' profit orientation by showing their participation in speculative enterprises. Francis Filkin's Dutchess County account book describes the arrangements he made in November 1743 (along with Anthony Yelverton) for the purchase of wheat for bolting. From five wheat producers, Filkin and Yelverton bought future rights to a fixed quantity of wheat (a total of 184½ bushels) at a fixed price (3s. 6d. per bushel), to be delivered the next summer. They agreed to buy the wheat crops of two other farmers "as the pris Goas in April." From another farmer, Captain Lester, they agreed to buy 500 bushels of wheat for 3s. 11d., specifically stating in the account book the understanding of the parties: "what it is Les when I sell the wheat or flower than Lester most Lose it and what it is more I most Lose it."[16] Because of the scarcity of rural account books, however, such evidence of speculation is too scattered to provide a measurable basis for assessing market orientation. Thus, although some information can be gleaned from probate inventories and account books, none of the available sources for colonial New York discussed so far provides an ideally useful, measurable indicator of market orientation.

Debt Litigation and the Spread of Market Relationships

There is, however, an excellent source for measuring the extent of involvement in the market: court records. Debt litigation provides an extremely useful measurable behavioral correlate of market orientation. The fact that many urban and rural New Yorkers alike turned to the courts to collect payments is a significant indicator of the arm's-length nature of economic relationships in the eighteenth century. From the earliest days of colonial settlement there were some kinds of exchanges of goods. During the early years these exchanges took place between family members, friends, and neighbors. Even if they were marked in an account book, they were distinctly personal exchanges within a close and mutually dependent community. While such personal debts might show up on the decedent's estate inventory if still outstanding at the time of death, they would be unlikely to appear in the court records. People do not sue to collect money from those with whom they have close personal ties (family members or members of a small, tight-knit, forgiving community). Economic relationships with such people are based on trust, mutual dependence, and tolerance. A market economy, in contrast, is characterized by arm's length, depersonalized relationships between buyers and sellers. People sue to collect money from those with whom they have such more distant, more impersonal relationships. Unless the underlying relationship is a distanced one, not only will they be reluctant to initiate lawsuits with the intent of immediately pressing for collection of debts, but also they will hesitate even to initiate lawsuits just for the purpose of recording debts for later collection.

Christopher Clark found that in late eighteenth- and early nineteenth-century western Massachusetts there was a sharp difference between the ethics of local exchange and long distance, or market, trade. "Whereas in long-distance trade creditors assumed the right to press for repayment and sue when debts were not settled," he wrote, "the local exchange ethic emphasized restraint, caution, and consideration of debtors' means to pay." Indeed, within the local area, "pressing for settlement could cause offense by implying lack of trust, or could be seen as an attempt to take advantage," and "to go to law to seek repayment of these debts was still regarded as a violation of 'neighborhood' well into the nineteenth century." Clark found that in many towns in early rural Massachusetts "lawsuits for debt were brought by one townsman against another only infrequently." Even in the early nineteenth century, "[s]uits between neighbors were still comparatively rare." Instead, "[m]ost debt actions were between strangers who lived at a distance from one another."[17]

Other economic historians of early America agree that people do not sue to collect on "personalized" credit transactions within a close, trusting, forgiving, "traditional" community; they go to court only to collect less personalized debts.[18] Court records, therefore, probably give a more accurate picture than probate records do of comparative levels of business credit and debt in a region.

Sociologist Donald Black has found that the amount of "law" in a society, including the amount of litigation, varies directly with the degree of economic complexity, specialization, and stratification of that society. In addition, the lower the degree of intimacy between people engaged in transactions with one another, the more likely they are to sue one another.[19] Black's study relies almost exclusively on studies of a variety of contemporary societies rather than on change in one society over time. It is evident, however, that the same principles apply to longitudinal studies.

The rate of litigation will rise as people in a society extend their economic relationships. Economic growth leads to an increased number of commercial transactions, which means an increased number of potential disputes.[20] In particular, it leads to an increased number of business relationships among people from a wider geographic range, people from different colonies, different areas of the province, and different groups in society. Lacking common neighborhood ties, these people turn to the courts for resolution of disputes arising out of those relationships.

In urban areas of the eighteenth century, for example, merchants sued those who bought but failed to pay for their goods (mostly craftsmen), those who were supposed to transport their merchandise carefully (ship captains), those who delivered defective goods to them (craftsmen), those who were supposed to sell goods in the domestic or foreign market on their behalf and failed to send them the proceeds of the sales (their agents), and those to whom they had lent money (other merchants, craftsmen). Craftsmen, meanwhile, most often sued those who failed to pay for craft work. Mariners sued ship captains and merchant-shipowners for wages. Ship captains sued mariners who failed to complete their terms of duty on board ships and merchants and craftsmen who failed to pay for goods delivered or services rendered. Lawyers and doctors sued those who had not paid for services rendered. Tavern keepers and innkeepers sued those who failed to pay for food and lodging. In rural areas, merchants sued those who bought but did not pay for their goods (mostly farmers and dual-occupation craftsmen-farmers). Farmers sued for repayment of money lent. In some cases rural debts were payments owed for the expenses of setting up or expanding a farm. Landlord-tenant relationships also often ended up in court, as landlords attempted to collect overdue rent and remove unlawful occupants from their land.

As the society becomes more commercial and the economic and legal culture change, not only do people take distant trading partners to court, they also become increasingly willing to take even their neighbors to court. Growth in the economy also increases the cumulative monetary value of business transactions, so disputes that emerge out of the transactions are worth taking to court. There is more to win—and more to lose. Furthermore, the inadequate supply of money may become more acute as the economy grows, as people buy more things, so the vast majority of the new kinds of commercial exchanges will be based on credit. The larger number of debts outstanding and larger number of credit instruments in circulation mean an increased potential number of debt cases in court. Recourse to the courts is needed to ensure collection of debts between people no longer connected by close family and neighborhood ties.

The following sections analyze men's experience in litigation and the market economy. They describe the increased volume and rate of litigation in urban and rural courts between 1690 and 1760 and the increasingly more widespread participation in litigation by a variety of groups of men in colonial New York, which indicates the general spread of depersonalized, market relationships into new classes of men in both urban and rural areas. Thus the data from colonial New York show that by the eighteenth century, urban and rural male New Yorkers were routinely using formal legal process to collect their debts, even from their neighbors.

The Increasing Rate of Debt Litigation

Early in the colonial period, rural villages had constituted their own separate communities, whose members knew one another well and depended on one another's reliability and honesty. But it was not just farmers who had their own separate communities. Merchants, too, constituted a close community of men who knew one another personally, dealt with one another on a regular basis, and relied on trust and reputation to enforce financial arrangements among themselves.[21] For some time merchants were able to bridge the gap in a limited way between their own community and the communities of potential consumers and suppliers of materials for export by choosing representatives of those communities to work through. They relied on trust and reputation to support their relationship with those representatives, the shopkeepers who would collect produce from farmers and sell imported goods to them. The shopkeepers thus served as the connectors between communities. They were well known in their hometowns, where they opened their shops, but they were also well known to the merchants from New York City. The presence of a small number of shopkeepers as known intermediaries allowed trust to provide a basis for a small degree of selling and buying even between communities. But real economic integration of communities, and real economic expansion, required more.

First, merchants needed to develop direct economic relationships outside the small merchant/shopkeeper community—direct relationships with farmers and craftsmen—and they also needed to relate to a larger number of shopkeepers as demand grew and interest in selling to and buying from the market became more widespread. Second, as it became increasingly difficult to rely on trust, New Yorkers had to base more of their economic exchanges on formal contracts subject to court enforcement. The courts at this time increasingly held men to the strict terms of their contracts in a wide variety of settings and relationships. Not only farmers but merchants, too, had had their own insulated community in which economic transactions had been protected by trust, and merchants, too, now needed courts to protect their expansion of relationships outside their own community—an expansion necessary for a true consumer revolution.

The very establishment of the Court of Common Pleas in Dutchess County in 1716 indicates the need for court-sponsored resolution of disputes in the early eighteenth century, which suggests that the rural economy had reached a stage at which financial matters had to be handled in a more businesslike way than the typically informal, unhurried, face-to-face, nonlegal approach taken in a noncommercial society. The increased number of cases as the eighteenth century progressed in rural Dutchess County, as in urban New York City, reflected the growing commercialization of the whole colony of New York; as men turned to the courts to enable them to extend their economic relationships, the rate of litigation rose dramatically. It should be noted, though, that the litigation rate remained lower in rural Dutchess County than in New York City, reflecting greater market orientation in the city than in the countryside.

The civil litigation rate in the New York City Mayor's Court doubled from the late 1690s to the late 1740s, although not in a steady, linear fashion. From 1698 (litigation rate 0.91 per 100 people) to 1749 (1.88 per 100 people), there was a 107% increase in the litigation rate. Over a longer period, from 1698 to 1756, the increase was 75%.[22] Specifically, in the five years around 1698 (1696–1700), the annual average number of cases was 45; in 1756 the annual average had grown to 207 cases. The rural litigation rate also increased—and even more dramatically—during this period. After about 1730 the number of cases in the Dutchess County Court of Common Pleas increased gradually over time, peaking in 1753. The litigation rate grew from .35 cases per 100 people in 1731 to 1.23 cases per 100 people in 1756—an increase of 250%. Between 1731 and 1756, the annual average number of cases rose from 10 to 196. The rise in litigation in this period parallels the rise in the population of the county, but the number of cases increased even faster than the population. The rate of litigation in the Supreme Court of Judicature, the highest court in the province, rose from .19 cases per 100 people in the province of New York in the 1690s to .35 cases per 100 people in the 1750s, an increase of 84%. The actual number of cases increased from an annual average of 28 between 1694 and 1696 to 342 between 1754 and 1756.[23]

The vast majority of these cases were debt related. Since the minute books do not systematically indicate the form of action for each case, it is impossible to know exactly what percentage of cases fell into each litigation category. Analysis of the Richmond County Court of Common Pleas minutes, which are unique in stating the form of action, provides some clue to the New York pattern. Those minutes indicate that between 1721 and 1747 debt-related actions constituted 86% of Richmond County cases.[24] If anything the percentage was probably somewhat higher in New York City, and it probably increased slightly between 1747 and the Revolution. As a rough estimate, then, approximately 90% of all litigation was debt litigation. The rising litigation rate represented most of all a rise in debt-related lawsuits.

The dramatic growth in the litigation rate occurred after commercial values were already fairly widely accepted and the number of commercial transactions had increased. The overall litigation rate increased not because of temporary conflicts of values during incipient commercialization but because of the permanent changes caused by the consumer revolution: people were buying more goods, incurring more debt, finding themselves unable to pay debts to more distant creditors, and being pulled into the courts in increasing numbers. Nor was the rising litigation rate prompted by lawyers eager to make profits. Rather, the higher litigation rate had a broader economic basis, and lawyers responded to the demand for more lawsuits.

The increased litigation rate in colonial New York is consistent with conclusions of studies focusing on other colonies. Scholars of colonial Massachusetts, William E. Nelson and David Thomas Konig, have found that that colony became progressively litigious during the colonial period as the growth of commerce, religious pluralism, and ethnic diversity led to a need for a more objective, predictable, certain, powerful, and precise form of adjudication of disputes than the local community could offer. A. G. Roeber has described an increase in debt cases in Virginia during the eighteenth century. In colonial Connecticut, Richard Bushman has described a rise in debt and debt litigation as the economy of the colony grew during the first half of the eighteenth century, and Bruce Mann has found that as disputants were more likely to be relative strangers to one another, there was a shift from resolution of disputes within the community to formal resolution in legal forums. Peter Hoffer identified a swell of cases in colonial America in the early years of commercialization, between 1710 and 1730.[25] The increased rate of litigation reflected the expanding market economy.

Widespread Participation in Debt Litigation

Close examination of New York legal records reveals that men from all wealth, occupational, and ethnic categories appeared in court, the institution that enforced and reinforced their economic relationships. Widespread litigation is a significant indicator of widespread involvement in the market. The colonial courtroom was not the exclusive realm of the wealthiest, most commercial people. Instead, as is shown in the following discussion of the residential, wealth, occupational, and ethnic makeup of litigants, the courtroom was familiar to a broad range of men.

Residence. Even in rural Dutchess County, creditors were turning to the courts not only to collect debts from strangers but also to collect from their own neighbors. Storekeeper Hendrick Schenk, for example, sued 50, or about 5%, of the local customers listed in his account book from 1763 to 1770.[26] Taking debts to court is a sign that those debts were regarded as business debts rather than personal debts. The larger legal pattern is consistent with data from Schenk's account book: analysis of residences of plaintiffs and defendants in the Dutchess County Court of Common Pleas in 1754 and 1755 shows that creditors often used the legal system to collect debts from neighbors. In 338 cases between Dutchess County residents in that two-year period the precinct of residence is known for both the plaintiff and the defendant. In 46% (154) of those cases the litigants were from the same precinct. Therefore, 308 residents of Dutchess County—or approximately 14% of the 2,181 taxpayers—were involved in litigation against someone from the same precinct in the two-year period 1754–55. Since the number of taxpayers in each precinct averaged 312 (ranging from 89 in Northeast Precinct to 451 in Crum Elbow), many of these litigants were indeed "neighbors," and all of them can reasonably be considered part of the same "community." Thus rural

New Yorkers were willing to sue even neighbors, people living within the same precinct. Not all were restrained by a "local exchange ethic" from pressing neighbors for repayment.

The evidence makes clear that men's relationships with other men in the same precinct often took on an arm's length, distanced quality suggestive of market transactions. Market relationships in rural New York were not limited to a thin layer of commercialized merchants at the top of society. Instead, such relationships were beginning to extend to more average men in both rural and urban counties.

It should also be noted that in the two-year period from 1754 through 1755 alone, at least 16 residents of New York City brought suits in the Dutchess County Court of Common Pleas to collect debts there, and at least 19 Dutchess County people initiated suits in the city's Mayor's Court. At least 6 additional Dutchess County residents appeared as defendants in the Mayor's Court. (These numbers do not include 15 Dutchess County people whose names are so common as to make it impossible to know for sure that the Mayor's Court litigants of those names were the Dutchess County people and not city dwellers of the same name.) The appearance of city people in Dutchess County courts and Dutchess County residents in city courts indicates commercial ties between the urban and rural regions.

Wealth. Analysis of the court records in conjunction with tax assessment lists reveals that litigants in the Mayor's Court and the Dutchess County Court of Common Pleas came from a wide range of wealth categories. Even in rural Dutchess County, one-third of 1735 taxpayers litigated at some point in their lives. Of the 428 taxpayers on the 1735 tax list, 141 (33%) appeared at least once as a litigant between 1721 and 1755: 79 (18%) appeared as a plaintiff and 98 (23%) appeared as a defendant.[27] This large number of rural dwellers litigating means that a large proportion of them—presumably even more than one-third—were involved in market relationships. The one-third figure counts only economic relationships that went wrong, which was only a fraction of all relationships. Thus the one-third figure represents the minimum percentage of those involved in such relationships. The total actual figure would have been even higher.

Furthermore, the percentage of Dutchess County taxpayers who litigated over failed economic arrangements increased over time. Between the 1730s and the 1750s the proportion of taxpayers who litigated during a two-year period doubled: the percentage of taxpayers suing increased from 3% to 6% and the percentage of taxpayers being sued increased from 5% to 11%. In urban New York City, the percentage of taxpayers who litigated was higher than in rural areas: in the 1730s, 7% of taxpayers appeared as plaintiffs (more than twice the percentage of Dutchess County taxpayers), and 6% appeared as defendants. Unfortunately, because of the gap in city tax records after 1735, however, one cannot examine change between the 1730s and the 1750s.

The availability of Dutchess County tax records from both the 1730s and the 1750s allows one to study other aspects of change over time. As the eighteenth century progressed, lower wealth groups became more likely to participate in the legal system, indicating greater involvement in market relationships. The availability of Dutchess County tax lists from the 1750s as well as the 1730s allows a comparison to be made for that rural county. In the period 1734–35, 0% of taxpayer-plaintiffs and 26% of taxpayer-defendants came from the bottom third of taxpayers, but twenty years later 10% of taxpayer-plaintiffs and 36% of taxpayer-defendants were from the bottom third. During the same period, the percentage of plaintiffs from the top third dropped from 83% to 74%, and the percentage of defendants from the top third dropped from 44% to 28%.[28]

The average number of cases involving by Dutchess County taxpayers increased during the twenty-year period: each taxpayer who appeared as a plaintiff in 1734–35 sued an average of 1½ times, and those who were defendants were sued an average of just under 1½ times. In comparison, each taxpayer who appeared as a plaintiff in 1754–55 sued an average of almost 3 people, and those who were defendants were sued an average of 2 times. Thus not only were more men gaining exposure to the courtroom experience as litigants, but they were obtaining repeated experiences; they were returning to court as experienced litigants. Furthermore, the fact that rural New Yorkers participated in a larger number of cases indicates that those who engaged in market-type relationships were involved in a larger number of economic transactions.

Participation in litigation by rural men of modest means is exemplified by the profile of those who were sued in Dutchess County in the 1750s for payment of money owed for goods purchased. In 22 of those cases, a detailed accounting of the goods is extant, so we know exactly what the basis of the lawsuit was: we know that these men were brought into court because of their consumer activity. Examination of their taxpayer records shows that they were fairly ordinary men, farmers with insubstantial assets. Fifteen of the 22 debtor-defendants were listed as taxpayers in 1754 in Dutchess County. Their average tax assessment was only between £1 and £2 (compared to an average of about £23 for the 19 seller-plaintiffs who were Dutchess County taxpayers). Even in the rural counties, neither the purchase of consumer goods nor participation in the legal system was limited to the wealthy classes.

Occupation. Analysis of litigants by occupation further reveals the widespread participation in formal economic and legal relationships by a wide variety of people. Colonial New York was comprised of a wide range of occupations. It is difficult to determine precisely what proportion of the population fell into each occupational group in New York City, but the work of Bruce Wilkenfeld, along with lists of taxpayers and freemen of the city, permit a rough estimation.[29] Craftsmen were probably approximately 60% of the male taxable population between 1700 and 1760, merchants and shopkeepers about 15%, laborers 10%, farmers and gentlemen 5%, mariners and captains 5%, professionals (doctors, lawyers, and ministers) 3%, and tavern keepers 2%. In Dutchess County, the vast majority of male residents—about 90%—were yeoman farmers. The rest of the male population were craftsmen, dual-occupation craftsman-farmers, gentlemen, professionals, merchants, and laborers.

Since the minute books, with only a few exceptions, do not provide any information about litigants, one must turn to other sources to identify litigants' occupations; approximately three-quarters of litigants in the Mayor's Court and two-thirds of litigants in the Court of Common Pleas could be identified. Tables 4.1 and 4.2 show the occupational distribution of identifiable male litigants in 1754–55 in the New York City Mayor's Court and the Dutchess County Court of Common Pleas, respectively.

As the tables illustrate, a substantial proportion of plaintiffs were merchants (in both urban and rural areas) and craftsmen (in urban areas), while craftsmen (in urban areas) and farmers (in rural areas) predominated as defendants. In both courts, the percentage of plaintiffs who were merchants was significantly higher than merchants' proportion of the population. In the Mayor's Court craftsmen were a smaller proportion of plaintiffs and defendants than of taxable or freeman population. In the Court of Common Pleas, farmers and craftsmen together were represented among defendants in numbers proportionate to their population but were significantly underrepresented among plaintiffs.

Sources available to identify New York City litigants make it possible to evaluate change over time. Between the 1690s and the 1750s, merchants significantly declined as a proportion of defendants while craftsmen constituted a significantly larger percentage of both plaintiffs and defendants. The increases in the proportion of litigants who were crafts-

Table 4.1

Male Litigants by Occupational Group, New York City Mayor's Court, 1754–1755

Occupation	Plaintiffs		Defendants		Plaintiff/ Defendant Ratio
	%	N	%	N	
Merchant	29	172	15	77	2.2
Professional	8	47	3	16	2.9
Farmer/gentleman	7	41	6	32	1.2
Craftsman★	33	195	42	219	0.9
Mariner/captain	8	45	11	57	0.8
Tavernkeeper	14	81	18	94	0.9
Laborer	2	14	5	28	0.5
Total	101	595†	100	523†	

Sources: "The Burghers of New Amsterdam and the Freemen of New York, 1675–1866"; "Abstracts of Wills on File in the Surrogate's Office, City of New York, 1665–1800"; Rita Gottesman, *Arts and Crafts in New York, 1726–1776* (New York, 1935); *Genealogical Data from New York Administration Bonds, 1753–1799*, Kenneth Scott, abstracter; Isaac Newton Phelps Stokes, ed., *The Iconography of Manhattan Island, 1498–1909*; and Edmund B. O'Callaghan, ed., *Calendar of Historical Manuscripts in the Office of the Secretary of State, Albany, N.Y.*, 2 vols. (Albany, 1866).

Note: The numbers include only litigants who sued or were sued on their own behalf. That is, the figures exclude litigants who were in court as executors of estates or in an official capacity (e.g., suing as a collector of liquor excise taxes). Such litigants are excluded because the kind of cases they got involved in, the characteristics of their adversaries, and the courtroom experience revolved primarily around the nature of the office they held or around the characteristics of the deceased person rather than around the litigant's own personal characteristics.

★ The category "craftsman" includes dual-occupation craftsmen-farmers.

† Some cases had more than one plaintiff or more than one defendant.

men reflect both the growing numbers of craftsmen and their developing market orientation—both as sellers and buyers—during the colonial period. Early in the period most New York families neither sold nor bought many goods or services outside a close personal community, but by the end of the period there had developed more specialization, a greater frequency of transacting business with strangers, and an increased inclination to buy consumer goods. This shift is associated with an increase in debt, a greater willingness to go to court against strangers, and a greater tendency to measure commodities in monetary terms. In general, the participation in litigation by a wide range of occupational groups indicates how widespread distanced, market-type relationships were in eighteenth-century New York.

William Offutt did the only comparable study of occupational makeup

Table 4.2

Male Litigants by Occupational Group, Dutchess County Court of Common
Pleas, 1754–1755

Occupation	Plaintiffs		Defendants		Plaintiff/ Defendant Ratio
	%	N	%	N	
Merchant	51	199	1	4	49.8
Professional	9	37	1	5	7.4
Gentleman	13	51	5	16	3.2
Farmer	17	68	77	265	8.3
Craftsman	8	32	16	54	0.6
Laborer	1	3	1	2	1.5
Total	99	390	101	344	

Source: Anc Doc.

of the colonial litigant population.[30] He focused on four rural Delaware
Valley counties: Bucks and Chester Counties in Pennsylvania and Burlington and Gloucester Counties in West Jersey. Farmers were 45% of all
litigants in Dutchess County courts, and Offutt's data show that farmers
were 43% of male litigants in the Delaware Valley courts. If farmers
constituted the same proportion of the population in both regions, then
they had a similar level of participation in distanced economic relationships.[31] His farmers, though, were about equally likely to be plaintiffs as
defendants, whereas Dutchess County farmers were much more likely to
be defendants, that is, debtors. It could be that as a group Delaware Valley farmers were wealthier and more established than Dutchess County
farmers so they not only had more cash to lend but also had less need to
borrow to buy tools, equipment, and land and perhaps also had less opportunity to develop new lands, so they lent money.[32]

Merchants and shopkeepers were 28% of all litigants in Dutchess
County and 11% of litigants in the Delaware Valley. More significantly,
merchants were 51% of plaintiffs (creditors) in Dutchess County but
only 16% in the Delaware Valley. Their greater presence in the Dutchess
County Court reflects their greater role as providers of credit in the
county compared to the Delaware Valley. Between 1754 and 1755, 85%
of the defendants (debtors) being sued by merchants in Dutchess County
were farmers. This suggests that there were more credit-debt relationships between the merchant community and the farmer community that
dominated the population in Dutchess County than there were in the

Delaware Valley. The interconnection, or economic integration, of those two occupational groups in Dutchess County is evident from the litigation figures.

Ethnicity. Economically related factors, such as occupation and wealth, it turns out, were more important than ethnicity in determining people's legal behavior. The percentage of litigants in the Mayor's Court who were Dutch fell in the 25–40% range during the seventy-year period from 1690 to 1760, which appears to be comparable to their percentage in the city's population. During most of the period, English and Dutch litigants in the Mayor's Court were about equally likely to be plaintiffs; approximately half the litigants of each group were plaintiffs and half were defendants. Dutch litigants also appeared in court approximately as frequently as non-Dutch people in the Dutchess County Court of Common Pleas.

Other ethnic groups rarely appeared in the Court of Common Pleas and were represented in the Mayor's Court in smaller numbers. People with a French background (who constituted approximately 11% of the white population of New York City in 1695) made up about 2% of litigants. Germans, who did not arrive in the colony in significant numbers until the early eighteenth century, constituted between 1 and 2% of litigants in the mid-eighteenth century. Jews, who came from a variety of countries and constituted approximately 1% of the white population of New York City in 1695, were about 2% of litigants during the first half of the eighteenth century. Other religious groups—members of the Anglican, Dutch Reformed, French, Quaker, Presbyterian, Baptist, and Lutheran churches—appeared in court in numbers that paralleled their immigration patterns.[33]

Conclusion

Debt litigation provides the most useful measure of distanced, impersonal, market-type relationships. As shown in this chapter, in eighteenth-century New York the debt litigation rate increased significantly, reflecting the expansion of the market economy. Debt litigation, an indicator of impersonal or purely business relationships, was not exclusively the province of the commercial elite of New York. Men from the whole range of wealth categories, occupational groups, and ethnicities participated in the legal system and were increasingly willing to sue people they knew personally, people from the same precinct. Those litigation patterns reveal the extent of the spread of market relationships in colonial New York, providing evidence that participation in such relationships was not limited to wealthy merchants but, rather, extended throughout the society. With the essential support of the courts, men from different communities—wealthy and poor, merchants and farmers, merchants and craftsmen, English and Dutch—were brought together in economic relationships. The legal system enabled these various groups to connect with one another, thus allowing different elements in the economy to become integrated. Because resort to an outside enforcer—the courts—was available, men from different occupational and geographic communities could do business with one another. In particular, merchants could engage in market relationships with farmers and craftsmen, whether from their own neighborhood or from another county.

PART III

The Economic Marginalization
of Women

CHAPTER 5

Women, the Courtroom,
and the Marketplace

The increased rate of litigation among men and the greater range of men participating in debt litigation indicated their greater involvement in market-type relationships. The opposite was true for women, however. Their low rate of debt litigation reflected their low level of independent participation in the distanced, businesslike relationships that formed the foundation of the expanding market economy.

While contractualized relationships backed by the courts allowed men to pursue expanded opportunities in the market as merchants, shop-keepers, and tavern keepers buying and selling goods, ship captains and mariners transporting goods, artisans making craft goods for the market, and farmers selling agricultural products into the market,[1] the opportunities for women were far more limited. Married farm women found a broadening niche in the production of butter and cheese for the market, but the vast majority of other women functioned only on the edges of the market economy, either in a merely supportive role alongside their husbands or in low-paying, subsistence-level "women's work."

This chapter begins by describing women's litigation rates in urban and rural courts and then gives a portrait of women's economic functions outside the home as the market economy expanded in the eighteenth century. Although some attention is paid to married women, especially married women in rural areas, the main focus is on widowed women who had no male support and who therefore had to find a place for themselves in the market-based economy. There were few opportunities for autono-mous enterprise by married women, but there was of necessity a place for women on the edges of the market economy once they were widowed; there were ways for many of them to earn cash when they no longer had a husband to support them. Although historians have previously described many aspects of women's economic roles in the northern colonies, those studies have not contrasted the urban and the rural experience as this study does. This chapter not only shows how men and women had different opportunities in the market economy but also describes how rural and urban women had distinctive experiences in the market economy.

Women and Litigation

Although the debt litigation rates of men of different wealth and occupational groups increased as they became integrated into the market economy in the eighteenth century, women's litigation rates declined as the rest of society became more commercialized and contractualized. Their low litigation rate reflected their exclusion from the business relationships that formed the foundation of the new market economy.

Women constituted only a small percentage of litigants in New York courts, and their percentage decreased over the course of the eighteenth century. In comparing urban and rural courts, one finds that women constituted a slightly larger proportion of litigants in the city than in the countryside. The vast majority of civil litigants in all early New York courts, though, were men. The number of women who came into court on their own, and on their own behalf, was small and declining.

The decline is particularly evident in the New York City Mayor's Court minutes, which cover more years and with fewer gaps, than the minutes of the other courts. Nonexecutor, single women comprised only 6% of all plaintiffs and 4% of all defendants in the approximately 600 civil cases in that court during the first decade of the eighteenth century. Of the approximately 1,500 cases brought in the middle decade of the century, the 1740s, single, nonexecutor women were still 6% of all plaintiffs but had declined to only 2% of all defendants. By the last decade, in the approximately 15,000 cases, such women were only 3% of plaintiffs and 1% of defendants.[2] These percentages are much smaller than the percentage of women not only in the population but also among city taxpayers (14% in 1734), which provides some indicator of the numbers of legally independent women in colonial New York City.

Other women came into court with their husbands, or as executors to conclude the business of their deceased husbands. In the highest court in the colony, the Supreme Court of Judicature, and in the second layer of civil courts, the New York City Mayor's Court and the Courts of Common Pleas of the rural counties, between one-fifth and one-quarter of female plaintiffs and defendants were in court as the executor of a deceased husband's estate, suing or being sued on the basis of *his* debts or credits, and approximately one-quarter of female litigants were married women suing or being sued along with their husbands. Thus only about half of female plaintiffs and defendants were single, nonexecutor litigants. If one includes in the analysis of litigators women who sued as executors or with their husbands, the numbers also show a decline. Women were 10% of plaintiffs in the New York City Mayor's Court in the 1700s, 10% in the 1740s, and 7% in the 1790s. They were 8% of defendants in the 1700s, 3.5% in the 1740s, and 3.5% in the 1790s.

We do not have minute books from all the rural county courts, and, furthermore, those courts went into operation later in the eighteenth century than the Mayor's Court did, so the same three periods cannot be analyzed. It is evident from the records that are available, however, that in the eighteenth century women's participation in those courts was even lower than in New York City. Between 1721 and 1760, only about 2% of the approximately 6,600 civil cases in the Courts of Common Pleas of Dutchess, Orange, and Westchester Counties had female plaintiffs, and only .5% had female defendants.[3] Apparently, women were not significantly more likely to appear before the local justices of the peace: fewer than 3% of plaintiffs and 1% of defendants who appeared before JP Roswell Hopkins in Dutchess County in 1764 and 1765 were women—and one woman, the widow Mary Gillet, accounted for almost two-thirds of those plaintiff appearances and one-half of the defendant appearances.[4] There are long gaps in the records of the Supreme Court of Judicature, but the minutes that are available also suggest a low litigation rate for women. In the 1,026 civil cases in that court between 1754 and 1756, for example, women were just under 8% of plaintiffs and 2% of defendants.[5]

The only comparable study of women's litigation rates in colonial America mirrors the findings of this study. Cornelia Hughes Dayton's analysis of New Haven County, Connecticut, revealed that women participated (as either a plaintiff or a defendant) in 17% of civil cases between 1670 and 1719, 10% of cases between 1720 and 1749, and 5% between 1770 and 1773.[6]

Note that in all the New York courts studied women were a larger proportion of plaintiffs than of defendants. Dayton found a similar pattern in the New Haven County Court. Of her female litigants in debt cases between 1670 and 1719, 56% were plaintiffs; from 1720 to 1749 and from 1770 to 1773 approximately 79% were plaintiffs. She explains that propertied women did not borrow money often, presumably because they rarely engaged in entrepreneurial ventures; therefore they were unlikely to appear in court as debtor-defendants except in their capacity as executors or administrators of their husbands' estates. Meanwhile, because of their discomfort with the increasingly technical nature of the legal process, poorer women actively resisted being dragged into court as debtors. They made great efforts to persuade their creditors to settle privately. Finally, Dayton notes, creditors following biblical prescriptions may have simply forgiven the debts of poor and elderly women, thereby allowing them to avoid litigation.[7]

Because men were regarded as the legally relevant parties, on occasion women were not named parties in lawsuits arising from their own activities. An example of such a case comes from the Dutchess County records. In 1753 Johannis Snyder sued Henry Bartlett for £2 12s. owed in part for one-half an ox sold to Bartlet and in part for the work, labor, and attendance of Snyder's wife as a midwife for Bartlet's wife, "done and performed at the request of Henry." Here the case involved a woman (indeed, two women), but the woman herself was not named as a litigant.[8] An example of a different sort is mentioned in attorney Joseph Murray's precedent book. He describes a 1735 action in trespass by Frederick Williams against Charles Beekman, Jr. The trespass: getting Williams's daughter pregnant, which deprived Williams of her services and brought scandal on the family.[9] The number of women appearing as litigants is therefore somewhat smaller than the number whose activities led to lawsuits, though it is impossible to determine to what extent. There is, it should be noted, no evidence that clerks neglected to mention female co-litigants, that is, women who were formally joined in the suit. For example, whenever a case name included a woman once, it would consistently include that woman in other minute book references to the case; one does not see cases that sometimes include the female litigant but sometimes carelessly do not. In any event, failure to include women in lawsuits that involved their activities is a sure indication that such women were functioning under the control of their husbands, not as independent entrepreneurs.

One cannot calculate exactly what percentage of each kind of case involved female litigants because the court clerks did not routinely note the form of action in the minute books. Women do appear to have constituted a higher proportion of litigants in cases involving personal injury—for example, slander, assault, and trespass—than in cases involving money owed. Women were, for example, a higher proportion of litigants in cases that went to trial than of all cases, which indicates their greater propensity to be involved in the nondebt actions that were most likely to be contested. Specifically, in the Mayor's Court between 1691 and 1760, there was a female plaintiff in 15% of the trials (112 out of 751 trials) and a female defendant in 13% of the trials (95 out of 751).[10]

Slander cases provide a useful example of women's high level of participation in contested personal injury cases. Of the 31 slander cases that went to trial in the Mayor's Court between 1690 and 1760, 17 (55%) involved a female litigant: 13 (42%) had a female plaintiff, and 10 (32%) had a female defendant.[11] Forty-six percent of cases with a female plaintiff (the alleged victim of slander) also had a female defendant (the alleged slanderer), and 60% of cases with a female defendant also had a female plaintiff.

Of the 13 cases in which a woman was the alleged victim of slander, the nature of the slanderous statement can be determined from the records in 9 cases. The slander against the woman involved sexual misconduct in 6 of those cases and illegal or dishonest conduct in 3 cases.[12] Yet all trial cases involving male victims of slander involved illegal or dishonest conduct; none involved sexual misbehavior. To be accused of sexual misconduct apparently caused no significant damage to a man's professional success or to his reputation in the community. A different standard of morality applied to women, who were particularly vulnerable to slanderous statements about their virginity or their sexual loyalty.[13]

Women were a higher proportion of trial litigants in cases of this nature than in debt-related cases. As debt litigation soared in the eighteenth century, bringing increasing numbers of men into the courtroom, women constituted a declining percentage of litigants. As the legal system narrowed into a more rigid rights-based conception of law in the colonial period, and as it came to focus on the interests of people engaged in long-distance and more capital-intensive economic relationships, women were increasingly marginalized from the courtroom.

In the twentieth century women have made significant progress through reliance on arguments based on rights. In fact, Sally Engle Merry's work has shown that in recent years women's relative powerlessness in personal relationships and reluctance to resort to violence have made them more likely than men to take their personal problems to court, at least to a mediation-oriented local court.[14] In the increasingly individualistic eighteenth century, however, the "individual" who held rights was a man.[15] Furthermore, the legal changes of the eighteenth century, which were designed to help people resolve their commercial disputes more quickly and predictably, made the courts even less hospitable to close interpersonal disputes than they had previously been. Straightforward, all-or-nothing litigation that dealt as much as possible only with yes-no questions (e.g., that a defendant had or had not repaid money owed) was more efficient than judicial activity that carefully balanced personal concerns.[16] Women were more likely to find resolution of personal problems outside the formal courtroom.

Overall, then, women's participation in litigation declined during the eighteenth century, while at the same time men's litigation rates soared and a broader range of men were involved in lawsuits. Women's low litigation rate is correlated with their low level of independent participation in market activities, and their lower rate of litigation in rural counties than in New York City reflects their slightly higher level of independent involvement in market relations in the city than in the countryside. As will be seen in the next section, the women who produced most successfully for the market were married rural women; their family legal issues and litigation would have been handled by their husbands. At the same time, unmarried women, who would have appeared independently as litigators, were less involved in the kind of market activities that might have led to litigation.

Rural Women

Although the subject of women's economic roles in colonial New York has received little scholarly attention, studies of other colonies, especially in New England, have yielded portraits of early American women that have many parallels to the women of New York. Thus we already know from the recent work of Laurel Thatcher Ulrich as well as the older books of Alice Morse Earle and Alice Clark that in the northern colonial household, women were commonly responsible for child care, food preparation, vegetable and herb gardening, dairying, making cider and brewing beer, smoking and salting meat, spinning, making cloth and clothing, laundering, feeding animals, and making soap, candles, and medicines. These chores would be done by the wife of the owner of the house and farm, but often also with the assistance of her daughters or female domestic servants. In addition, a colonial woman typically assisted her husband in his work as a farmer, craftsman, or shopkeeper.[17]

Rural women also participated in the economy outside the household in colonial America. Laurel Thatcher Ulrich's work provides an excellent description of women's economic exchanges in colonial New England.[18] Evidence of rural women's economic activities in New York is scarce because rural towns did not have their own newspapers and few rural account books have survived, but in one surviving account book one can see similar transactions by women in mid-eighteenth-century rural New York.

The account book of Francis Filkin, a Dutchess County storekeeper, illustrates three ways in which married women engaged in economic transactions with neighbors and storekeepers in rural colonial New York. On a number of occasions Francis Filkin's wife, Cathrena, acted as her husband's agent, delivering or collecting payments. For example, in connection with Bartholomew Crannel's running account, Filkin recorded in November 1745 that "Crennel paid in mony to my wife [£]1.4.0.," and in December 1736 he recorded that "my wife had of [Mindert] [V]and[en]bogert in new york 2 busals of bockweat @ 3/4." Filkin's daughter Trintie also acted on his behalf, as illustrated by an entry of September 1743: "I sant with [T]rintie the @14/6 of strakland to Constables wife and it is paid."[19] As suggested by Trintie Filkin's delivery to "Constables wife" (rather than to the man himself), other men's wives also acted as agents for them. Filkin recorded in August 1741 that "I paid to [Augustinus] [T]urcks wife by his ordr for Geting my Gon mended @26/," and in October 1746 he recorded in connection with Abraham Freer's account that "Freers wife Give me mony a long to york."[20]

A second way in which women participated in economic relationships was by providing services to neighbors in exchange for goods or money. For example, in connection with the Widow Doyo's account Filkin recorded in May 1745 that "She weft for me 49 Els @6p and sum at 7½." Widow Doyo's weaving (at least 56 ells, or 70 yards) for Filkin recorded that month credited a total of £1 9s. 7½d. to her running (mostly barter based) account with Filkin. In 1742 Francis Filkin noted "than my three Childeren begon to go scoll by Elisabeth Keps att 6/ pr qur pr ps." Along with her household duties, Elisabeth Keps was apparently serving as a schoolteacher. In August 1745, Maritie ten Broeck made four vests and some britches for Francis Filkin and his sons Baltus and Peter, at a total cost of £1.5s. 8d.[21]

Third, women participated in economic relationships by producing surplus products that they could trade with neighbors or local storekeepers for other items needed by the household. Most notable was farm women's role in making and selling butter and textiles. The analysis of probate inventories described in chapter 1 revealed the increased ownership of equipment used by women to produce textiles and dairy goods in the home. In the earliest period studied, 1680–99, 32% of decedents owned at least one spinning wheel, 3% owned a loom, and 24% owned dairying equipment. By the end of the colonial period (1760–75), 55% owned a spinning wheel, 22% owned a loom, and 60% owned dairying equipment.

Thus at a time when fabrics were widely available in country stores, the equipment for making fabric also became more easily obtainable. Depending on the composition of a household by gender and age, the decision might be made to continue (or commence) home production of fabrics for family use or for sale to others in the local community. Indeed, some of the fabric that the rural storekeeper offered for sale might have been produced by local women, not imported. Ulrich's description of Martha Ballard's household makes it clear that even at the very end of the century large amounts of fabric were produced in the home, at least a home that included a large number of daughters or female servants.[22]

The sharp decline in rural households owning sheep (62% of inventories between 1680 and 1699, down to 36% in 1760–75) indicates that fewer families engaged in producing the wool itself, an activity that would entail a significant amount of male work (including shearing). At the same time, however, the proportion of rural inventories that included flax increased from 12% to 35%. Though the inventory does not always make it apparent whether the flax was grown or purchased by the family, in most cases it does appear to have been produced by the household. Men often helped make flax, but most of the tasks were considered primarily women's work, so linen, unlike wool, could be made almost exclusively through female labor.[23] Making cloth of linen rather than wool thus probably entailed less male labor, allowing men's time and energy to be devoted to other agricultural activities.

The increased ownership of butter churns, milk tubs, and cheese presses—so that by the end of the colonial period 60% of rural New York households contained at least one piece of dairying equipment—reflected rural women's increased production of dairy products, not only for their own families but also for sale to others. Although the percentage of families owning cows declined somewhat between 1680–99 and 1760–75, in the later period three-quarters of rural households still owned cows, which was enough to make dairying a very common activity for women in the countryside. Joan M. Jensen has described the importance of household butter production in the mid-Atlantic states in the early nineteenth century.[24] Farm women devoted significant amounts of time not only to producing butter but also to marketing it. To a large extent, Jensen notes, their profitable dairying work came to supplant their textile production, particularly when factories began producing fabrics. Between 1750 and 1850, dairying became a central part of mid-Atlantic farm work. Men made a contribution to buttermaking by caring for the cows (e.g., by building barns to shelter the animals and harvesting hay to feed them), but women did most of the actual dairying work themselves. Butter was in fact to become mid-Atlantic rural women's most significant contribution to the market economy.

Francis Filkin's account book mentions examples of women's sales of their own products. For example, he noted in January 1736 that he had received from Mary de Graef some eggs and six pounds of butter, and he later recorded that he received from the Widow Pels two gallons of honey in October 1741 and a pig in October 1743.[25] Filkin's account book is filled with references to the trading of butter, cider, and beer, all products typically made by women.

The heavy tasks of farming were considered men's work, and it was difficult and thus unusual for a woman to carry on her husband's farm-work after his death. Some widows did, however, engage in commercial agriculture. An example is the Widow Allen of Dutchess County. Francis Filkin's account book reveals that Allen was one of five partners who promised in November 1743 to deliver 184½ bushels of wheat the next summer for bolting by Filkin and Anthony Yelverton.[26]

The Widow Allen was unusual, however. A rural woman who did not remarry when her husband died and who had grown children was more likely to become a member of her son's household than to support herself independently from farmwork. Frequently a man's will passed the house to his oldest son, allowing the widow to occupy one room and requiring the son to provide her with firewood and food.[27] Although the woman would have little autonomy in such a situation (which would be nothing new to her anyway), she at least would not have to support herself. Because there was more likely to be room in a child's home for a widow in a rural area than in an urban area, probably there were fewer rural widows than urban widows who had to work to support themselves independently. That was just as well, since the low population density in rural areas probably made it more difficult for rural colonial women to find a sufficiently large market for their services for self-support. The income earned by the women mentioned in Filkin's account book as described above was supplementary to other household income, not the sole family income. Overall, while it was fairly routine in rural areas for a married woman to make products (like butter and cheese) for the market, it was unusual for a rural widow to support herself through independent participation in a market economy. In contrast, in urban areas there were fewer opportunities for married women to produce goods for the market in the home, yet at the same time many more women lived alone and had to find a way to support themselves.

Urban Women on the Edges of the Market Economy

Like rural women, urban women participated in the market economy as their husbands' assistants in craft shops or small stores. That married women were sometimes active (if subordinate) partners in their husbands' businesses is indicated, for example, by the fact that they were sometimes jointly charged with crimes relating to the business. For example, both bookbinder Joseph Johnson and his wife Catherine were indicted for counterfeiting money in 1735, and both tavern keeper John Webb and his wife Anne were indicted in 1712 for entertaining and trading with slaves.[28] But the evidence suggests that it was unusual, not typical, for a colonial woman to be fully involved in and informed about her husband's business. Probably the best indicator of women's functions in the market economy is Mary Beth Norton's study of the claims of 468 loyalist women after the Revolution. Norton's study revealed that, with only a few exceptions, these late eighteenth-century women were ignorant about family financial matters. Norton's findings reflect colonial women's common lack of participation in household economic decision making.[29]

Probate inventories indicate that urban women were less equipped to produce goods for the market than rural women were. As noted in chapter 1, urban decedents were much less likely than rural decedents to own the kinds of equipment that women used to make textiles and dairy products. In the earliest period analyzed, 10% of the urban households owned a spinning wheel, and none of them owned a loom or any dairying equipment. Even by the end of the colonial period, only 7% of urban decedents owned spinning wheels, 4% owned looms, and only 10% had dairying equipment (compared to 55% of rural decedents owning a spinning wheel, 22% owning a loom, and 60% owning dairying equipment). Most likely it was farming families in the more rural Out Ward of New York City who owned this equipment rather than people living in the center of town.

The significantly lower percentage of households owning the kinds of equipment that women used meant that urban women could produce less in the home than rural women could. Most notably, their lesser opportunities for dairying meant that they were unable to contribute to the trade in butter that was so crucial for rural women. There was no directly comparable product successfully and independently made in the home for the market by urban women. Thus it was difficult for urban women to find a productive niche in the expanding economy of the eighteenth century. There was room for them only at the periphery of the economy.

Although most married women in New York City did not contribute goods and services to the market economy, some women who were on their own were forced to participate independently in the economy outside the home. Some urban widows were able to support themselves, at least at a subsistence level, doing low-paid "women's work" for others on the edges of the market economy. Although there were some rural widows as well who engaged in these activities, low-paid women's work appears to have been much more common in the city than in the countryside.

Urban women who had no male supporter usually had to find a way to bring in income that did not require ownership of property, particularly since urban households were less likely than rural homes to contain income-producing equipment suitable for women. The small number of urban widows who did have textile-making equipment available to them could do "putting out" work at home for merchants, but most urban women who made fabric did so outside the home by contributing their labor to new "manufactories." Thus they could earn money without owning equipment.

A 1767 advertisement in the *New York Gazette or the Weekly Post-Boy* announced the sale of products of a "linnen manufactory" that had hired poor women to do weaving and spinning:

> Society for Promoting Arts.—Whereas it has been found, that the Society for promoting Arts, &c. has answered great and valuable purposes, particularly in the Encouragement of raising Flax and manufactoring Linnen. And besides what has been done by them for that laudable Purpose, there was some Time since, put into the Hands of those Gentlemen and Trustees, the Sum of Six Hundred Pounds, to encourage the Linnen Manufactory in this City, which Sum they put into the Hands of Mr. Obadiah Wells, to employ Weavers and Spinners; which Trust, they believe, he has honestly and faithfully performed, by employing above Three Hundred poor and necessitous Persons for 18 Months past in this City, in the above Business. As the said Trustees have at present, to the Value of £600, in Linnens manufactored in this City and County, to dispose of, which while lying on Hand, disables them from farther prosecuting the benevolent Purposes; they intend therefore to send them about the City, to be sold and distributed, hoping that the good and

charitable Inhabitants will purchase them; by this Means, the Linnen Manufactory may again be carried on, the publick Interest greatly promoted, many penurious Persons saved from Beggary, and great Expence to the Corporation, by relieving Numbers of distressed Women, now in the Poor-House. And the Publick may be assured, that the said Linnens have been manufactured on as low Terms as possible, and are now ordered to be sold with out any Advance, with the Price of the Cost per Yard, marked on each Piece.

The fact that the cloth had been "manufactured on as low Terms as possible" suggests that the main purpose of the manufactory was profit, not charity. In other advertisements, linen manufactory manager Obadiah Wells offered ready money for a large quantity of flax and offered to buy fifty spinning wheels, all for the factory. In the *New York Gazette* on May 8, 1766, Wells notified spinners in New York that every Tuesday, Thursday, and Saturday afternoons he would be available "to give out Flax and receive in Yarn."[30] Another factory, established by the St. Andrew's Society, advertised in 1762 for "poor scots Women" to be employed in spinning flax, wool, or cotton; advertisers also mentioned other clothing manufactories in the 1760s and 1770s.[31] As manufacturing efforts expanded in the late eighteenth century and in the nineteenth century, increasing numbers of capitalists employed women's services on a putting-out basis, producing a wide variety of goods. Later, rural women, too, would find opportunities to do putting-out work and even to work in factories, but in the colonial period such work was rare in the countryside.[32]

Other market activities were possible for propertyless women because they did not require ownership of special equipment, so no capital investment was required. For example, some women in New York City offered laundering and sewing services from their own homes in the eighteenth century. At the end of the century Keziah Parker published the following advertisement in a city newspaper: "Washing done in the best Manner, Also Mending, and all kinds of Sewing Work, by the Widow, Keziah Parker. Mrs. Parker has particular Recommendations, from Persons of Character, as an honest, industrious woman, and as she has no other means of getting an honest livelihood for herself and family, begs Employment in this Line from such Ladies & Gentlemen as wish to have their work done reasonably and expeditiously, by the dozen or single piece."[33] Elizabeth Boyd offered to mend stockings, gloves, and mittens in a 1751 advertisement, Mary Callander offered to wash silk stockings in 1759, and Mary Campbell offered to do washing in 1773.[34] Recently widowed Mrs. Ridgely advertised her midwife services in the *New York Gazette* in

1765; that many women served as midwives is evident from statutory regulation of the profession.[35] Lydia Rose is an example of a widow who earned income as a nurse.[36] Widows or other single women who had no small children to hamper them might become domestic servants, doing traditional women's work in other people's households.

Other widows brought in income by selling simple homemade products. Sarah Sells advertised her muffins and crumpets for sale in 1768; the widow Magdalen Salnave was also a baker. A few years before the Revolution widow Hetty Hays advertised the sale of pickled and preserved cucumbers, peaches, and other goods. In 1769 Mary Morcomb sold dresses; Judith Brasher made and sold starch in New York City in 1737. In 1736 Mrs. Edwards advertised the sale of a homemade "Beautifying Wash" that "makes the Skin soft, smooth and plump" and "takes away Redness, Freckles, Sun-burnings, or Pimples, and cures Postures, Itchings, Ring-Worms, Tetters, Scurf, Morphew, and other like Deformities of the Face and Skin."[37]

Widows who inherited at least a possessory interest in a house might open a tavern or an inn, thus doing homemaking for travelers. Female tavern keepers and innkeepers in colonial Albany and New York City included Eve Scurlock, Martha Vernon, the Widow Brett, Elizabeth Jourdaine, Catherina Post, Ann Stockton, Mary Van Gusen, Mary Broughton, and Mary Harris.[38]

Those who had the requisite skills could use an inherited house as a boarding school. In 1747, for example, Sarah Hay announced in the *New York Gazette or the Weekly Post-Boy* the opening of a boarding school "in the house where she formerly lived." She would teach young ladies to read English and sew and would instruct them "in the strictest principles of religion and morality and in the most polite behaviour." Mary Bosworth, Mrs. Edwards, and Maria Gibbons also advertised as teachers. Mrs. Mary Gray, Mrs. Carroll, Isabella Jones, Clementina and Jane Ferguson, and Mrs. Cole all offered to teach young ladies sewing skills. At a more esoteric level, in 1731 Martha Gazley offered to teach "the following Curious works, Viz. Artificial Fruit and Flowers, and Wax-work, Nunswork, Philligree and Pencil Work upon Muslin, all sorts of Needle-Work, and Raising of Paste, as also to Paint upon Glass, and Transparant for Sconces, with other Works."[39]

Thus most urban widows who needed income to support themselves and their families stayed within the female sphere, bringing in cash by doing "women's work" in their own homes or in others' households. Women's work, though, was not well-paid work. Carole Shammas estimates that women's wages were one-third to one-half those of men doing comparable work. She found that in Philadelphia those doing women's work—schoolmistresses, seamstresses, washerwomen, and the like—had property assessments of zero. Their meager income allowed them only to scrape by.[40]

Only a few widows ended up doing "men's work" after their husbands died. Precisely because they had entered the male sphere those women were most likely to turn up in public records, but their prominence and significance should not as a result be exaggerated. Nor should it be assumed that they earned substantial incomes. Although a few widows— like the female mortgage lenders mentioned in chapter 2—were quite wealthy, most women doing "men's work," like those doing "women's work," lived very modestly.

Occasionally, widows of commercial farmers or craftsmen were able to take over the businesses of their deceased husbands. Margaret Norton, who became a butcher after her husband died, and Catherine Zenger, who managed her husband's newspaper publishing business for a year until her stepson could take over, are examples of such widows. Widows Hester Kortright and Tryntie Remsen were both listed as bakers in court records in 1751.[41] But such women were rare. Even if they did inherit sufficient ownership rights (which most did not), few widows had the skills necessary to take over artisanal shops.

It was easier for women to support themselves by selling goods than by making goods; shopkeeping required less specialized training than craft work. Financially comfortable widows of shopkeepers could sometimes continue their husbands' businesses. Indeed, as Patricia A. Cleary, Jean P. Jordan, and Elisabeth Dexter have shown, a number did so quite successfully in colonial New York. Jordan found 106 female retailers in business between 1660 and 1775, while Cleary counted 179 between 1740 and 1775 alone, a majority of them widows whose husbands had been merchants or shopkeepers.[42] Running a business did not always translate into wealth, however. Carole Shammas's study of Philadelphia women shows that 40% of female retailers had tax assessments of zero. She further observes that men constituted over 95% of the customers of merchants who supplied retailers with dry goods, which suggests that most female retailers ran small shops with limited inventories.[43] In any case however, as Joan Hoff Wilson points out, shopkeeping, like innkeeping, was "sex-role based in that most of the early retail stores and taverns were located in private homes and simply represented an extension of normal household duties." Craft work, in contrast, was "not always related to traditional domestic tasks," so women who engaged in craft work were genuinely breaking gender lines.[44]

Furthermore, as Edwin Perkins, Amy Erickson, and Julie Matthaei have pointed out, even women who did men's work were typically neither functioning the same as men nor perceived the same as men. Perkins has noted that "such women are best viewed as persons functioning primarily as trustees for future generations of males," that is, not as people expressing independent entrepreneurial motives but as family members who are simply "conserving and expanding assets for male progeny or male relatives until some future date." With regard to English women and inheritance in the early modern period, Erickson observed that "[f]rom the point of view of a legal system in which property was controlled by men, a woman was a conduit—nothing but the intervening stage between her father's and her husband's and her son's ownership."[45] As Matthaei has written with regard to colonial American women, although

> within the family economy women were, under special family circumstances, recruited into men's work—work that involved the producer/retailer/and/or manager in a business whose goal was the accumulation of wealth . . . such a woman never became the same as a man, nor was she seen as a man: her primary concern remained the well-being of her family. She did not seek self-advancement in a worldly career, but rather entered and left the masculine sphere as dictated by the needs of her family. Hence, the manly activities of these women did not undermine the sexual division of labor and did not challenge the category of "men's work." . . . Society understood and accepted such a woman as Mr. X's widow or daughter.[46]

Clearly, although there were some urban women who participated in the market economy, more commonly women remained outside the commercial world. Women's very invisibility makes it difficult to describe their role, but the scarcity of references to women in sources that systematically list artisans, merchants, and members of other occupational groups is itself evidence of their low rate of involvement in skilled and professional enterprises. Most notably, no women were admitted as freemen of New York City after 1728, and, technically at least, one had to be a freeman in order to engage in a trade in the city.[47] Fewer than 10% of the women in Mary Beth Norton's study of Loyalist women stated an occupation.[48] There are no letters addressed to—or even any references to—female merchants among the commercial correspondence of such New York businessmen as Gerard Beekman.[49] In short, although widows sometimes supported themselves by doing women's work or, more rarely, by filling men's shoes (usually on a temporary basis), urban women as a whole did not participate significantly in the eighteenth-century economic expansion. Despite the successes of some widows in supporting themselves independently, in general, even as a vigorous market economy developed for men, women's economic opportunities outside the home remained very limited.

Conclusion

While men's increasingly active involvement in businesslike market relationships is reflected in their increasing debt litigation rate, women's declining litigation rate shows their peripheralization from the expanding market. Women's slightly higher participation in litigation in urban areas than in rural areas suggests their marginally greater independent involvement in the market in the city than in the countryside.

Examining other sources, one can see that the economic experiences of rural and urban women differed in important ways. During marriage, a rural woman was more likely than an urban woman to produce goods for the market economy in the home. As a widow, a rural woman was probably more likely to be able to continue to live in her home; even if the house and farm had been inherited by her son, there would more likely be an extra room for her to live in with adequate provision for her food and fuel. Consequently, a rural widow was probably less likely to need to support herself by selling goods or services to others. In urban areas there were more widows independently supporting themselves by doing laundry or sewing for neighbors, by working in one of the new textile manufactories, or by opening schools, boarding houses, shops, or taverns. The urban trend was the pattern of the future, since as New York's economy continued to become more commercialized in the eighteenth century and into the nineteenth century, a larger percentage of New Yorkers lived in urban areas and thus a larger proportion of women were in the position of the colonial urban woman: few opportunities to contribute products to the market economy during marriage but a greater likelihood of having to rely on income from market transactions once widowed.

CHAPTER 6

Women, Law, and Money

The experiences of women in the eighteenth-century market economy, as described in the preceding chapter, were very different from those of men, who enjoyed greater opportunities to sell their goods to distant purchasers and enhanced opportunities to borrow money to build up their businesses and finance their investments in land. The distinct economic experiences of men and women are attributable to their different positions under the law; law was crucial in defining both men's and women's economic experiences in the expanding economy of the eighteenth century.

While the rules of law furthered the economic integration of men, as described in chapters 3 and 4, those rules constrained women economically. That is, whereas the legal system allowed men to participate in expanding trading networks in the eighteenth century, the law worked to marginalize women from the growing economy. The rules of coverture and inheritance in particular played an important role in limiting women's economic functions. While married women faced the legal barriers of coverture, widowed women encountered a lack of access to financial resources that was largely due to inheritance provisions.

Legal Constraints on Women

The only full-length study of women in the colonial legal system is Cornelia Hughes Dayton's excellent, extensive study of court actions in the New Haven County Court between 1639 and 1789.[1] Dayton is more interested in the broad topic of gendered justice than in women's role in the economy, but she does provide a valuable analysis of women's shifting experience in the legal system. She emphasizes changing cultural prescriptions as a major factor changing women's courtroom experiences more than this book does, primarily because gender expectations were particularly important in shaping women's legal experiences relating to four of her topical focuses—illicit consensual sex, rape, slander, and divorce—that are outside the purview of this book on economic history. When Dayton discusses her fifth topic, debt, there is somewhat less emphasis on cultural limitations and thus more relevance to this study of colonial New York. As will be seen, in several ways her conclusions mirror my findings. The present study makes it clear, though, that an additional crucial factor not discussed by Dayton—indeed, the key factor in explaining women's legal and economic roles—was women's inability to make enforceable contracts in a period when economic relationships were becoming increasingly contractualized.

It is particularly important to examine women's position under the law in this study because it was through legal instruments and legal process that men were able to expand their economic opportunities and foster greater integration of their communities. Women and men had a different relationship with the state, and law and the legal system played a different role in their lives.

Without her husband's participation a married woman—a *feme covert*—in early America could not write a will, sue or be sued, spend money she earned, or sell property she brought to the marriage. Furthermore, as a matter of traditional common law, women did not share men's ability to make contracts.[2] Blackstone, the most widely read explicator of eighteenth-century Anglo-American law, described married women's legal status, coverture, as follows in 1765:

> By marriage, the husband and wife are one person in law: that is, the very being or legal existence of the woman is suspended during the marriage, or at least is incorporated and consolidated into that of the husband: under whose wing, protection, and cover, she performs everything.

Blackstone added:

> But though our law in general considers man and wife as one person, yet there are some instances in which she is separately considered; as inferior to him, and acting by his compulsion. And therefore all deeds executed and acts done, by her, during her coverture, are void, or at least voidable.[3]

No casebooks or law reports recording judge-enforced law exist for the eighteenth century, but we can see even in the early nineteenth century the continuation of legal limitations on women's ability to participate in economic transactions. The rules of coverture did not change much between the seventeenth and nineteenth centuries.[4] Eighteenth-century New York courts applied the same legal principles of coverture as in the nineteenth century; they just did not formally articulate them. Therefore, the law as stated in the early nineteenth century reflects also the state of the law in the colonial period.

In the early nineteenth century, the chief justice of the New York Supreme Court stated explicitly that "[i]t is a settled principle of the common law that coverture disqualifies a *feme* from entering into a contract or covenant, personally binding upon her." That is, a married woman cannot enter into a contract. One finds other justices ruling that a married woman could not bind herself by a promissory note so as to be liable at law, that a married woman was incapable of conveying real estate by deed, and that when husbands and wives cosigned on deeds, the husbands were bound by their promises but the wives were not. If a married woman in early New York could not be bound by her contractual promises, whether in deeds or in promissory notes, then she could not effectively engage in contractual economic relationships at all.

While an exception could be made for property legally designated the woman's "separate estate" (e.g., property she may have inherited from her first husband), as a general rule women did not have control over property in seventeenth-, eighteenth-, or early nineteenth-century America. Married women were not regarded as owners of the marital property or as people entitled to spend its proceeds. New York justices specifically stated that the common law rule remained in effect: upon marriage the property of a woman passed to her husband.[5]

How Real Were Legal Constraints in Practice?

Formal litigation based on the common law was not the only form of official justice available in colonial New York. Petitions to the governor provided an alternative avenue to justice, especially for women. Under special circumstances, the petitionary process could mitigate the harshness of common law. That is, although formal law provided women with few rights, through petitions to the governor some women were able to obtain official protection of their economic interests and solutions to their economic problems. The less formalized petitionary process for remedying economic grievances, which existed alongside the formal court system, complemented the portion of the early American economy that was based primarily on personal, local exchange—exactly the kinds of economic relationships that women were engaged in. Most often the women who appealed to the governor for discretionary help were in a difficult, even desperate, situation. Often they were extremely poor women lacking financial support, as exemplified in the discussion of women's financial position in the next section (which includes references to women's petitions for permission to beg, for financial support, for possession of their deceased husbands' property, and for protection against men on whom they were directly dependent for financial support).

Even in situations when men would turn to the law courts, women often petitioned the governor for help. For example, whereas most men would bring an ejectment action in court to assert title to land occupied by another, a replevin, detinue, or trover and conversion action to regain or obtain possession of personal property wrongfully held by another, or an assumpsit action to obtain payment for services rendered, the records reveal numerous circumstances in which women instead petitioned the governor for help. For example, in 1699 Lydia Rose petitioned the governor for his help in collecting payment owed to her for services she had rendered to another, rather than bringing an assumpsit action in court to collect the money. She requested the governor's help in collecting payment for nursing and maintaining Jacob Smith, the son of Jacob Smith and Mary Griggs, both deceased. She pointed out in the petition that she was a "poor widow" with "nothing to depend on but the payment of this debt for her future maintainance." The governor ordered the executors of Mary Griggs's will, John Buckley and William Bickley, to appear before the council to answer Rose's petition. Evidently her claims were eventually allowed, though she continued to have trouble actually collecting the money: eleven years later Rose petitioned the governor to order the attorney Jacob Regnier to pay her money collected on her behalf from William Bickley. We cannot always take literally people's claims to poverty—petitions, like pleadings, tended to share a common rhetoric. Whether or not Lydia Rose (or any other particular widowed petitioner) was in fact poor, however, the reality of colonial life was that many widows were left in poverty and unable to support themselves; that widows regularly tried to achieve their goals by portraying themselves as helpless is a reflection of that societal reality.[6]

Women, more often than men, chose the petitioning process for resolution of their problems. The process had disadvantages: unlike litigation, the petition process itself required and reinforced deference and subservience on the part of the petitioner. Furthermore, the opportunities for obtaining petitionary justice appear to have declined as the legal system became more formalized in the eighteenth century to suit the needs of commercial people. Petitionary justice was often successful, however, so in a small number of special situations, especially cases involving the poorest and most vulnerable women, it did offer a way around the formal restrictions and technicalities of the common law.[7]

Common law was also tempered to some extent by the Chancery Court. Women used New York's Chancery Court only rarely, however, contrary to the argument of legal historian Richard Morris and women's historian Mary Beard. Richard Morris asserted that although English women were confined by a strict adherence to the common law on marriage and property, the legal position of women was better in America than in England because the marriage contract was viewed as a reciprocal agreement and because women enjoyed enhanced property rights. Morris stressed the use of antenuptial contracts, separation agreements, and *feme sole trader* status. He also noted that in practice common law rules restricting married women's legal rights were not always enforced in the colonies. Mary Beard, too, argued that the availability of equitable remedies substantially diminished women's subjugation.[8]

While colonists undoubtedly made some exceptions to common law rules, Morris vastly overrated women's legal position when he concluded that his evidence demonstrated "the extent to which married woman in the American colonies had achieved emancipation in the law."[9] As Linda Kerber has written, equitable modification of common law rules of coverture was exceptional, limited, and often conservative in intent throughout the colonies.[10] Certainly in eighteenth-century New York, the use of antenuptial contracts, separation agreements, and *feme sole trader* status were rare exceptions, not the rule. Though a few married women may have unofficially acted as *feme soles,* New York did not have a *feme sole trader* statute, and private empowerment acts or other official permission to act independently were rare. Moreover, there is only a handful of references to antenuptial agreements or separate estates in the wills of male New Yorkers or in the Chancery Court records. Although a substantial proportion of equity courts' business in England may have involved married women's property, this was not the case in colonial New York, where only a few women—and typically only wealthy women, not ordinary women—took their legal or economic problems to the Chancery Court. The absence of references to women's independent actions in official sources does not mean that women were never able to act independently, but it does suggest not only that such independent action was rare but also that it was dependent on men's continuing goodwill. It should be noted that the creation of separate property for women or *feme sole* status usually required the consent of the husband. Husbands did sometimes allow their wives to control property or to conduct a business, but because married women's independent authority was a rare privilege rather than a right, it was often insecure and vulnerable to challenge. Government officials sometimes allowed women who had been deserted by their husbands and left in poverty to take legal actions ordinarily prohibited to married women, but only infrequently and in extreme circumstances. In short, although at times a Chancery Court was available to New Yorkers in the colonial period, in practice it only rarely alleviated the weight of common law restrictions on women.[11]

It is clear that by the eighteenth century at least, New Yorkers adhered fairly closely to common law rules regarding married women, finding exceptions through petitionary justice and equity law infrequently and only in special circumstances. The exceptions to the common law appear to be rare. Sources from the colonial period show, for example, that married women did not appear individually (without their husbands) in the minute books of the Supreme Court of Judicature of the Province of New York, the Dutchess County Court of Common Pleas, or the Mayor's Court of New York City. Nor did they appear individually in extant bonds, mortgages, or deeds. Only widows and single women were included in tax lists. In short, there is no evidence that eighteenth-century New York deviated significantly from common law restrictions on married women. Furthermore, when there were such deviations, they were founded on the goodwill of men, not on women's entitlements. The system as a whole severely restricted women and kept them in a firmly dependent position.

Certainly there were some women in colonial New York who conducted their own businesses as shopkeepers, but they were almost all widowed women who had broader legal rights than married women, and all of them were wealthy women who had inherited money from their husbands. Scholars who have studied such women have sometimes ignored the larger context of female economic activities and consequently have created an exaggerated view of women's independence and autonomy in the colonial economy. Lisa Wilson and Patricia Cleary, for example, argue that colonial women were far more than "deputy husbands" and were actively engaged in business both during marriage and as widows.[12] No doubt women who were privileged enough to be able to engage in trade conducted their businesses capably, competently, and knowledgeably, but it is doubtful that their experiences exemplified colonial women's genuine independence. Studies like Wilson's and Cleary's tend to minimize the limits on married women's legal and economic autonomy. As Marylynn Salmon has pointed out, "Colonial women of business have been heralded without a comprehension of the rules of contract governing their activities."[13] While it is interesting to observe the minor shifts in the amount of leeway that husbands gave wives or that society allowed wealthy widows—for example, to count the number of female shopkeepers at any particular time—such shifts have little real significance in the face of women's continuing lack of genuine autonomy.

Ordinary women, the 90% of women who were married plus the large proportion of widows who were poor or of middling means, had few opportunities for engaging in market relationships beyond local, domestic exchanges. The ordinary woman was subordinate to a husband's legal and economic authority or was a widow with inadequate training or resources to engage in lucrative market relations. As Salmon notes, "Although a woman's legal rights constitute only one of several strands necessary for defining her status, control over property is an important baseline for learning how men and women share power in the family." To understand women's position, it is essential to understand formal rules of law, she writes.[14] Ignoring the legal context can lead to a distorted understanding of women's real experience. Although people sometimes made exceptions to laws or managed to circumvent them, they were in fact constrained by the rules of law. The reality was that under the common law married women could not make contracts or control property without their husbands' consent. That underlying reality must be taken into account in assessing women's position in colonial society. Although married women participated in the informal local exchange economy, then, they could not do business entirely independently of their husbands, nor did they have any legal right to the proceeds of their sales. They did not, in short, have legal and economic rights independent of their husbands.

In sum, women's limited legal rights acted as a very real constraint on their legal and economic activities. Early in the colonial period petitionary remedies tempered the impact of the strict common law in special cases. Furthermore, the chancery court supported a handful of antenuptial agreements, allowing a few women greater control over property than the law entitled them to. But, contrary to the influential arguments of historians Richard Morris and Mary Beard, the overall impact of these exceptions was actually minimal in New York, especially by the eighteenth century. The effect of the legal constraints was consequently very real for colonial women.

Women's limited legal rights and peripheral status in the legal system acted as a severe restraint on their economic activities. That constraint became relatively more significant in New York as the economy became increasingly dependent on law. As the economy expanded in the eighteenth century, women's participation was limited by their inability to make contracts that courts would enforce. In particular, since married women could not be sued for debt, lenders were hesitant to lend money to them. Without formal credit, it was difficult for a woman to participate freely in the expanded market economy.

As the economy became more integrated through the use of court-enforced contracts between people from different communities, women's lack of contractual rights increasingly became a significant barrier to economic participation. Even as colonial New York became more commercialized, with the free-willed, legally accountable individual at the foundation of an expanded contractualized economy, the principles underlying freedom to contract were still not applied to women. Whereas men were legally able to keep up with the contractualization of society, women were handicapped by that development. In the eighteenth century, while men were increasingly reworking their economic relationships into contractualized form and thus expanding their economic networks, the 90% of women who were married were legally unable to do the same.[15] Women had been able to participate in a local economy that was based on trust between neighbors who knew one another personally. With rare exceptions they were not financially independent, but they were able to buy and sell products and services within their local communities. Their limited ability to turn to the courts to buttress relationships outside the local community, however, constrained their ability to take part in such expanded relationships. Since extended relationships were the basis for the expanding market economy, married women's effective exclusion from that realm by the laws of coverture reduced their role in the economy.

Women's Financial Position

Women's participation in the market economy was affected not only by their limited ability to participate in the contractualized market economy but also by their limited control over resources. While the inability to make independent contracts hampered the economic activities of the 90% of women who were married, limited financial resources were a problem shared by all women. Lack of control over property meant that it was rare for women to own and control land for the production of agricultural goods for the market and difficult for them to accumulate enough capital and other assets in their own names to launch profitable small craft or retail shops, much less invest in large trading, banking, or manufacturing ventures. Women who were single or widowed often had to scramble to find a means of support, whether they lived in the city or the country. The polarization of wealth had a gender dimension as well as a class dimension.

To a large extent women's limited ownership of property was, like their limited contractual rights, determined by law. As observed above, husbands were the legal owners of family property. Furthermore, when men died, their widows' property ownership was shaped by inheritance law; even when their husbands died, women still did not gain control over all the family property. When a man died intestate, his widow inherited a life estate (not full ownership) in one-third of his real property, plus one-third of the personal property. A man could leave more to his wife by will if he so chose, but many bequeathed only the minimum amount—or less. If the widow rejected her husband's will because its provisions were inadequate, she inherited as her dower right a life estate in one-third of the real property only.[16] Daughters, too, tended to be slighted when their fathers died—typically their brothers inherited the income-producing assets.[17] In short, married women did not control the family property, single women were unlikely to inherit adequate means of support from their fathers, and widows typically did not gain full ownership rights over income-producing land or other assets.

Thus, as long as they were married, women shared the improved standard of living that their husbands' expanded market relationships permitted: they enjoyed the greater variety of consumer goods that most New York households acquired during the eighteenth century. Women who were single, separated from their husbands, or widowed, however, were less likely to enjoy the benefits of the rising consumer society. Being married was so important to a woman's financial status that many widows, particularly younger widows with small children, remarried quickly and were thereby able to preserve a satisfactory standard of living. One sees, for example, women who have already remarried probating their deceased first husbands' estates.[18] Remarriage, however, was not always possible.

In the eighteenth century, at any one time approximately 10% of adult white women were widows.[19] The widow's inheritance was intended to provide her with basic necessities of shelter and food. The life estate typically inherited by a widow gave her the right to occupy and draw income from real property for life rather than ownership and control of the property itself. To the extent that it was possible to earn income from inherited property, a widow's inheritance could serve as a kind of annuity, although a somewhat unstable annuity, for her support. If a woman was fortunate, an annuity was made explicit and direct, that is, stated as a fixed annual sum.[20] The widows who received such explicit annuities may have been in a better, somewhat more autonomous, position than those who were left only with the right to occupy space in their sons' homes; at least they could spend the fixed monetary amount as they chose. On the other hand, as Lisa Wilson Waciega points out, a fixed cash annuity lost value in times of inflation, whereas income from property was more likely to keep pace with inflation and bequests of fixed annual amounts of farm produce at least assured a widow of food to eat even in times of economic depression.[21]

Although inheritance rules were designed to provide widows with sufficient shelter and food so that they would have no need to support themselves, often a woman was left without adequate support. Yet at the same time both laws and societal conventions presumed that widows would be taken care of by male relatives and allowed few opportunities for them to participate independently in the economic world outside the home. Therefore, if a woman did not inherit sufficient property and an adequate income stream for her support, it was difficult for her to live comfortably on her own. Although, as described in the preceding chapter, some urban widows managed to scrape by on the edges of the market economy, many women sank into poverty upon the deaths of their husbands, and most women experienced some decline in their financial position when they became widows. Inherited property rarely allowed a widow to maintain the lifestyle she had enjoyed as a married woman.

Inheritance laws, male decedents' preference for leaving property to sons rather than wives, the diminution of estates by the repayment of debts owed,[22] and other barriers to widows' ability to gain control over family property left rural and urban women alike living in significantly reduced financial circumstances after their husbands died. When weaver John Dewsbury of Oyster Bay, Queens, died in 1698, his inventoried estate was worth £149, which placed him in the middle third of wealth categories, well above the median of £110 for that time period. But when his widow Jane Dewsbury died five years later, her inventoried estate was worth only £11, which fell in the lowest third of wealth categories. Most notably, while John Dewsbury owned three weaver's looms and a variety of types of farming equipment with which to support himself and the family, Jane Dewsbury owned none of those items. Similarly, when Suffolk County farmer Christopher Youngs died in 1727, his estate was valued at £138, which was exactly the median for that time period. When his wife died two decades later—no longer owning the farming equipment, livestock, weaver's looms, spinning wheels, and sides of leather listed in her husband's inventory—her estate totaled only £11, which put her in the lowest third of estate inventories. When Westchester County farmer William Pinckney, Jr., died in January 1747, his inventoried estate totaled £230, which placed him in the middle third of estates at that time and significantly above the median of £144. When his wife Sarah Pinckney died in September of the same year, her estate totaled only £76, which ranked in the lowest third of estates.[23]

Some widows of wealthy men were able to maintain a strong economic position. For example, Mary Teller inherited a substantial amount from her wealthy husband, William Teller, Sr. When merchant William Teller died in August 1701, his personal property (before debts) was valued at £910, which placed him in the top tenth of inventories; he was also owed over £1,000 in bonds and mortgages at the time of his death. When Mary Teller died the next year, her inventory totaled £758 (£669 of it in cash) plus £500 in debts still owed to the estate. When merchant William Cox died in 1689, his estate was worth over £1,400 even before debts owed to him. When his widow Alice Cox died five years later, her inventory totaled £423, a very comfortable amount (in the top third of inventories).[24] The female mortgage lenders described in chapter 2 are additional examples of widows who were left in very comfortable financial positions.

Carole Shammas's study of Bucks County showed, however, that the overall pattern was that widows of wealthy men were even less likely than widows of poor men to inherit the full intestacy share, so although they may have been financially comfortable, they tended to own far less than their husbands had. Shammas reports that during the Revolutionary War era, the mean net wealth of widows in Massachusetts and Pennsylvania was only about one-quarter of that of their deceased husbands; over 60% of Bucks County husbands left their wives even less than the intestacy law provided.[25] Christine Tompsett found that widows' tax assessments were often "considerably less" than one-third of their husbands' last assessment, and the widows' assessments tended to decline over time.[26] Although some of the wealth not bequeathed to wives went to daughters instead, except in very unusual circumstances as soon as daughters married control of that property passed to their husbands. Thus any increase in bequests to daughters resulted in no net increase in control over property by women.

Tax records and probate inventories illustrate that men controlled most of the resources in colonial New York. Overall between 1680 and 1770, New York's probate inventories show that women owned less than 5% of inventoried wealth. The inventories did not include real property, only sometimes enumerated debts owed to a decedent, and rarely indicated debts owed by decedents. Since women were less likely than men to borrow or lend money or to own land, women's inventories were more likely than men's to include all, or almost all, of the decedent's property. Even when inventoried property alone is considered, however, women owned far less than men did. The figures in Bucks County, Pennsylvania, were similar: Carole Shammas reports that in that county women owned 5.3% of wealth between 1685 and 1755 and 7% between 1791 and 1801. In comparison, Alice Hanson Jones found that in 1774 women owned 2.1% of the personal wealth in Massachusetts and 11.4% in Virginia and Maryland.[27] If real property, credits, and debts were also included in the calculations, the figures would show control of an even higher proportion of total property by men. Overall, men probably owned and controlled about 95% of all property in the colonial period.

The tax records also indicate a significant disparity between women's and men's control of property in colonial New York. No tax records are available for New York City for the 1750s, but in Dutchess County by the mid-1750s women owned less than 2% of the taxable wealth. In the mid-1730s, women had owned almost 13% of taxable wealth in New York City and almost 6% in Dutchess County.[28]

It should be noted that widows' annuities would neither be reflected in tax lists nor show up on probate inventories; and widows typically were entitled to the use of property that they did not own, and that would therefore not be included in inventories when they died. Assets are therefore not always equivalent to wealth or material well-being. Both tax records and inventories do, however, fairly closely reflect the amount of property over which a woman really had power. Those documents provide clear evidence that women controlled very little property in colonial New York. Furthermore, the evidence suggests that as the colonial period advanced and mid-Atlantic society became more commercialized, women controlled less and less property. Christine Tompsett has described the declining economic status of New York City widows as the colonial period advanced. Carole Shammas, Marylynn Salmon, and Michel Dahlin have observed that men became less likely to appoint their wives executors of their estates in the later decades of the colonial period.[29] David Narrett has shown that as English inheritance law replaced Dutch law in colonial New York and as New York society became more competitive and profit oriented, widows were given less control over the property of their deceased husbands and property was instead placed under the earlier control of sons. Similarly, Carole Shammas has found that as the colonial period progressed, male testators in Bucks County, Pennsylvania, gave their widows less property; increasingly, they bequeathed their wives less property than was provided in intestacy laws.[30] Thus a number of women in the late eighteenth century lived in straitened economic circumstances. Although married women gained numerous material benefits from the commercialization of New York society, their financial position as widows became more precarious.

Many women slipped into poverty after the deaths of their husbands, particularly in urban areas. Perhaps widows were more likely in the countryside than in the city to receive the support of families, possibly because there was a deeper sense of family responsibility in rural areas that led people to take care of the elderly, but more likely because there was more room in farmhouses than in townhouses and a greater abundance of home-produced food and fuel on farms than in city dwellings. Or perhaps there were more poor women in the cities because poor rural women migrated there to take advantage of urban poor relief or to seek a denser market for their services. In any case, as Amy Erickson has pointed out, the "feminization of poverty" is nothing new: "poverty has been thoroughly feminized for at least four hundred years."[31] Of the 62 people mentioned on the New York City tax list of 1734 whose assessment was £0, 35 were widows or other single women.[32] Furthermore, Christine Tompsett found a number of widows listed in the New York City poorhouse records whose names did not appear on the tax lists, and Elaine Forman Crane reports a general colonial American pattern of increasing numbers of women living in poorhouses.[33] Carole Shammas's study of female heads of families (virtually all of whom were widows) in two Philadelphia wards found that 59% in one ward and 70% in the other were exempted from paying taxes due to poverty.[34]

Newspaper advertisements asking for charitable contributions to "Poor House Keepers, Widdows, and other necessitous People as may stand most in Need of Relief" reflect some women's desperate financial plight in the mid-eighteenth century.[35] The arrest in 1753 of 22 "Ladies of Pleasure" from "several Houses of Ill Repute" indicates the lengths to which some women had to go to support themselves.[36] Criminal court records also mention prostitutes, such as Mary Lawrence and Bridget Williams, both appearing in the New York City Court of General Sessions in the 1730s.[37]

The difficulty experienced by women who had children but no male supporter is evidenced by the women who turned to the government to ensure their support. Poor widows and women who were separated from their husbands found themselves in a difficult financial position if they had to support children, as exemplified by the situations of Mary Barnet (a widow with four children and no home), Elizabeth Collins (whose husband was off at sea), and Elizabeth Pugsley (who had been abandoned by her husband); all appealed to the state for help. Both Barnet and Collins petitioned the governor for permission to beg; Pugsley requested that her husband be ordered to support her and the children.[38] Pregnant single women whose male partners had abandoned them also came before government officials to force the fathers of their children to support them.[39] Criminal court records and newspaper accounts report at least eight cases of infanticide by poor pregnant single women, further suggesting unattached women's strained financial circumstances.[40]

The extent of some poor women's dependence and economic vulnerability is suggested by their pleas for protection against those on whom they were directly dependent for financial support, particularly their masters and their husbands. Servants and slaves who were victims of abuse at the hands of their masters sometimes brought petitions to the governor requesting that their obligation of service be terminated because of abuse, and free women whose husbands were abusing them also appealed for protection.[41]

These poor women were not typical of female New Yorkers, of course; their numbers remained fairly low in the prerevolutionary period. Nor was it only women who suffered financial difficulties in colonial New York. As described in chapter 1, when New York became more commercialized, wealth became more polarized. Thus there were poor men too.[42] Women, however, suffered from special disabilities in the commercializing world. Women's lack of financial resources also affected their access to the legal system. Their options for pursuing justice in the courts were limited by the high cost of litigation. Although some women did have the resources to use courtroom procedures, as a group women were more likely than men were to be poor, so the impact of the class factor fell more heavily on women. The lack of property and financial resources therefore not only made it less likely that women would be involved in the kinds of economic relationships that might lead to litigation but also made it more difficult for them to pay for legal services when they were necessary.[43]

In short, those women who did not have a man (whether husband, father, or brother) to depend on, and who were not fortunate enough to inherit sufficient wealth to maintain them, were in a difficult position. Because it was harder for women to support themselves, they faced challenges beyond those experienced by men with few financial resources. Furthermore, women's lack of control over property limited the extent to which they could profitably invest in market opportunities in the eighteenth century.

Cultural Expectations of Women

Although women's low rate of litigation and low level of participation in the commercial world was determined primarily by their limited contractual rights and control of property, to some extent it was also affected by cultural gender prescriptions. Women were deterred from entering the courtroom and the marketplace by the prevailing gender assumptions of eighteenth-century culture and society. As Cornelia Hughes Dayton notes, women's decreased participation in the legal system is attributable in part to new notions of gentility and divergent expectations of men's and women's sexual behavior (factors that affected their role in cases relating to slander, illicit consensual sex, rape, and divorce more than their role in debt-related cases) and also to women's increasing reluctance to enter the public sphere.[44]

As one writer in a New York newspaper observed in 1734, women should stay out of public affairs. "Policks is what does not become them," he wrote, "the Governing Kingdoms and Ruling Provinces are Things too difficult and knotty for the fair Sex." The problem was not only that women were incapable of understanding political and economic matters but also that dealing with such issues would make them less feminine: "It will render them grave and serious, and take off those agreeable Smiles that should always accompany them." Women should stick to their domestic duties, he concluded, rather than "Discommoding their pretty Faces with Passion and Resentment."[45] The next month a poem, submitted by an anonymous man and entitled "Advice to a Lady," expressed similar sentiments. Women should not strain themselves trying to understand complex matters: "Nor make to dangerous Wit a vain Pretence: / But wisely rest content with common Sense," he wrote, "For Wit, like Wine, intoxicates the Brain, / Too strong for feeble Women to sustain." Nor should they abandon their feminine qualities of modesty ("Seek to be good, but aim not to be great"), passivity ("A Woman's noblest station is Retreat; / Her fairest Virtues fly from public Sight"), and eagerness to please others ("Bless'd is the Maid, and worthy to be bless'd / . . . [who] asks no Power but that of pleasing most").[46] Clearly the courtroom, like the legislative meeting hall, was considered a primarily male, not a female, place. In the social environment of early New York, therefore, litigation was not consistent with expected female behavior.

Within the appropriate female sphere women could, however, appeal to discretionary justice. In the social environment of early New York it was considered more appropriate for women to seek redress not as litigants invoking rights but as petitioners asking for male protection. One can easily understand why women in the colonial period would be more likely to get what they wanted if they took an approach that was consistent with their assigned roles and presumed characteristics as women and that was not threatening to the basic social order because it implicitly acknowledged the established gender hierarchy.[47] Thus women could more comfortably use petitionary justice than formal courtroom justice.

Similarly, women's continued participation in informal economic exchanges on the local level complemented their social networks and fit comfortably with their social roles. Engaging in larger-scale business ventures outside the community social network, however, was regarded as entering the male public sphere. The domesticity and dependence of women were important cultural values. In her book on witchcraft in colonial New England, Carol Karlsen has noted the ways in which Anglo-American men expressed their fear of independent, propertied women.[48] Men shaped the laws of coverture and inheritance to ensure that women remained dependent, and where the law left gaps, social prescriptions were expected to limit women's autonomous economic behavior.[49]

The Idealization of Colonial Women's Status

Scholars who have argued that legal constraints on colonial women's contract and property rights were so tempered in practice that they were ineffectual, and those who have focused on the exceptional colonial women who achieved financial success and have ignored the difficult economic situation experienced by most independent colonial women, have fed into a general idealization of the colonial period for women. The work of Mary Beth Norton, Marylynn Salmon, and others has undermined the simplistic view that the colonial period was a golden age for women.[50] Nevertheless, sometimes elements of the concept creep into scholarship on early American women and into surveys of American women's history. Even as recently as the mid-1990s, women's historian Carol Berkin observed that the assumption of the golden age has stayed with us, still affecting how we see the colonial period; she was still admonishing historians to break free of the golden age thesis, demonstrating that it still has a hold on scholars of early America.[51]

The argument that the colonial period was a golden age for women has been primarily based on two correlated assumptions: that wives in fact wielded significant authority and power within the home because their economic contribution to the household was equally as important as their husbands' and that only the coming of industrialization, which eliminated most of women's production at home and put men's work on a wage basis, brought inequality in practice between husbands and wives.[52] That idealized image of women in the colonial period does not reflect the reality. As Mary Beth Norton and Carol Berkin have pointed out, equality of economic contribution in a household does not mean equality of power.[53] At the extreme, for example, a slave may contribute more labor to a plantation economy than the master, but the master retains complete power over that slave. Similarly, while wives' contributions to the household were substantial, necessary, and even appreciated, they did not translate into increased power in the household. Women held an inferior position already in the colonial period; industrialization did not create that inferiority. Even if men respected their wives' contributions and were sometimes influenced by their wives' advice, legal limitations, buttressed by social norms and religious prescriptions, meant real constraints on women's authority. Men made the ultimate decisions in the household about the use and allocation of resources and labor, and women had to obey; men represented the family in the outside world while women remained invisible in the public sphere. In short, men did in practice dominate colonial households.

There has been a notable lack of consistency of argument among some scholars who have judged the progress or decline of women between the seventeenth and nineteenth centuries. Curiously, those who take seriously the advantages and benefits of nineteenth-century True Womanhood tend to be those who also deny the importance and the empowerment of colonial women's domestic roles and the consequent existence of equality between colonial husbands and wives. At the same time, the argument that True Womanhood did not actually mean enhanced authority for women because in fact men remained the bosses has frequently been paired with the argument that in practice women wielded power in early colonial households despite formal legal and political limitations. That is, in the search for clear linear patterns and trends, arguing for women's decline seems to have meant evoking an empowered colonial woman to contrast with the pure but weak True Woman of the antebellum period, whereas arguing for improvement in women's status seems to have meant portraying the colonial period as negative for women so that their nineteenth-century position and role appear more advantageous. But surely it is more consistent to see continuity, that is, to doubt women's genuine empowerment throughout the entire period. As long as men controlled resources and constituted the sole political voice, women did not have significant power.

Commercial capitalism and industrialization may have provided women with a few more options for wage work outside the home. Some widowed women, especially in urban areas, found ways of trading goods and services for cash, but their work tended to be low paying. Therefore, it was difficult for women to support themselves independent of a man. Marriage continued to be women's only real source of financial stability and comfort; wage work did not provide a stable and sufficient economic alternative to marriage. As for married women, the social pressure for middle- and upper-class women not to work outside the home was intense, and legal limitations on women in the contractualized economy made it almost impossible for a married woman to engage in independent shopkeeping or otherwise to participate independently in the market economy. At times husbands allowed their wives some leeway, such as selling surplus butter or functioning as a shopkeeper, but the husbands retained ultimate control over proceeds, credit, and allocation of labor. Thus, although certain changes in women's experience took place between the early colonial period and the antebellum period, at bottom the most important reality remained the same: men managed women's labor and property.

Women may have exerted informal influence in both the colonial period (as household producers) and the antebellum period (as moral guardians of the home), but in neither period did women enjoy genuine autonomy as individuals. Women may have had opportunities in one period that they did not have in the other. For example, women probably did engage in a wider range of skilled functions during the colonial period than they did later when most forms of production shifted from the home to the factory and certain occupations became more professionalized; and middle-class women probably did play a more substantial role in bringing up their sons in the antebellum period than they had previously (not to mention that their lives were probably easier overall than they had been in the first two centuries of European settlement). But those respective advantages in the two periods did not mean real autonomy for women. Women lacked autonomy in both periods.

Although the overall picture is one of continuity (women's continuing lack of autonomy), this book points to one way in which women experienced a decline relative to men. The intent is to describe that decline without idealizing the period that came before, that is, without suggesting that there was a golden age before the contractualization of the economy when women were significantly more empowered. The book does not judge whether women's lives overall became "better" or "worse" as the colonial period progressed—indeed, as Mary Beth Norton and Carol Berkin have pointed out, it is not even clear by what (or whose) standards and values one would make such a broad judgment.[54] The study just judges one aspect of women's lives and concludes that certain legal and economic developments of the eighteenth century had a negative effect on women's economic roles, position, and power relative to men.

Women's economic opportunities relative to men's declined in the eighteenth century. More specifically, the commercialization and contractualization of the economy and the formalization of law meant that women were excluded from participation in certain new economic opportunities and relationships outside the household while men were increasingly integrated into the expanded economy. The result was a progressively clear distinction between women's and men's opportunities, and thus between male and female spheres.

From the time of the first European settlement men had been the official public representatives of the family unit.[55] From the beginning men had also had more educational options available to them, making it easier for them to acquire the training necessary to enter craft specialties and such professional fields as law and the ministry. Their ownership of family property meant that they controlled the economy of the colonial household. But the growth of a market economy opened up new economic possibilities—possibilities that were largely closed to women—and thus made the gap between women's and men's opportunities significantly wider.

The expansion of the market had a major impact on women that was quite different from its effect on men. First, that expansion began the shift toward labeling men's work as "economic" work and women's work as outside the economic sphere. Jeanne Boydston has observed that although women's work did not actually change much during the colonial period, because the context shifted their work came to be perceived differently by the eve of the Revolution. Women's household labor became devalued during the eighteenth century as extrahousehold work acquired a cash value. During the early colonial period, "husbands' and wives' work were understandable in the same economic terms": both labored directly to ensure the "material viability" of the household, and therefore the work of both was seen as economic. When money came to be a significant determinant of success and status, and economic work came to be seen as an individualistic activity serving a money-making function, women's unpaid household labor declined in status and came to be seen as outside the economic sphere.[56]

Second, as shown in this book, the expansion of the market economy peripheralized women from the economy outside the home. Although the legal system provided a mechanism of economic integration for male

New Yorkers, the elevated importance of formal law in the economy resulted in the peripheralization of women from the core of economic relations. Once contractual arrangements became the basis of economic exchanges, married women's inability to make enforceable contracts became a substantial barrier to involvement in the economy. They were no longer able to depend on mutual trust to support their economic arrangements, nor was informal justice easily available to them any more. In addition, women's limited control over financial resources further hampered their ability to participate in the expanding economy. Thus commercialization and contractualization had a dramatic impact on women.

In fact, the disparate effect of commercialization on women and men in the eighteenth century was sharper than the impact of industrialization in the nineteenth century: while industrialization in practice gave job opportunities to a small number of married women, in the commercial economy of the eighteenth century strict legal limitations meant that married women as a group could not independently participate in commercial opportunities. There was more room for women in the industrial economy than in the commercial economy. Thus commercialization more significantly widened the gap between women's and men's economic opportunities than industrialization did. While industrialization limited women most substantially through social pressure and custom, commercialization limited women more directly through law.

The disparate impact of commercialization on women and men significantly divided the sexes. The separation of spheres that most scholars attribute to industrialization and locate in the nineteenth century actually began in the colonial period. Most historians, following Nancy Cott, have attributed the separation of male and female spheres to industrialization.[57] The household economy of the colonial period, they point out, had depended upon equal contributions of men and women; industrialization offered unequal opportunities to women and men. Although women were eligible for a few wage-earning jobs, most occupations were open to men only. Consequently, men had economic opportunities that were denied to women, leaving women on the domestic front excluded from full participation in the economy. Closer analysis shows, however, that the division of male and female spheres in fact predated those developments. The differential between women's and men's economic opportunities widened substantially in the eighteenth century as women were excluded from full participation in the commercial economy that preceded the industrial economy. While men's work continued to be deemed economic, women's labor came to be seen as outside the economic sphere. Gender inequality was not, though, caused by capitalism itself. Rather, it was the result of continuing patriarchal attitudes and practices, particularly as embodied in law.

The division of spheres along gender lines existed well before the nineteenth century and helped lay the foundation for nineteenth-century economic developments. If one accepts the view that women's maintenance of the domestic sphere as a place of traditional values was necessary to anchor industrialization, then the legal and economic developments of the colonial period—which had the effect of excluding women from the core of economic relationships—could be seen as helping to provide an essential social structure for industrialization.

Women's Behavior and Women's Nature

There is another way of idealizing women: some scholars have interpreted women's apparent lack of embrace of capitalism and the adversarial legal system as heroic resistance based on women's naturally anticompetitive nature. Those scholars attribute women's past and present economic and legal behavior to their natural qualities as women. They maintain that women are by nature communally oriented, concerned about connections and relationships between and among people, and imbued with the values of caring and responsibility to others, whereas men, in contrast, are individually oriented, concerned about autonomy, and imbued with the values of rights and competition.[58] Although they usually refrain from claims of biological difference, some scholars argue that the different socialization of men and women results in a different mentality. Their theories have been used to speculate that a female-constructed legal system and economic system would work differently from the male systems that have existed throughout our history—that the female structure would be more communal and less individualistic and rights oriented. They have argued that women have historically resisted participating in our adversarial legal system and in our capitalist economic system because they do not feel comfortable with the values and assumptions of those systems, and they have maintained that women's concepts of mutuality provide an alternative model of justice and of exchange relations. But close analysis shows that women's legal and economic behavior in early America was not merely an expression of inherent, gender-based inclination. In both the legal and economic domains, women's actions were to a large extent determined by external conditions.

Although this study of early New York supports the assertion of many scholars of feminist jurisprudence—such as Carrie Menkel-Meadow, Joan Hoff, Lucinda M. Finley, Eve Hill, Suzanna Sherry, and Ann C. Scales—that women and men approach law, conflict, and justice differently, it provides no evidence that men's and women's different approaches to law are attributable to fundamentally different natures or attitudes, as is often suggested by those scholars.[59] This debate over gender differences has obscured the more important factor of external constraints that hinder women from behaving economically and legally the way men do. Because in practice early New York's economic and legal system privileged men at the expense of women, it does not really matter (and we cannot tell) whether there is anything fundamentally male about formal, rules-based, universalized, abstract justice or anything fundamentally female about informal, contextualized justice, and because in practice men benefited from their rights as individuals, it does not matter (and we cannot tell) whether there is anything fundamentally more male about individualism or a focus on rights. Certainly women in colonial New York behaved differently than the men did, but there is no evidence that that was because they were different by nature. Rather, women's legal behavior was clearly determined by external conditions, by their different legal, social, and economic position. Indeed, women had little choice. Finding themselves unprotected by the law, limited by societal expectations that women be passive and subordinate, and lacking in financial resources, early American women found little support in the formal court system.

If women did not participate as extensively as men did in commercialism and capitalism, it was also not as a matter of choice. In her 1993 review article on "Gender and the Transition to Capitalism in Rural America," Nancy Grey Osterud writes that "gender had profound consequences for rural people's acceptance of or resistance to the penetration of capitalist social relations," that "women's conception of mutuality provided farm movements with an ideological alternative to capitalism," and that therefore "[g]ender relations . . . are central . . . to the history of capitalism in the countryside."[60] Such statements suggest that women by nature resisted capitalism. But there is no evidence of such a natural inclination. In fact, if women did not participate actively in capitalism it was because they were not truly given the option. Women were not a natural bulwark against capitalism; women did not help men resist capitalism. Women were largely excluded from capitalism.

Thus although cultural prescriptions affected women's economic and legal behavior, there is no evidence that women's essential nature determined their role in eighteenth-century economic and legal systems.

Instead, women's low level of involvement in the expanding market economy and in courtroom litigation is attributable primarily to legal limitations on their contractual rights and property rights.

Women, in comparison to men, did not participate as actively in the market economy, did not as eagerly embrace the early rise of capitalism, were more likely to resort to informal paths to justice, and were less likely to participate in formal litigation. This behavior was not merely an expression of inherent, gender-based inclination. In both the legal and economic domains, women's actions were to a large extent determined by external conditions: women controlled few financial resources, were constrained by cultural expectations of proper female behavior, and were excluded from the opportunity to engage in the contractualized relationships that formed the foundation for the expanding eighteenth- and early nineteenth-century economies. Because women had so little autonomy and so little free choice in early America, women's behavior at that time cannot be presumed to reflect women's nature. Scholars may want to interpret women's low level of participation in capitalist economic relations or in an adversarial legal system as evidence of their active resistance to oppressive systems that did not reflect women's values. But it is clear that essentialist arguments do not provide useful explanations of colonial women's legal and economic behavior. The reality is that social, legal, and economic constraints, not women's inherent qualities, determined women's marginal status in colonial New York.

Conclusion

The expansion of the market economy in New York, while providing fantastic new opportunities for men, had a negative impact on women. Exclusion from legal rights denied most women court support of extended economic relationships in the eighteenth century. Before the development of an integrated market economy, the fact that women were denied many legal rights did not as significantly affect their participation in the economy as it would later. When economic relationships are based on trust and mutual dependence rather than on contract, it matters less that married women cannot independently make contracts or sue in court. As an economy changes, however, and trading relationships rely on legal sanctions for enforcement, women are necessarily at a greater disadvantage. Women were excluded from the contractualized relationships that formed the basis of the new economy. Such exclusion affected them both outside the home and in the home. Self-support in the market at a subsistence level was possible for widows, but women as a group were denied the opportunity to participate in more profitable distanced economic relationships by their legal inability to enforce contracts. While men were being integrated into a growing economy, women were increasingly being excluded from it.

The denial of equal access to the legal system, the institution of economic integration, began the peripheralization of women from the market economy. Thus the often-heralded separation of working spheres that occurred with industrialization in the nineteenth century only continued the process of marginalization, a process that began with eighteenth-century commercialization. And peripheralization from the core of all these forms of capitalist relations was not a matter of choice for women. It was not an expression of women's innate antimaterialistic or anticompetitive qualities. On the contrary, it reflected social attitudes and legal and economic limitations of the time.

CHAPTER 7

The American Revolution and Beyond

As the War for Independence approached, Americans began to vocalize more vigorously their discomfort with the changes discussed in this book. Their concerns about consumption of luxuries, commitment to community versus pursuit of self-interest in a free market, and the role of jury trial in the legal process often conflicted with or challenged the legal and economic developments that occurred during the first half of the eighteenth century.

As shown in chapter 3, when writers praised the sanctity and importance of juries in the 1760s and 1770s, the jury had already substantially declined in importance and was no longer part of the typical dispute resolution process in either urban or rural courts. The decline of jury trial in colonial New York by the 1750s is particularly significant in light of the American patriots' claims a decade later that jury trial was essential to the preservation of British liberties. During the controversy provoked by the *Forsey v. Cunningham* case in 1764–65, New Yorkers almost unanimously protested the clear threat to the sanctity of jury verdicts. In 1765 the New York Assembly resolved that "Trial by Jury is the Right of the Subject not only by the common Law, by Statute Law and the Laws of this Colony, but essential to the Safety of their Lives, Liberty, and Property."[1] The Stamp Act Congress of 1765 asserted that "trial by jury is the inherent and invaluable right of every British subject in these colonies"; the First Continental Congress of 1774 protested all statutes that "deprived the American subject of trial by jury"; and the Declaration of Independence of 1776 charged the King with "depriving us in many cases of the benefits of trial by jury."[2] The revolutionaries vigorously supported jury trial in order to ensure American control over politics and justice, even

though their position conflicted with commercial people's efforts to avoid
jury trials in economic matters and even though their pleas came at a time
when trials were in practice rare in New York courts. By 1750 the civil
jury trial rate in the Mayor's Court was one-sixth of what it had been in
1700, and other courts mirrored the pattern.

Furthermore, the increased frequency of lawsuits between men from
the same geographic community, as described in chapter 4, reinforces
a substantial body of evidence that the idealized, tight-knit, traditional
community had declined by the time of the American Revolution. Men
from all wealth and occupational categories appeared in court as litigants
in debt-related actions. Even in rural Dutchess County, one-third of all
taxpayers listed in 1735 litigated at some point in their lives. Since most
commercial agreements did not end up in court, far more than one-third
of rural male New Yorkers must have been involved in such agreements.
That is, far more than one-third of rural men must have been participating in distanced, market relationships. Relationships became more
contractualized, and courts increasingly enforced the explicit terms of
contractual arrangements. Although creditors sometimes tolerated late
payments on debts, they also showed a keen willingness to use the courts
to force repayment, even if it meant that their debtors ended up in jail.
Even neighbors, people who lived in the same precinct, sued each other
for repayment of debts, reflecting the depersonalization of local relationships as the market spread. Yet the pamphleteers of the Revolution chose
nevertheless to use the persuasive communal rhetoric of civic virtue and
republicanism as the foundation of their cause.

Finally, as shown in chapter 1, the American colonists were buying
luxury goods in increasing numbers in the decades preceding the Revolution. By the 1760s about two-thirds of urban and rural decedents died
owning candles and looking glasses, more than one-third of them owned
such luxuries as teaware and forks and knives, and between one-quarter
and one-third of them owned china, clocks, and pictures. Travelers recorded the widespread ownership of luxuries, newspapers advertised
hundreds of imported products for sale, and there was at least one store in
every large village. Furthermore, a large percentage of New Yorkers was
involved in borrowing and lending money to pay for those purchases. By
the end of the colonial period, 60% of urban and rural decedents died
with assets that included debts owed to them. Those investments—debts
recorded in the form of bonds, notes, or book debts—suggest the beginning of a capital market in colonial New York. Yet in the middle of the
consumer revolution and particularly during the American Revolution
one heard loud laments about the corruption brought about by luxuries,
debt, and commercialization.

Some historians have argued that the revolutionary pamphleteers' laments about loss of virtue were not genuine. Certainly there were political advantages to the rhetorical positions taken on such issues as luxuries, debt, juries, communal values, and the pursuit of self-interest during the revolutionary era: the purchase of luxuries could convincingly be shown to be bad because it increased American economic dependence on England, the source of manufactured goods; portraying luxuries, debt, and promotion of self-interest as exemplifying English moral corruption allowed Americans to take the high ground and promote their own unity; and juries could persuasively be portrayed as the colonists' voice to counterbalance pro-English tendencies of judges appointed by the governor.

Whatever the real role of economic factors in the coming of the American Revolution, however, the politically advantageous arguments used to explain and justify it were not necessarily disingenuous. Although the views expressed by revolutionary pamphleteers were not always consistent with the way many Americans in fact experienced community, consumer goods, or the legal system by the late eighteenth century, those views were nevertheless legitimate and genuine expressions of uncertainty by people who were grappling with economic change. Those who assume that political arguments were made merely to mask economic concerns disregard an important element of human nature: often the loudest arguments against offensive behavior or practices are heard as a society is making a transition to those very practices. They are often a nostalgic—and genuine—expression of uneasiness about change at a time when dominant forces in the society have in fact already accepted the new practices. It is apparent that revolutionary era rhetoric in opposition to luxuries and the pursuit of self-interest and in favor of juries and communal values was significantly shaped by uneasiness about societal changes and nostalgia for a remembered—or imagined—more comfortable past.

After the American Revolution and into the nineteenth century, the consumer revolution continued with increasing intensity, cases continued to be resolved without jury trial, and individualism and the pursuit of self-interest came to dominate economic life—despite rhetoric against all three during the revolutionary era. In short, though the revolutionaries may have praised republicanism, in practice, as this study has shown, many of them had already moved on to live lives based more on the principles of liberalism. So how were Americans to retain the values of community that were necessary for holding the society together?

The solution grew out of the distinct rights and responsibilities of women and men. Women, who were effectively excluded from the new economic opportunities because of their inability to make binding contracts in a progressively contractualized commercial environment, were to be the bearers of the old values that were necessary to hold the society together, the values of community, selflessness, and morality.[3] After arguing for community during the revolutionary era, men went back to enjoying the benefits of economic liberalism after the Revolutionary War, and the more individualistic they became the more they relied on women to support the old values. The appropriate spheres of men and women became more sharply distinguished, with men taking the public sphere and women assigned to the home. Women's marginalization from official justice—which had come to embody the new, more individualistic, economic mentality—could be seen as part of their separation from the public sphere. Women's peripheralization from the economy further reinforced their domestic orientation.

Moreover, despite revolutionary rhetoric against the king as patriarch—and contrary to the assertions of Mary Ryan, who describes the late eighteenth and early nineteenth centuries as a period of "patriarchy in disarray," and Glenna Matthews, who refers to the "erosion of patriarchy" in that period—the developments of the late eighteenth century actually reinforced and strengthened patriarchal authority in the home.[4] Although economic changes may (as Matthews and Ryan argue) have made sons less dependent on fathers, and may even have allowed women to choose husbands independent of their fathers' will, neither the American Revolution nor commercial capitalism genuinely liberated women from men's patriarchal authority. Those women who had more say in choosing a husband still had to submit to their husbands' dominance in the household. Perhaps parental authority over women became weaker, but men's more important authority as husbands continued.

Some scholars point to the rise of "companionate marriage" as undermining patriarchal attitudes and increasing women's power and autonomy in America and Europe.[5] But Amy Louise Erickson has aptly noted that "one man's 'companionate marriage' is another woman's 'gentle tyranny'"; that is, the new "romantic ideals were simply a new means of maintaining male dominance at a time when overt demands of submission were no longer acceptable."[6] In short, despite rhetoric of love and partnership, the structure of power in the family did not change in law or in practice in the eighteenth century.

The male revolutionaries managed to limit the application of their rhetoric of self-governance and independence to propertied white males, granting women no improved political rights in the new nation.[7] Moreover, even though commercial capitalism eventually led to the displacement of the male-controlled household as the primary locus of production and led to the recognition of a distinct female domestic sphere, men still remained the family patriarchs: they still legally controlled the family's resources and still monopolized political representation. Toby Ditz has written that women's moral role under the cult of domesticity allowed them to become the new "mediators" between the private and public spheres, but in fact women's increased connection to the public sphere was minimal. Women may have been perceived to have a moral influence on the nation, but that was in no way the equivalent of enjoying actual representation in policymaking bodies. Men retained the exclusive privilege of speaking on behalf of the family in the public sphere.[8]

"Republican motherhood" and the "cult of domesticity" may have defined the moral education of children as an area of female influence, but it did not enhance women's real power. Indeed, one of the chief attributes of the antebellum "True Woman" was submissiveness.[9] True Womanhood in practice meant selflessness, subservience, and obedience, not independence, authority, or power. Thus although revolutionary rhetoric criticized patriarchal authority and slavish dependence, and it applauded traditional values—such as communalism, selflessness, morality—that later would be viewed as characteristically female qualities, the War for Independence neither liberated nor empowered women. In fact, more political and economic freedom for men was possible only because, in a time of expanding suffrage and entrepreneurial opportunities, societal order was maintained by men's maintaining authority over their households and by women's sacrificing their own individuality and autonomy.

Conclusion

American economic history, legal history, and women's history do not begin with the American Revolution, though historians often seem to assume otherwise. Not only were developments of the nineteenth century continuations of processes that began in the colonial period, they also were built on those earlier foundations.

First, the high level of consumption, debt, and debt litigation in colonial New York, and the extent of convergence of urban and rural patterns for the three factors, show that colonists in both regions participated in the consumer revolution, produced surplus exchangeable goods, and were involved in businesslike credit relationships. That is, both urban and rural New Yorkers were interested in more than a subsistence existence, and they had moved beyond regarding economic relationships as personal and communal. They were prepared to enter the industrial economy as consumers and wage-earners.

Second, by the end of the colonial period the legal system worked to promote business. Mutuality and trust may have provided adequate support for exchanges that took place within the early colonial family or close community, but as the economy expanded beyond the local arena, people could not rely on communal ties to enforce economic arrangements, so the courts took the place of personal trust. By serving as a connector between different communities of men—merchants and farmers, merchants and craftsmen, and urban and rural dwellers—law became the essential foundation for an integrated economy. Such integration allowed a true market economy to emerge and later was to be essential to nineteenth-century economic expansion on the national level. Furthermore, the law encouraged commercial investments by making legal agreements predictably enforceable. The legal system firmly supported the contracts that formed the basis of the market economy, allowing ambitious, risk-taking entrepreneurs to gain the advantage of their speculative ventures and thus begin to build up the capital that their sons and grandsons would use to establish manufacturing plants. Thus colonial legal developments not only promoted and fostered commercial growth in the eighteenth century. By buttressing long-distance economic relationships, sustaining and encouraging the growing demand for consumer goods, and providing legal support for the accumulation of capital, eighteenth-century legal changes laid an essential foundation for the industrial revolution.

Third, by the end of the colonial period there was a sharp distinction between men's and women's economic opportunities. While men were able to engage in impersonal, distanced relationships with men from other communities as part of an expanding market economy, women's position under law typically confined them to personal, domestic, and local relationships. Gender distinctions were important in the transition to capitalism because men could become independent producers in a market economy only by relying on the nonmarket services of the women in their households. And gender relations were important because women, through the denial of legal rights, were forced to base their interactions on trust rather than guarantees, and thus were forced to maintain a more communal environment. Without women maintaining "traditional" values—both within their families and with other women—contractualization and individualization would have atomized society into isolated and alienated pieces. Maintenance of traditional values in the home provided a comforting, loving, caring place for the capitalist man to retreat to from the harsh commercial world, and maintenance of traditional values between women helped keep separate families (and thus the society as a whole) connected. In commercial and industrial economies, men could act as individuals only because women remained connected. The gender distinctions that existed by the end of the colonial period with regard to economic opportunities and spheres thus supplied a crucial foundation for nineteenth-century economic developments.

In short, it was the interrelationships between merchants and farmers, between urban and rural regions, between law and economy, and between women and men that provided the basis for the market economy and later for industrialization. One cannot write the full story of early American economic development without considering all those factors and intertwining the study of economic history, legal history, and the history of gender.

The findings of this study show that the colonial period needs to be more fully incorporated into the analysis by scholars in all three fields of history. Developments of the nineteenth century had their roots in the colonial period. Capitalism did not arise abruptly in the nineteenth century; the process was well under way in the colonial period. Law did not suddenly begin playing an active role in economic development in the nineteenth century; that relationship existed during the colonial period. And women were not suddenly displaced from the core of economic relationships in the nineteenth century; their peripheralization was clearly evident in the colonial period. Historians should stop searching for the rise of capitalism, an instrumentalist legal system, and the roots of women's economic marginalization in the nineteenth century. The search must be redirected to focus on the seventeenth and eighteenth centuries, even if it may mean that we lose our idealized image of the colonial period.

Appendix

Table A.1

Population of New York County in the Eighteenth Century

Year	1698	1713	1723	1731	1737	1746	1756
Population	4,937	7,248	8,622	10,664	11,718	13,294	13,040
% increase		47	19	24	10	13	−2

Sources: Doc Hist, 1:467–74; and Evarts B. Greene and Virginia D. Harrington, *American Population before the Federal Census of 1790* (New York, 1932), 92–101.

Table A.2

Population of Dutchess County in the Eighteenth Century

Year	1713	1723	1731	1737	1746	1756
Population	500	1,083	1,727	3,418	8,806	14,148
% increase		117	90	99	158	61

Sources: See table A.1.

Table A.3

Dutchess County Mortgages, 1754–1770, Occupations of Mortgagors and Mortgagees

	Mortgagors				Mortgagees			
	Crum Elbow Precinct		Rombout Precinct		Crum Elbow Precinct		Rombout Precinct	
Occupation	%	N	%	N	%	N	%	N
Yeoman/farmer	77.7	140	59.0	39	8.0	16	18.8	13
Gentleman/esquire	2.8	5	1.5	1	14.5	29	20.3	14
Merchants	4.4	8	0.0	0	50.1	101	37.7	26
Shopkeeper	0.6	1	0.0	0	0.0	0	0.0	0
Trader	0.6	1	0.0	0	0.0	0	1.4	1
Merchant	2.8	5	0.0	0	50.1	101	29.0	20
Merchant/esq.	0.0	0	0.0	0	0.0	0	7.2	5
Tavern keeper	0.6	1	0.0	0	0.0	0	0.0	0
Widow	0.0	0	0.0	0	16.0	32	8.7	6
Widow (no occup.)	0.0	0	0.0	0	13.5	27	8.7	6
Widow/merchant	0.0	0	0.0	0	2.5	5	0.0	0
Professional	1.1	2	0.0	0	1.5	3	1.4	1
Minister	0.0	0	0.0	0	0.5	1	0.0	0
Attorney	0.0	0	0.0	0	1.0	2	1.4	1
Clerk	1.1	2	0.0	0	0.0	0	0.0	0
Doctor	0.0	0	1.5	1	3.5	7	0.0	0
Craftsman	12.8	23	36.0	24	3.0	6	11.6	8
Blacksmith	5.0	9	3.0	2	0.0	0	4.3	3
Carpenter	0.6	1	6.0	4	0.5	1	1.4	1
Cooper	1.1	2	3.0	2	0.0	0	0.0	0
Cordwainer	2.8	5	7.6	5	1.5	3	1.4	1
Currier	0.6	1	0.0	0	0.0	0	0.0	0
Joiner	0.0	0	0.0	0	0.0	0	1.4	1
Miller	0.6	1	7.6	5	1.0	2	0.0	0
Painter	0.0	0	1.5	1	0.0	0	0.0	0
Surveyor	0.6	1	0.0	0	0.0	0	0.0	0
Tailor	0.0	0	3.0	2	0.0	0	1.4	1
Tilemaker	0.6	1	0.0	0	0.0	0	0.0	0
Turner	0.0	0	1.5	1	0.0	0	0.0	0
Upholsterer	0.6	1	0.0	0	0.0	0	0.0	0
Weaver	0.6	1	1.5	1	0.0	0	1.4	1
Wheelwright	0.0	0	1.5	1	0.0	0	0.0	0
Laborer/mariner	1.1	@	1.5	1	1.0	2	0.0	0
Carman	0.0	0	0.0	0	0.5	1	0.0	0

(Continued)

Table A.3

(*Continued*)

Occupation	Mortgagors				Mortgagees			
	Crum Elbow Precinct		Rombout Precinct		Crum Elbow Precinct		Rombout Precinct	
	%	N	%	N	%	N	%	N
Miner	0.6	1	0.0	0	0.0	0	0.0	0
Mariner	0.6	1	1.5	1	0.5	1	0.0	0
Executor	0.0	0	0.0	0	2.0	4	0.0	0
Trustee	0.0	0	0.0	0	0.0	0	1.4	1
Unknown occup.		51		22		31		19
Total	100.5	231	99.7	88	99.6	231	99.5	88

Sources: William McDermott, ed., *Eighteenth Century Documents of the Nine Partners Patent, Dutchess County, New York*, vol. 10 of *Collections of the Dutchess County Historical Society* (Baltimore, 1979), 333–498; and Helen Wilkinson Reynolds, ed., *Eighteenth Century Records of the Portion of Dutchess County, New York, that was included in Rombout Precinct and the original Town of Fishkill*, vol. 6 of *Collections of the Dutchess County Historical Society* (Poughkeepsie, 1938), 127–207.

Note: Percentages are of mortgagors and mortgagees of *known* occupation.

Table A.4
Dutchess County Mortgages, 1754–1770, Residences of Mortgagees

Residence	Crum Elbow		Rombout	
	%	N	%	N
Dutchess County	29.3	66	56.3	45
Crum Elbow Precinct	7.1	16	2.5	2
Beekman Precinct	0.4	1	0.0	0
Northeast Precinct	0.0	0	0.0	0
Oblong	0.0	0	0.0	0
Philips Precinct	0.0	0	1.3	1
Poughkeepsie Precinct	4.0	9	5.0	4
Rhinebeck Precinct	13.8	31	0.0	0
Rombout Precinct	2.2	5	45.0	36
No precinct named	1.8	4	2.5	2
Outside Dutchess County	70.7	159	43.8	35
Albany County	0.9	2	0.0	0
Kings County	0.0	0	5.0	4
New York County	60.9	137	36.0	29
Orange County	0.0	0	1.3	1
Queens County	3.1	7	0.0	0
Richmond County	0.0	0	1.3	1
Suffolk County	1.3	3	0.0	0
Ulster County	2.2	5	0.0	0
Westchester County	0.9	2	0.0	0
New Jersey	0.4	1	0.0	0
Connecticut	0.9	2	0.0	0
Residence unknown		6		8
Total number		231		88

Sources: See table A.3.

Note: Percentages are of mortgagees of known residence 225 Crum Elbow mortgages and 80 Rombout mortgages).

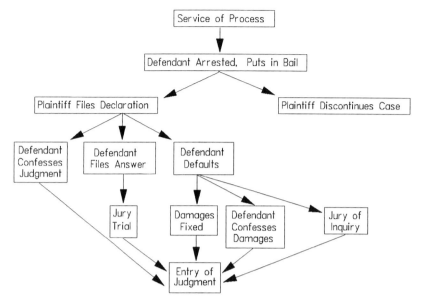

Figure A.1 Procedure in New York Courts

Sources: MC Min, SC Min, DCCCP Min.

Table A.5

Cases Resolved by Jury Trial as Percentage of All Cases in
Each Category, Mayor's Court of New York City

Plaintiff–defendant	1714–1715	1754–1755
Merchant–merchant	0★	0★
Craftsman–craftsman	18	2
Merchant–craftsman	11	2
Craftsman–merchant	25	19

Sources: MC Min.

★ For the whole period from 1690 to 1760, this figure is actually slightly
over 0%. Merchant-merchant litigative pairs did occasionally go to jury
trial in the early eighteenth century.

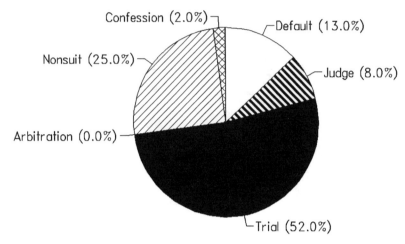

Figure A.2 Cases Resolved in Supreme Court, 1694–1696

Source: SC Min.

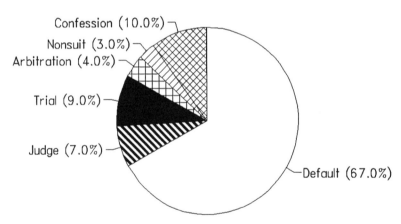

Figure A.3 Cases Resolved in Supreme Court, 1754–1756

Source: SC Min.

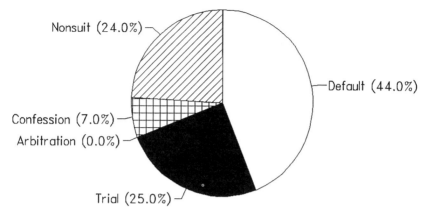

Figure A.4 Cases Resolved in Mayor's Court, 1694–1695

Source: MC Min.

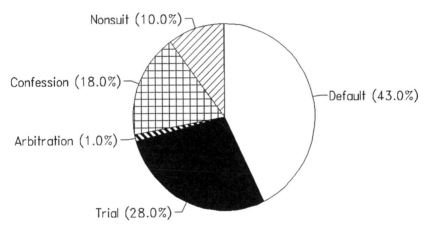

Figure A.5 Cases Resolved in Mayor's Court, 1714–1715

Source: MC Min.

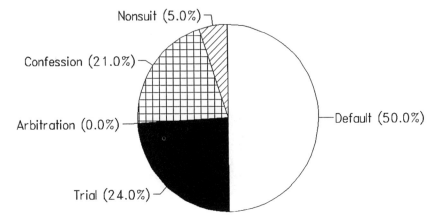

Figure A.6 Cases Resolved in Mayor's Court, 1734–1735
Source: MC Min.

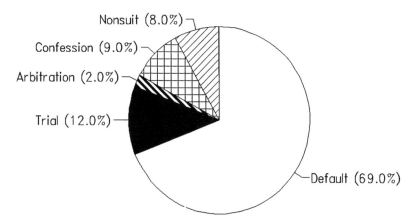

Figure A.7 Cases Resolved in Mayor's Court, 1754–1755
Source: MC Min.

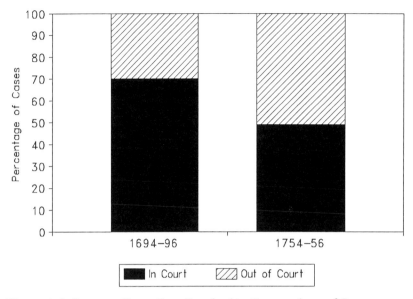

Figure A.8 Supreme Court Cases Resolved in Court and out of Court

Source: SC Min.

Figure A.9 Mayor's Court Cases Resolved in Court and out of Court

Source: MC Min.

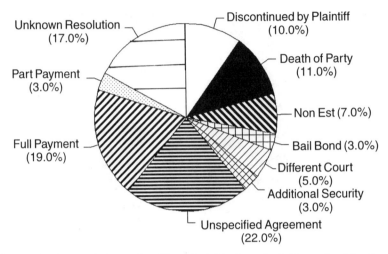

Figure A.10 Resolution of William Smith's Cases Left Unresolved in Court Minute Books

Source: William Smith, Jr., "A Supream Court Register," Manuscript Division, New York Public Library, New York.

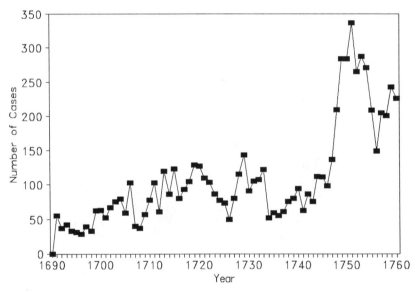

Figure A.11 Volume of Litigation, New York City Mayor's Court

Source: MC Min.

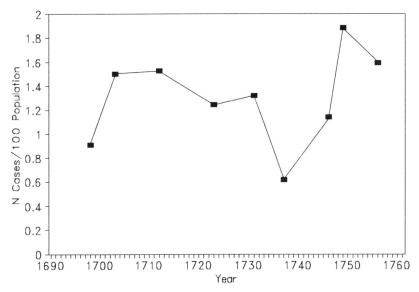

Figure A.12 Rate of Litigation, New York City Mayor's Court

Source: MC Min.

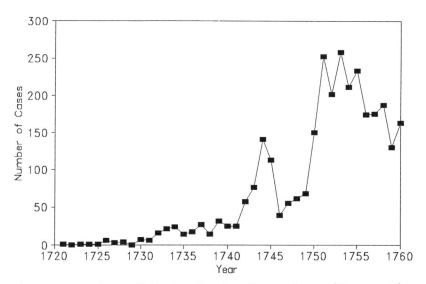

Figure A.13 Volume of Litigation, Dutchess County Court of Common Pleas

Source: DCCCP Min.

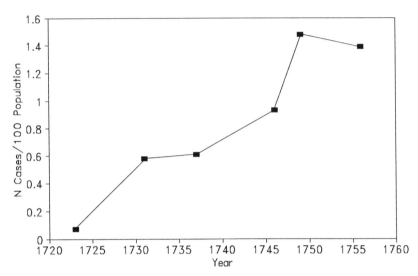

Figure A.14 Rate of Litigation, Dutchess County Court of Common Pleas

Source: DCCCP Min.

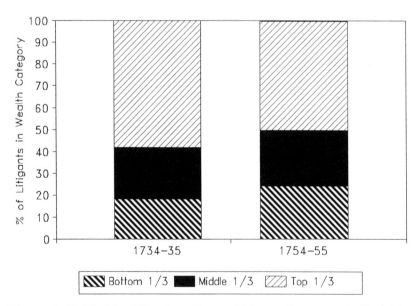

Figure A.15 Wealth of Dutchess County Litigants, Percentage in Each Tax Category

Source: DCCCP Min and Dutchess County Tax Lists, Dutchess County Clerk's Office, Poughkeepsie, N.Y.

Table A.6
1735 Tax Assessments of Dutchess County Litigants, 1721–1755

	Plaintiffs	Defendants
N of taxpayers appearing as litigants	79	98
% of taxpayers appearing as litigants	18	23
Average N of cases involved in 1734–35	6.6	3.4
·Average tax assessment	£34	£12

Sources: DCCCP Min and Dutchess County Tax Lists.

Table A.7
1735 Tax Assessments of Dutchess County Litigants, 1734–1735

	Plaintiffs	Defendants
N of taxpayers appearing as litigants	12	21
% of taxpayers appearing as litigants	3	5
Average N of cases involved in 1734–35★	1.5	1.3
Average tax assessment	£33	£13

Sources: DCCCP Min and Dutchess County Tax Lists.

★ The first column represents the average number of cases plaintiffs were involved in as plaintiffs; the second column represents the average number of cases defendants were involved in as defendants.

Table A.8
1754 Tax Assessments of Dutchess County Litigants, 1754–1755

	Plaintiffs	Defendants
N of taxpayers appearing as litigants	134	225
% of taxpayers appearing as litigants	6	11
Average N of cases involved in 1754–55	2.8	2.0
Average tax assessment	£18	£4

Sources: DCCCP Min and Dutchess County Tax Lists.

Table A.9
1734 Tax Assessments of Mayor's Court Litigants, 1734–1735

	Plaintiffs	Defendants
N of taxpayers appearing as litigants	105	86
% of taxpayers appearing as litigants	7	6
Average N of cases involved in 1734–35	1.5	1.5
Average tax assessment	£57	£19

Sources: MC Min and New York City Tax Lists, New York State Library.

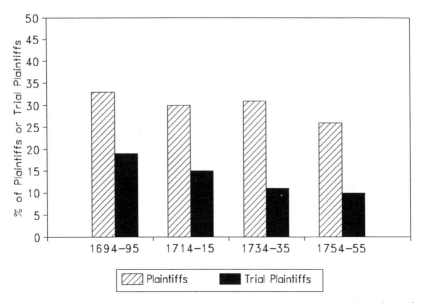

Figure A.16 Merchants in Mayor's Court, Percentage of Plaintiffs and Trial Plaintiffs

Source: MC Min.

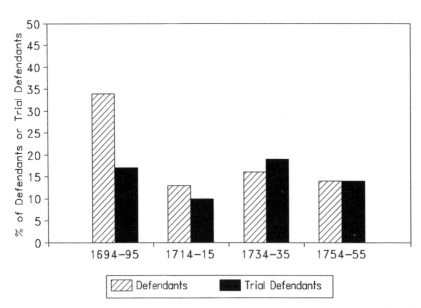

Figure A.17 Merchants in Mayor's Court, Percentage of Defendants and Trial Defendants

Source: MC Min.

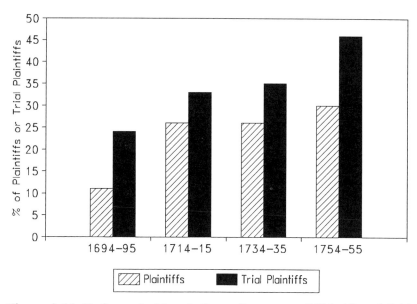

Figure A.18 Craftsmen in Mayor's Court, Percentage of Plaintiffs and Trial Plaintiffs

Source: MC Min.

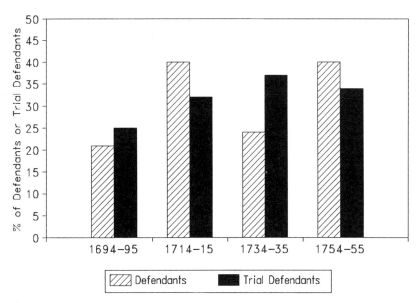

Figure A.19 Craftsmen in Mayor's Court, Percentage of Defendants and Trial Defendants

Source: MC Min.

Figure A.20 Litigants in Mayor's Court Jury Trials, Percentage of Cases Won, by Occupation

Source: MC Min.

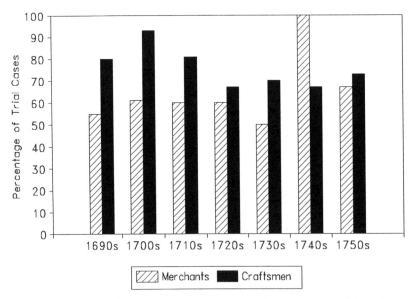

Figure A.21 Plaintiffs in Mayor's Court Jury Trials, Percentage of Cases Won, by Occupation

Source: MC Min.

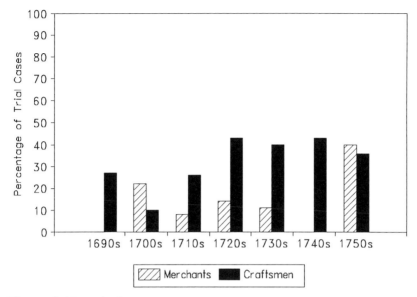

Figure A.22 Defendants in Mayor's Court Jury Trials, Percentage of Cases Won, by Occupation

Source: MC Min.

Table A.10

Residential Matchups by Precinct of Litigants in Dutchess County Court of Common Pleas, 1754–1755

Plaintiff	Defendant								
	CE	RH	B	RO	PO	S	Semitotal	D	Total
CE	63	1	30	9	7	6	116	5	121
RH	16	7	7	4	5	1	40	1	41
B	7	1	33	4	1	4	50	2	52
RO	5	0	14	32	9	10	70	6	76
PO	14	3	16	8	15	1	57	3	60
S	0	0	0	1	0	4	5	1	6
Total	105	12	100	58	37	26	338	18	356

Source: DCCCP Min.

Note: CE = Crum Elbow, RH = Rhinebeck, B = Beekman, RO = Rombout, PO = Poughkeepsie, S = Southern, D = Other Dutchess County (precinct unknown).

Table A.11

Residential Matchups by County of Litigants in Dutchess County Court of Common Pleas, 1754–1755

Plaintiff	Defendant							
	CE	RH	B	RO	PO	S	D	Total
D	114	12	115	64	39	26	18	388
U	1	0	0	0	8	0	0	9
O	0	0	1	0	0	0	0	1
W	0	0	0	1	0	0	0	1
N	5	2	3	2	2	0	0	14
Q	1	0	0	0	0	0	0	1
CT	2	0	2	0	0	2	0	6
Total	123	14	121	67	49	28	18	420

Source: DCCCP Min.

Note: CE = Crum Elbow, RH = Rhinebeck, B = Beekman, RO = Rombout, PO = Pough-keepsie, S = Southern, D = Other Dutchess County (precinct unknown), U = Ulster County, O = Orange County, W = Westchester County, N = New York County, Q = Queens County, CT = Connecticut.

Because of jurisdictional requirements, all defendants had a Dutchess County residence.

Notes

Introduction

1. Michael Zuckerman, *Peaceable Kingdoms: New England Towns in the Eighteenth Century* (New York, 1970); Kenneth Lockridge, *A New England Town: The First Hundred Years: Dedham, Massachusetts, 1636–1736* (New York, 1970); Philip J. Greven, *Four Generations: Population, Land, and Family in Colonial Andover, Massachusetts* (Ithaca, N.Y., 1970); and John Demos, *A Little Commonwealth: Family Life in Plymouth County* (New York, 1970).

2. See reviews of the literature on the transition to capitalism in Allan Kulikoff, *The Agrarian Origins of American Capitalism,* intro. and chap. 1; Winifred Barr Rothenberg, *From Market-Places to a Market Economy: The Transformation of Rural Massachusetts, 1750–1850,* chap. 2; and Christopher Clark, *The Roots of Rural Capitalism: Western Massachusetts, 1780–1860,* chap. 1. Those reviews of the literature take different views of the historiographical development. They do agree, however, that the view of a precapitalist colonial period came to dominate in the 1970s and 1980s, which may tell us more about the last few decades than about the seventeenth and eighteenth centuries. Social historians' uneasiness about apparently increasing materialism and greed and immoral, unethical, and selfish behavior in their own society, accompanied by a perceived decline in the family, could partially explain the recent increased interest in the topic of the transition to capitalism.

3. Carole Shammas, "How Self-Sufficient Was Early America?"; Shammas, *The Pre-industrial Consumer in England and America;* Gloria L. Main, "The Standard of Living in Southern New England, 1640–1773"; Gloria L. Main and Jackson T. Main, "Economic Growth and the Standard of Living in Southern New England, 1640–1774"; Lois Green Carr and Lorena S. Walsh, "Changing Lifestyles and Consumer Behavior in the Colonial Chesapeake," in Carson, Hoffman, and Albert, eds; *Of Consuming Interests: The Style of Life in the Eighteenth Century;* Alice Hanson Jones, *Wealth of a Nation to Be: The American Colonies on the Eve of the American Revolution;* T. H. Breen, " 'Baubles of Britain': The American and Consumer Revolutions of the Eighteenth Century"; Karen Ordahl Kupperman, *Providence Island, 1630–1641: The Other Puritan Colony;* John Frederick Martin, *Profits in the Wilderness: Entrepreneurship and the Founding of New England Towns in the Seventeenth Century;* Mary M. Schweitzer, *Custom and Contract: Household, Government, and the Economy in Colonial Pennsylvania;* Richard L. Bushman, *From Puritan to Yankee: Character and the Social Order in Connecticut, 1690–1765;* Bushman, "Family Security in the Transition from Farm to City,

1750–1850"; Daniel Vickers, *Farmers and Fishermen: Two Centuries of Work in Essex County, Massachusetts, 1630–1850;* Rothenberg, *From Market-Places to a Market Economy: The Transformation of Rural Massachusetts, 1750–1850;* James T. Lemon, *The Best Poor Man's Country: A Geographical Study of Early Southeastern Pennsylvania;* Charles S. Grant, *Democracy in the Connecticut Frontier Town of Kent;* James T. Lemon, "Household Consumption in Eighteenth-Century America and Its Relationship to Production and Trade: The Situation among Farmers in Southeastern Pennsylvania"; and Duane Eugene Ball and Gary M. Walton, "Agricultural Productivity Change in Eighteenth-Century Pennsylvania."

4. Thomas M. Doerflinger, *A Vigorous Spirit of Enterprise: Merchants and Economic Development in Revolutionary Philadelphia;* Virginia D. Harrington, *The New York Merchant on the Eve of the Revolution;* Bernard Bailyn, *The New England Merchants in the Seventeenth Century;* and David Hancock, *Citizens of the World: London Merchants and the Integration of the British Atlantic Community, 1735–1785.*

5. Clark, *Roots of Rural Capitalism;* Christopher Clark, "Household Economy, Market Exchange and the Rise of Capitalism in the Connecticut Valley, 1800–1860," *Journal of Social History* 13 (1979): 169–189; Michael Merrill, "Cash Is Good to Eat: Self-Sufficiency and Exchange in the Rural Economy of the United States"; Merrill, "Self-Sufficiency and Exchange in Early America: Theory, Structure, Ideology"; Steven Hahn, *The Roots of Southern Populism: Yeoman Farmers and the Transformation of the Georgia Upcountry, 1850–1890;* Kulikoff, *Agrarian Origins of American Capitalism;* James A. Henretta, "Families and Farms: *Mentalité* in Pre-Industrial America."

For descriptions of continuing "traditional," noncommercial, and communal values in eighteenth- and nineteenth-century America, see also Robert E. Mutch, "Yeoman and Merchant in Pre-Industrial America: Eighteenth-Century Massachusetts as a Case Study"; Thomas S. Wermuth, " 'To Market, To Market': Yeoman Farmers, Merchant Capitalists and the Development of Capitalism in the Hudson River Valley, 1760–1820"; Wermuth, "Were Early Americans Capitalists? An Overview of the Development of Capitalist Values and Beliefs in Early America"; Wermuth, " 'To Market, To Market': Yeoman Farmers, Merchant Capitalists, and the Transition to Capitalism in the Hudson River Valley, Ulster County, 1760–1840"; and Nancy Grey Osterud, *Bonds of Community: The Lives of Farm Women in Nineteenth-Century New York.*

6. Stephen Innes, *Creating the Commonwealth: The Economic Culture of Puritan New England;* Michael A. Bellesiles, *Revolutionary Outlaws: Ethan Allen and the Struggle for Independence on the Early American Frontier* (Charlottesville, Va., 1993); Christine Leigh Heyrman, *Commerce and Culture: The Maritime Communities of Colonial Massachusetts, 1690–1750;* Jack P. Greene, *Pursuits of Happiness: The Social Development of Early Modern British Colonies and the Formation of American Culture.* The main point of Greene's book is that a model derived from the experience of New England is not appropriate for analyzing all the colonies. While New England societies were falling apart after 1660, those of the other colonies were coming together and becoming more settled and cohesive; that is,

although New England went from coherence to incoherence, the rest of the colonies went from incoherence to coherence. Between 1713 and 1763, Greene says, New England and the rest of the colonies converged as the colonies south of New England moved from individualism toward communalism and the New England colonies moved from communalism to individualism at the same time. Other scholars taking an intermediate position on the communalism-capitalism debate include Bettye Hobbs Pruitt, "Self-Sufficiency and the Agricultural Economy of Eighteenth-Century Massachusetts," and T. H. Breen, *Tobacco Culture: The Mentality of the Great Tidewater Planters on the Eve of the Revolution* (Princeton, N.J., 1985).

7. Morton J. Horwitz, *The Transformation of American Law, 1780–1860;* William E. Nelson, *Americanization of the Common Law: The Impact of Legal Change on Massachusetts Society, 1760–1830;* and Nelson, *Dispute and Conflict Resolution in Plymouth County, Massachusetts, 1725–1825.*

8. Bernard Bailyn, "General Introduction: The Transforming Radicalism of the American Revolution," in Bailyn, ed., *Pamphlets of the American Revolution, 1750–1776* (Cambridge, Mass., 1965); Bailyn, *Faces of Revolution: Personalities and Themes in the Struggle for American Independence* (New York, 1990); Gordon S. Wood, *The Creation of the American Republic, 1776–1787* (Chapel Hill, 1969); Wood, *The Radicalism of the American Revolution* (New York, 1991); J. G. A. Pocock, *The Machiavellian Moment: Florentine Political Thought and the Atlantic Republican Tradition* (Princeton, N.J., 1975); and Robert E. Shallhope, "Republicanism and Early American Historiography," *William and Mary Quarterly,* 3d ser., 39 (1982): 334–56.

9. Edwin J. Perkins, "The Entrepreneurial Spirit in Colonial America: The Foundations of Modern Business History"; Richard Hofstadter, "The Myth of the Happy Yeoman," *American Heritage,* April 1956, 43–53; Hofstadter, *The Age of Reform From Bryan to FDR* (New York, 1955), chap. 1; Louis Hartz, *The Liberal Tradition in America: An Interpretation of American Political Thought since the Revolution* (New York, 1955); and Carl Degler, *Out of Our Past: The Forces That Shaped Modern America* (New York, 1959), 2.

10. See James Hoffman Lewis, "Farmers, Craftsmen and Merchants: Changing Economic Organization in Massachusetts, 1730 to 1775"; Rona Stephanie Weiss, "The Development of the Market Economy in Colonial Massachusetts"; Peter C. Mancall, *Valley of Opportunity: Economic Culture along the Upper Susquehanna, 1700–1800* (Ithaca, N.Y., 1991); Grant, *Democracy in the Connecticut Frontier Town of Kent;* Stephen Innes, *Labor in a New Land: Economy and Society in Seventeenth-Century Springfield* (Princeton, N.J., 1983); and Thomas M. Doerflinger, "Farmers and Dry Goods in the Philadelphia Market Area, 1750–1860," in Hoffman, et al., eds., *The Economy of Early America: The Revolutionary Period, 1763–1790.* Rothenberg, *From Market-Places to a Market Economy,* focuses on the period after 1750 but does not presume a precapitalist economy before that date.

11. Rural people's resistance to capitalism has been described not only as reluctance to make the change from autonomous farmer to wageworking factory

worker but also as broader discomfort with and rejection of commercial values and the market economy. The first, loss of autonomy, is a plausible and reasonable cause for concern and resistance; there is less evidence for assertions that farmers resisted involvement in the market itself. On rural resistance to capitalism, see especially the essays in Steven Hahn and Jonathan Prude, eds., *The Countryside in the Age of Capitalist Transformation: Essays in the Social History of Rural America*. On the resistance of rural women, see in particular Nancy Grey Osterud, "Gender and the Transition to Capitalism in Rural America."

12. Raymond Williams, *The Country and the City*, 290.

13. See, for example, Stanley L. Engerman and Robert E. Gallman, eds., *The Cambridge Economic History of the United States*, and John J. McCusker and Russell R. Menard, *The Economy of British America, 1607–1789*. As J. R. Pole has noted with regard to early American history, "With a few worthy exceptions, one will search in vain the political and social histories of the period to find the legal process, when considered as a whole, or the role of juries within that system, properly integrated into the fabric of political, institutional, or economic development." J. R. Pole, "Further Reflections on Law in the American Revolution: A Comment on the Comments," *William and Mary Quarterly* 50 (1993): 594–99, at 597.

14. Bruce H. Mann, *Neighbors and Strangers: Law and Community in Early Connecticut*. See also Deborah A. Rosen, "The Supreme Court of Judicature of Colonial New York: Civil Practice in Transition, 1691–1760."

15. Clark, *Roots of Rural Capitalism;* Kulikoff, *Agrarian Origins of American Capitalism*.

16. On women's economic roles in seventeenth- and eighteenth-century northern colonies, see the following works by Laurel Thatcher Ulrich: *Good Wives: Image and Reality in the Lives of Women of Northern New England, 1650–1750;* " 'A Friendly Neighbor': Social Dimensions of Daily Work in Northern Colonial New England"; "Housewife and Gadder: Themes of Self-Sufficiency and Community in Eighteenth-Century New England," in Norton and Groneman, eds., *"To Toil the Livelong Day": America's Women at Work, 1780–1980;* "Martha Ballard and Her Girls: Women's Work in Eighteenth-Century Maine," in Innes, ed., *Work and Labor in Early America;* and *A Midwife's Tale: The Life of Martha Ballard, Based on Her Diary, 1785–1812*. See also Mary Beth Norton, "The Evolution of White Women's Experience in Early America," *American Historical Review* 89 (1984): 593–619; Alice Morse Earle, *Home Life in Colonial Days;* Alice Clark, *Working Life of Women in the Seventeenth Century;* and Mary Sumner Benson, *Women in Eighteenth-Century America: A Study of Opinion and Social Usage* (1935, repr. ed. Port Washington, N.Y., 1966); Nancy Woloch, *Women and the American Experience;* Glenna Matthews, *The Rise of Public Woman: Woman's Power and Woman's Place in the United States, 1630–1970;* Mary P. Ryan, *Womanhood in America, from Colonial Times to the Present;* Mary Beth Norton, *Founding Mothers and Fathers: Gendered Power and the Forming of American Society;* Julie A. Matthaei, *An Economic History of Women in America: Women's Work, the*

Sexual Division of Labor, and the Development of Capitalism; Patricia A. Cleary, " 'She Merchants' of Colonial America: Women and Commerce on the Eve of the Revolution"; and Cleary, " 'She Will Be in the Shop': Women's Sphere of Trade in Eighteenth-Century Philadelphia and New York."

17. Toby L. Ditz, *Property and Kinship: Inheritance in Early Connecticut, 1750– 1820;* David E. Narrett, *Inheritance and Family Life in Colonial New York City;* Marylynn Salmon, *Women and the Law of Property in Early America;* Lisa Wilson, *Life after Death: Widows in Pennsylvania, 1750–1850;* Linda Briggs Biemer, *Women and Property in Colonial New York: The Transition from Dutch to English Law, 1643–1727;* Joan R. Gunderson and Gwen Victor Gampel, "Married Women's Legal Status in Eighteenth-Century New York and Virginia"; essays by Salmon, Narrett, Daniel Scott Smith, Gloria L. Main, Carole Shammas, and Lois Green Carr in Ronald Hoffman and Peter J. Albert, eds., *Women in the Age of the American Revolution;* and Carole Shammas, Marylynn Salmon, and Michel Dahlin, *Inheritance in America from Colonial Times to the Present.*

18. Cornelia Hughes Dayton, *Women before the Bar: Gender, Law, and Society in Connecticut, 1639–1789.*

19. Richard B. Morris, *Studies in the History of American Law with Special Reference to the Seventeenth and Eighteenth Century Colonies;* Mary R. Beard, *Woman as Force in History: A Study in Traditions and Realities.*

20. On women in the revolutionary era see Mary Beth Norton, *Liberty's Daughters: The Revolutionary Experience of American Women, 1750–1800;* Linda K. Kerber, *Women of the Republic: Intellect and Ideology in Revolutionary America;* and Hoffman and Albert, eds., *Women in the Age of the American Revolution.* On American women in the late eighteenth century and into the nineteenth century see Suzanne Lebsock, *The Free Women of Petersburg: Status and Culture in a Southern Town, 1784–1860;* Nancy F. Cott, *The Bonds of Womanhood: 'Woman's Sphere' in New England, 1780–1835;* Jeanne Boydston, *Home and Work: Housework, Wages, and the Ideology of Labor in the Early Republic;* Gerda Lerner, "The Lady and the Mill Girl: Changes in the Status of Women in the Age of Jackson"; Osterud, *Bonds of Community;* Joan M. Jensen, *Loosening the Bonds: Mid-Atlantic Farm Women, 1750–1850;* and Barbara Welter, "The Cult of True Womanhood, 1820–1860."

21. Philip H. Smith, *General History of Duchess County from 1609 to 1876* (Pawling, N.Y., 1877). Most of the county was distributed as large land grants between 1685 and 1706. Dutchess County was organized by a 1683 statute but it remained provisionally attached to Ulster County until 1713, when it was deemed to have sufficient population to warrant having its own assembly representatives. In 1719 the county was divided into the North Ward, Middle Ward, and South Ward. Col Laws NY 1:1033–34, at 1034 (1719). In 1737 the county was redivided into seven precincts corresponding substantially with the original patents: Rhinebeck in the northwest corner along the Hudson River, Little Nine Partners (or Northeast) in the northeast corner, Crum Elbow (or Great Nine Partners) covering a large area in the middle of the county, Poughkeepsie and

then Rombout (or Fishkill) to the southwest of Crum Elbow and Beekman to
the southeast of Crum Elbow, and then South (or Philipse) Precinct from the
river to Connecticut in the southernmost portion of the county adjoining Westchester County. Col Laws NY 2:955–58. The Philipse, or South, Precinct was
separated from Dutchess County in 1812 and became Putnam County. The
precinct lines were extended to include the Oblong in 1743.

22. Frederick Jackson Turner, "Problems in American History" (1892) and
"The Significance of the Frontier in American History" (1893), in Everett W.
Edwards, ed., *The Early Writings of Frederick Jackson Turner* (Madison, 1938), 78–
79, 217–18; Turner, *The Rise of the New West* (New York, 1906), 29–30; Turner,
"Some Sociological Aspects of American History" (1895) and "The Develop-
ment of American Society" (1908) in Wilbur R. Jacobs, ed., *Frederick Jackson
Turner's Legacy: Unpublished Writings in American History* (San Marino, Calif.,
1965), 163–64, 177; Turner, *The United States, 1830–1850* (New York, 1935),
92, 94, 112, 138, 143; Woodrow Wilson, "The Proper Perspective of American
History," *The Forum* 19 (1895): 544–46; Wilson, "Mr. Goldwin Smith's 'Views'
on Our Political History," *The Forum* 14 (1893–94): 494–95; Wilson, "The
Course of American History," *Collections* of the New Jersey Historical Society 8
(1900): 186–89; Milton M. Klein, "Shaping the American Tradition: The Mi-
crocosm of Colonial New York," *New York History* 59 (1978): 173–97; Klein,
"New York in the American Colonies: A New Look"; and Patricia U. Bonomi,
"The Middle Colonies: Embryo of the New Political Order," in Alden T.
Vaughan and George A. Billias, eds., *Perspectives in Early American History* (New
York, 1973), 63–92. All citations to Turner and Wilson are drawn from the first-
cited Klein article.

23. Klein, "New York in the American Colonies."

24. Both Alice Hanson Jones and Gary Nash provide some data on wealth in
colonial New York, but there is no analysis of consumer goods purchased by
New Yorkers and thus no clear picture of what people had in their homes in the
seventeenth and eighteenth centuries. Jones, *Wealth of a Nation to Be;* Gary B.
Nash, "Urban Wealth and Poverty in Pre-Revolutionary America."

25. Wayne Bodle, "Themes and Directions in Middle Colonies Historiography, 1980–1994," *William and Mary Quarterly,* 364. Cornelia Hughes Dayton,
"Turning Points and the Relevance of Colonial Legal History," 8.

Chapter 1

1. On consumption patterns in early America, see esp. Cary Carson, Ronald
Hoffman, and Peter J. Albert, eds., *Of Consuming Interests: The Style of Life in the
Eighteenth Century,* and Carole Shammas, *The Pre-Industrial Consumer in England
and America.* For citations to scholars who have underestimated colonists' involvement in the consumer goods market, see the citations in n. 5 of the introduction.

2. The view that the American colonists were liberal and entrepreneurial in
orientation from the beginning has been expressed recently by Edwin J. Perkins,

who refers to colonial society as "a culture permeated with market values and capitalist principles." Perkins shows that not only merchants but also craftsmen, most farmers, indentured servants, and many young day laborers exhibited the entrepreneurial spirit. Perkins, "The Entrepreneurial Spirit in Colonial America: The Foundations of Modern Business History." The quotation is on p. 162. See also Richard Hofstadter, "The Myth of the Happy Yeoman," *American Heritage,* April 1956, 43–53, and Hofstadter, *The Age of Reform From Bryan to FDR* (New York, 1955), chap. 1; Louis Hartz, *The Liberal Tradition in America: An Interpretation of American Political Thought since the Revolution* (New York, 1955); Charles S. Grant, *Democracy in the Connecticut Frontier Town of Kent;* and Carl Degler, *Out of Our Past: The Forces That Shaped Modern America* (New York, 1959), 2. For the argument that colonists were limited by the absence of adequate markets, see Max George Schumacher, *The Northern Farmer and His Markets during the Late Colonial Period;* Percy Wells Bidwell and John I. Falconer, *History of Agriculture in the Northern United States, 1620–1860;* and Ulysses Prentiss Hedrick, *A History of Agriculture in the State of New York* (Albany, N.Y., 1933).

3. Peter Kalm, *Peter Kalm's Travels in North America: The English Version of 1770,* 335, 342, 618–19; Andrew Burnaby, *Travels through the Middle Settlements in North-America in the Years 1759 and 1760 with Observations upon the State of the Colonies.* For a contemporary description of trade, see the letter from Lord Cornbury to Mr. Secretary Hedges in London, July 15, 1705, in Doc Rel 4:1150–56. On the economy of colonial New York, see Samuel McKee, Jr., "The Economic Pattern of Colonial New York," in Alexander C. Flick, ed., *History of the State of New York,* 2:249–82. See also Michael Kammen, *Colonial New York: A History,* 161–76. On the economy of colonial America in general, see John J. McCusker and Russell R. Menard, *The Economy of British America, 1607–1789;* Edwin J. Perkins, *The Economy of Colonial America;* and Stuart Bruchey, *The Roots of American Economic Growth, 1607–1861: An Essay in Social Causation.*

4. On the rise of imports, see John J. McCusker, "The Current Value of English Exports, 1697 to 1800." The deficit balance of trade is indicated by the rising exchange rate between New York currency and pounds sterling (which is also approximately equal to the rate of exchange for bills of exchange drawn in sterling). An increasing exchange rate reflects a rising need for more currency to pay for the excess of imports over exports. On the shortage of specie, see Herbert Alan Johnson, *The Law Merchant and Negotiable Instruments in Colonial New York, 1664 to 1730,* p. 13 and n. 56, p. 61.

5. Col Laws NY 1:296–300 (1692).

6. Min Com Coun 4:108–10.

7. Peddlers and auctions were regulated by statute. On peddlers, see Col Laws NY 1:805–8 (1714), 1:999 (1718), 2:571–74 (1729), 2:758–59 (1732), 2:988–92 (1737), 3:60–63 (1739), 3:417–18 (1744), 3:873 (1751), and 4:388–91 (1759). On auctions, see Col Laws NY 1:692 (1709) [title of statute only], 1:789–91 (1713), 1:863–66 (1715), 1:904–7 (1717), 1:1021 (1719), and 2:34–36 (1720).

8. Kalm, *Peter Kalm's Travels,* 635.

9. *New-York Mercury,* June 5, 1753.

10. See McCusker, "Current Value of English Exports."

11. Shammas, *Pre-industrial Consumer,* 68. Her calculation was based on a per capita annual income of about £12 and a per capita annual expenditure of £3 6s. on imported goods.

12. The data in Table 1.1 are drawn from surviving accountings in the following cases: (1) *Jacobus DePeyster v. Johannes VanSteenberg* (Anc Doc 3355); (2) *Jacobus DePeyster v. George Cornell* (Anc Doc 2956); (3) *Charles LeRoux v. Gerrit Nostrant* (Anc Doc 3360); (4) *Mathew Dubois v. Samuel Fuller* (Anc Doc 3380); (5) *Mathew Dubois v. Enoch Earll* (Anc Doc 2954); (6) *Thomas Braine v. Thomas Linnington* (Anc Doc 3595 and 3473); (7) *James Duncan v. Abraham Lassing* (Doc 2958); (8) *Francis Filkin v. Johannes Gonsales* (Anc Doc 2961); (9) *Henry Filkin v. Ichabod Everitt* (Anc Doc 2959); (10) *Martin Hoffman v. Johannes Wilsie, Jr.* (Anc Doc 2947); (11) *Bartholomew Noxon v. Stephen Hicks* (Anc Doc 2962); (12) *Bartholomew Noxon v. Timothy Ricketson* (Anc Doc 3049); (13) *Dirck Brinckerhoff v. Daniel Sawyer* (Anc Doc 3060); (14) *Dirck Brinckerhoff v. Enoch Earll* (Anc Doc 2953); (15) *Dirck Brinckerhoff v. William Mosier* (Anc Doc 2955); (16) *Dirck Brinckerhoff v. Christian Zacharida* (Anc Doc 2949); (17) *Nicholas Delavergne v. Samuel Alger* (Anc Doc 2948); (18) *Nicholas Delavergne v. Timothy Buck* (Anc Doc 2950); (19) *Nicholas Delavergne v. Jonas Bull* (Anc Doc 2957); (20) *Nicholas Delavergne v. Richard Satterly* (Anc Doc 2951); (21) *Nicholas Delavergne v. Aaron Smith* (Anc Doc 2952); and (22) *Nicholas Delavergne v. Christopher West* (Anc Doc 3381).

13. Along with the shop merchandise and the usual consumer goods, Byvanck also owned one "electrical machine." Probate inventories of William Teller, Sr. (1701) and Evert Byvanck (1773). Colonial New York inventories are available on microfilm at the New-York Historical Society, New York, from the New York State Archives, Albany, N.Y., and from the Family Research Center at the Salt Lake City, Utah, headquarters of the Church of Jesus Christ of the Latter Day Saints. A statute of 1692 described probate and inventory procedures in New York. Col Laws NY 1:300–303.

14. Kalm, *Peter Kalm's Travels,* 190, 195, 346–47, 605. The quotation is on p. 190.

15. *New-York Mercury,* April 23, 1753.

16. Carl Bridenbaugh, ed., *Gentleman's Progress: The Itinerarium of Dr. Alexander Hamilton, 1744* (Chapel Hill, 1948), 54–55.

17. Ibid., 72.

18. For full discussion of potential biases in probate records, see Lois Green Carr and Lorena S. Walsh, "Inventories and the Analysis of Wealth and Consumption Patterns in St. Mary's County, Maryland, 1658–1777"; Gloria L. Main, "The Correction of Biases in Colonial American Probate Records," *Historical Methods Newsletter* 8 (1974): 10–28; Daniel Scott Smith, "Underregistration and Bias in Probate Records: An Analysis of Data from Eighteenth-Century Hingham, Massachusetts," *William and Mary Quarterly,* 3d ser., 32 (1975): 100–

110; Margaret Spufford, "The Limitations of the Probate Inventory," in John Chartres and David Hey, eds., *English Rural Society, 1500–1800* (New York, 1990), 139–74; and Toby L. Ditz, *Property and Kinship: Inheritance in Early Connecticut, 1750–1820,* 39–45 and 173–94.

19. Some residents of New York City, particularly those living in the Out Ward, were farmers; although their occupation was more typically rural than urban, they have nevertheless been included in the urban category because of their city residence. The proportion of rural inventories among the records studied (77%) is somewhat higher than the proportion of the province of New York that lived outside New York City and Albany, which ranged from about 65% to 69% during the first half of the eighteenth century.

20. For the period 1680–99, 108 inventories were studied, 87 from 1700–1719, 189 from 1720–39, 134 from 1740–59, and 82 from 1760–75.

21. All percentages are of inventories that actually list household items owned at the time of death; inventories that simply give a total value of "household goods" without itemizing them were not included in calculating the percentage of decedents owning particular goods.

22. In comparison, Kevin Sweeney's study of probate inventories from Wethersfield, Connecticut, found that in the 1750s 88% of decedents owned tables, 90% owned chairs, and 73% owned looking glasses. See Kevin M. Sweeney, "Furniture and the Domestic Environment in Wethersfield, Connecticut, 1639–1800," in St. George, ed., *Material Life in America, 1600–1860.* Other studies detailing colonial ownership of consumer goods include Shammas, *Pre-industrial Consumer;* Lois Green Carr and Lorena S. Walsh, "Changing Lifestyles and Consumer Behavior in the Colonial Chesapeake," in Carson et al., *Of Consuming Interests;* Gloria L. Main, "The Distribution of Consumer Goods in Colonial New England: A Subregional Approach," in Benes, ed., *Early American Probate Inventories;* Gloria L. Main, "The Standard of Living in Colonial Massachusetts"; Gloria L. Main and Jackson T. Main, "Economic Growth and the Standard of Living in Southern New England, 1640–1774"; Lorena S. Walsh, "Urban Amenities and Rural Sufficiency: Living Standards and Consumer Behavior in the Colonial Chesapeake, 1643–1777"; Lois Green Carr, "Diversification in the Colonial Chesapeake: Somerset County, Maryland, in Comparative Perspective," in Carr, Morgan, and Russo, eds., *Colonial Chesapeake Society;* Alice Hanson Jones, *Wealth of a Nation to Be: The American Colonies on the Eve of the Revolution;* Jack Michel, " 'In a Manner and Fashion Suitable to Their Degree': A Preliminary Investigation of the Material Culture of Early Pennsylvania"; Karen E. Andresen, "The Layered Society: Material Life in Portsmouth, N.H., 1680 to 1740," Ph.D. dissertation, University of New Hampshire, 1982; Steven R. Pendery, "Consumer Behavior in Colonial Charlestown, Massachusetts, 1630–1760," *Historical Archeology* 26 (1992): 57–72.

23. The index of amenities used in this study was modeled on the scheme described by Carr and Walsh in their article "Inventories and the Analysis of Wealth and Consumption Patterns."

24. The index of luxuries in rural areas was .03 in 1680–99, .17 in 1700–

1719, .50 in 1720–39, .59 in 1740–59, and 1.06 in 1760–75. The index of luxuries in urban areas was .29 in 1680–99, .66 in 1700–1719, 1.00 in 1720–39, 1.15 in 1740–59, and 1.57 in 1760–75.

25. The rural amenities score was 4.70 in 1680–99, 5.79 in 1700–1719, 6.76 in 1720–39, 5.43 in 1740–59, and 6.59 in 1760–75. The urban amenities score was 8.97 in 1680–99, 8.90 in 1700–1719, 8.65 in 1720–39, 9.46 in 1740–59, and 9.39 in 1760–75.

26. Carr and Walsh, "Changing Lifestyles and Consumer Behavior"; Main, "Distribution of Consumer Goods in Colonial New England."

27. See Carr and Walsh, "Changing Lifestyles and Consumer Behavior," 116–17; Main, "Distribution of Consumer Goods," 161; Michel, " 'In a Manner and Fashion,' " 11; and Shammas, *Pre-industrial Consumer,* 86–100.

28. Carr and Walsh, "Changing Lifestyles and Consumer Behavior."

29. Cary Carson, "The Consumer Revolution in Colonial British America: Why Demand?" in Carson et al., *Of Consuming Interests,* 483–697.

30. Kalm, *Peter Kalm's Travels,* 139, 344–45.

31. *New-York Weekly Journal,* November 19, 1736.

32. Letter to *New-York Weekly Journal,* March 3, 1735. On February 16, 1741, an article reprinted in the *Journal* from a London magazine argued that people were indulging in too many luxuries at the dinner table, that they were catering to taste and fashion rather than eating good, plain food. The author pleaded with the wealthy to stop the practice, which the "inferior Ranks" had come to imitate.

33. Tax data are drawn from the New York City Tax Lists, New York State Library (available on microfilm). That wealth was polarized in urban New York by the end of the colonial period is consistent with Gary Nash's work on eighteenth-century Philadelphia, Boston, and New York City, though this study shows that polarization existed well before the Revolution. Gary B. Nash, *The Urban Crucible: Social Change, Political Consciousness, and the Origins of the American Revolution.* On northern urban poverty, see also Billy G. Smith, *The "Lower Sort": Philadelphia's Laboring People, 1750–1800;* Robert E. Cray, Jr., *Paupers and Poor Relief in New York City and Its Rural Environs, 1700–1830;* and Douglas Lamar Jones, "The Strolling Poor: Transiency in Eighteenth Century Massachusetts."

34. See, for example, Jeffrey Williamson and Peter Lindert, *American Inequality: A Macroeconomic History* (New York, 1980).

35. Because no tax lists are available for colonial New York City after 1735, no comparison can be made between the city and Dutchess County in the 1750s. This study found a higher level of wealth polarization in Dutchess County, New York, than others have measured in Chester County, Pennsylvania. James Lemon found that, between 1693 and 1760, the top 10% of taxpayers in that county paid between 24 and 30% of the taxes. In his study of three Worcester County, Massachusetts, towns in 1717, 1732, and 1740, John L. Brooke found that the top decile of taxpayers owned 25, 27, and 34% of the wealth, respectively. Jackson Turner Main found that in colonial Connecticut the top decile of taxpayers

owned about 30% of taxable property in the early eighteenth century. On Chester County, see James T. Lemon, *The Best Poor Man's Country: A Geographical Study of Early Southeastern Pennsylvania,* 11; James T. Lemon and Gary B. Nash, "The Distribution of Wealth in Eighteenth-Century America: A Century of Change in Chester County, Pennsylvania, 1693–1802"; and Duane E. Ball, "Dynamics of Population and Wealth in Eighteenth-Century Chester County, Pennsylvania," *Journal of Interdisciplinary History* 6 (1976): 621–44. On Massachusetts and Connecticut, see John L. Brooke, *The Heart of the Commonwealth: Society and Political Culture in Worcester County, Massachusetts, 1713–1861* (New York, 1989), 43; and Jackson Turner Main, *Society and Economy in Colonial Connecticut,* 117.

36. Tax data are drawn from an analysis of Dutchess County Tax Lists, Dutchess County Clerk's Office, Poughkeepsie, New York.

37. On the limitations of tax lists as historical sources (especially for comparative purposes) see three articles published in the *Journal of Interdisciplinary History* in 1976 (vol. 6): G. B. Warden, "Inequality and Instability in Eighteenth-Century Boston: A Reappraisal," 585–620, at 604–9; Gary B. Nash, "Urban Wealth and Poverty in Pre-Revolutionary America," 545–84, at 547–48; and Jacob M. Price, "Quantifying Colonial America: A Comment on Nash and Warden," 701–9, at 704–6.

38. On the climbing price of land, see Thomas Cochran, *Business in American Life: A History* (New York, 1972), 57; and J. T. Main, *Society and Economy,* 31–33.

Chapter 2

1. John J. McCusker and Russell R. Menard, *The Economy of British America, 1607–1789,* 334; Edwin J. Perkins, *American Public Finance and Financial Services, 1700–1815;* Richard L. Bushman, *From Puritan to Yankee: Character and the Social Order in Connecticut, 1690–1765;* Bushman, "Massachusetts Farmers and the Revolution," in R. M. Jellison, ed., *Society, Freedom, and Conscience: The American Revolution in Virginia, Massachusetts, and New York* (New York, 1976), 77–124; John L. Brooke, *The Heart of the Commonwealth: Society and Political Culture in Worcester County, Massachusetts, 1713–1861* (New York, 1989); Mary M. Schweitzer, *Custom and Contract: Household, Government, and the Economy in Colonial Pennsylvania;* Thomas M. Doerflinger, *A Vigorous Spirit of Enterprise: Merchants and Economic Development in Revolutionary Philadelphia;* Julian Gwyn, "Private Credit in Colonial New York: The Warren Portfolio, 1731–1795"; Wilbur C. Plummer, "Consumer Credit in Colonial Philadelphia"; Bruce H. Mann, *Neighbors and Strangers: Law and Community in Early Connecticut;* Peter J. Coleman, *Debtors and Creditors in America: Insolvency, Imprisonment for Debt, and Bankruptcy, 1607–1900;* Alice Hanson Jones, *Wealth of a Nation to Be: The American Colonies on the Eve of the American Revolution;* and Jackson Turner Main, *Society and Economy in Colonial Connecticut.*

2. Anc Doc 143.

3. Francis Filkin, *Account Book of a Country Store Keeper in the 18th Century at*

Poughkeepsie; Hendrick Schenk Account Book, Ledger B, 1764–84, New York Public Library, Rare Books and Manuscripts Room, New York; Hendrick Denker Account Book, 1750–65, New-York Historical Society; Henry Smith Ledger, 1750–92, New-York Historical Society; and Charles Nicoll Ledger, 1759–65, New-York Historical Society.

4. Where possible (i.e, where the ledgers were fully legible), the sampling was random, e.g., every twentieth customer. For Henry Smith, only customers from the 1750s were used in the sampling; the sampling does not represent the entire period covered by the account book, 1750–92. I am indebted to Lafayette College student Byard Brogan for collecting and inputting the data from the account book of Hendrick Schenk.

5. In comparison, Thomas Wermuth found that in the same decade (the 1760s), Ulster County shopkeeper William Pick received 41.5% of his payments in cash, 26.1% in agricultural goods, and 32.2% in work. Thomas S. Wermuth, " 'To Market, To Market': Yeoman Farmers, Merchant Capitalists, and the Transition to Capitalism in the Hudson River Valley, Ulster County, 1760–1840," 66. See also Wermuth, " 'To Market, To Market': Yeoman Farmers, Merchant Capitalists and the Development of Capitalism in the Hudson River Valley, 1760–1820."

6. Contrast these figures for colonial New York with the percentages of payment by cash, goods, and labor in a colonial Springfield, Massachusetts, store between 1755 and 1767: 59% of payments were in cash, 31% in goods, and 10% in labor. Margaret E. Martin, *Merchants and Trade of the Connecticut River Valley, 1750–1820,* 149–56. See also studies of Virginia and Maryland described in Carole Shammas, *The Pre-Industrial Consumer in England and America,* 271.

7. When a currency is declared to be "legal tender," any seller or creditor is required by law to accept that currency in payment of amounts owed. The statutes issuing bills of credit in colonial New York routinely provided that "the tender of the said Bills for the payment And Discharge of any Debt or Debts, Bargains, Sales, Bonds, Bills, Mortgages And Specialties, whatsoever shall be as good and Effectuall in the Law to all Intents Construction and purposes, as if the Current Coin of this Colony had been offered and tendered to any person or persons whatsoever for the Discharge of the same or any part thereof."

8. Col Laws NY 1:666, 689, 695, 737, 815, 847, 938; 2:137, 173, 885, 911, 1015; 3:21, 548, 577, 660. Jour Gen Ass, 2:424. On the use of bills of credit in the colonial economies, see Perkins, *American Public Finance,* chap. 2; Perkins, "Conflicting Views of Fiat Currency: Britain and Its North American Colonies in the Eighteenth Century"; E. James Ferguson, *The Power of the Purse: A History of American Public Finance, 1776–1790* (Chapel Hill, 1961), chap. 1; and Curtis Putnam Nettles, *The Money Supply of the American Colonies before 1720.*

9. Jour Gen Ass, 2:696. See Leslie V. Brock, *The Currency of the American Colonies, 1700–1764: A Study in Colonial Finance and Imperial Relations,* 72.

10. Col Laws NY, 3:1038, 1078, 1131; 4:43, 60, 215, 317, 350, 398. On the

discussion as to whether these bills of credit would be made legal tender, see Doc Rel 6:840, 848; Jour Gen Ass, 2:411–12; Col Laws NY 3:1038.

11. Col Laws NY 1:71 (1665), and 1:153 (1684). The later New York laws are in *Laws of New York,* Gaines ed. (1774), c. 1327 (1767) and c. 1612 (1773). The English Promissory Note Act is at 3,4 Anne, c.0 (1704). See Herbert Alan Johnson, *The Law Merchant and Negotiable Instruments in Colonial New York, 1664 to 1730,* 35; Morton J. Horwitz, *The Transformation of American Law, 1780–1860,* 337, n. 4. On the history of bills and notes, see also James Stevens Rogers, *The Early History of the Law of Bills and Notes: A Study of the Origins of Anglo-American Commercial Law* (New York, 1995); William Cranch, "Promissory Notes before and after Lord Holt"; William S. Holdsworth, *A History of English Law,* vol. 8, 170–78; and Arthur Nussbaum, *A History of the Dollar* (New York, 1957), 15.

12. *New-York Weekly Journal,* May 26, 1740.

13. Joseph Murray, "Precedent Book," Columbia University Law Library, Special Collections, New York, 137–38.

14. Francis Baird to William Alexander, November 16, 1767, William Alexander Papers, New York Public Library, New York.

15. Examples can be found in the letterbooks of Gerard Beekman, John Sanders, and William Livingston. Philip L. White, ed., *The Beekman Mercantile Papers, 1746–1799,* vol. 1, 11–13, 24, 111, 200; John Sanders to James Bonbonous, November 10, 1755, and John Sanders to Champion and Heyley, November 9, 1755, John Sanders Letter Book, New-York Historical Society; William Livingston to Champion and Hayley, May 25, 1762. See also Livingston's letters of July 30, 1754, December 15, 1755, April 22, 1757, August 11, 1757, November 13, 1757, and October 31, 1758, William Livingston Papers, Letter Book.

16. Both bills of exchange and promissory notes represented an extension of credit as between the original parties, but once they passed to other people they became more like money, a medium of exchange. In that function, they are distinguishable from mere credit between buyer and seller: if a seller accepted a bill of exchange from a buyer, it functioned as a real payment of the amount owed, not an extension of credit, even though the actual money was not in the seller's hands.

17. Anc Doc.

18. There were no banks in New York until 1784. For a recent description of what is known about the colonial credit system, see Perkins, *American Public Finance,* chap. 3.

19. Virginia D. Harrington, *The New York Merchant on the Eve of the Revolution,* 103. British merchants provided most credit to colonial merchants. See Jacob Price, *Capital and Credit in British Overseas Trade: The View from the Chesapeake, 1700–1775* (Cambridge, Mass., 1980), and David Hancock, *Citizens of the World: London Merchants and the Integration of the British Atlantic Community, 1735–1785.*

20. See esp. Perkins, *American Public Finance.* The quotation is on p. 58. On

retailers' sales devices, see Richard L. Bushman, "Shopping and Advertising in America," in Cary Carson, Ronald Hoffman, and Peter J. Albert, eds., *Of Consuming Interests: The Style of Life in the Eighteenth Century*, 233–51; and Shammas, *Pre-Industrial Consumer*, chaps. 8, 9.

21. See Plummer, "Consumer Credit in Colonial Philadelphia" and Carl Bridenbaugh, *The Colonial Craftsman*, 153–54.

22. *New-York Weekly Journal*, June 11, 1739.

23. DCCCP Min 118, 187, 274, 279; Anc Doc 3502 and 3339.

24. St. John de Crèvecoeur, *Sketches of Eighteenth Century America: More "Letters from an American Farmer."* The editors concluded that these essays were probably written sometime between 1770 and 1774.

25. *New-York Weekly Journal*, May 2, 1737.

26. On the increasing price of land, see Thomas Cochran, *Business in American Life: A History* (New York, 1972), 57; and Main, *Society and Economy*, 31–33. On land development in early New England, see John Frederick Martin, *Profits in the Wilderness: Entrepreneurship and the Founding of New England Towns in the Seventeenth Century*.

27. Letter to *New-York Weekly Journal* from "John Farmer," May 20, 1734.

28. *New-York Mercury*, February 25, 1754.

29. Crèvecoeur, *Sketches of Eighteenth Century America*.

30. See *Abstracts of Wills on File in the Surrogate's Office, City of New York, 1665–1800*, in *Collections of the New-York Historical Society for the Years 1892–1908*.

31. The figures in the text are based on a study of 600 probate inventories available on microfilm at the New-York Historical Society in New York City, the New York State Archives in Albany, N.Y., and the Family Research Center at the Salt Lake City, Utah, headquarters of the Church of Jesus Christ of the Latter-Day Saints.

32. Consistent with these findings, Edwin Perkins's recent book concludes that "[m]ost households at every level of wealth had some financial assets and liabilities." *American Public Finance*, 59.

33. In comparison, both Alice Hanson Jones (on New England) and Jackson Turner Main (studying Connecticut) have found that by the eve of the Revolution credit extended constituted about one-fifth of net worth. Jones, *Wealth of a Nation to Be*, 128; Main, *Society and Economy*, 36.

34. Alice Hanson Jones's figures for the Middle Colonies indicate average credit assets of about £14 per person in the 1770s, which would mean an average of substantially less than £305 per family. Jones, *Wealth of a Nation to Be.*

35. The loan office was established by statute in 1737. Col Laws NY 2:1015–40 and 2:1040–47. Jean Peyer, "Jamaica, Long Island 1656–1776: A Study of the Roots of American Urbanism."

36. See statutory references to recording of deeds and mortgages in Col Laws NY 1:6–71, at 30–31 (1665), 1:141–42 (1683), 1:148–49 (1684), and 3:957 (1753). The Crum Elbow Precinct mortgage records are printed in William

McDermott, ed., *Eighteenth Century Documents of the Nine Partners Patent, Dutchess County, New York,* 333–498. The Rombout Precinct records are printed in Helen Wilkinson Reynolds, ed., *Eighteenth Century Records of the Portion of Dutchess County, New York, that was included in Rombout Precinct and the original Town of Fishkill,* 127–207.

37. Edwin Perkins suggests that many colonial mortgages were purchase money mortgages, securing purchase of the mortgaged land itself. He has found that such credit typically was extended to a young mortgagor by male relatives or other residents of the local community and that repayment was usually due in less than five years. Perkins, *American Public Finance,* 68.

38. McDermott, *Eighteenth Century Documents of the Nine Partners Patent;* and Reynolds, *Eighteenth Century Records of the . . . Rombout Precinct.* Crum Elbow borrowers relied heavily on New York City lenders: 61% of the Crum Elbow mortgages and only 36% of the Rombout loans came from city dwellers. Crum Elbow residents borrowed from New York City merchants Robert G. Livingston (31 loans), George Folliott (18 loans), Augustus Van Horne (11 loans), and Levinius Clarkson (5 loans), as well as from New York City merchants' widows.

39. Probate inventory of Sarah Arnold (1768).

40. William Livingston to Isaac Willet, March 14, 1755, William Livingston Papers, Letter Book 1754–70.

41. William Chester Jordan, *Women and Credit in Pre-Industrial and Developing Societies* (Philadelphia, 1993); Cornelia Hughes Dayton, *Women before the Bar: Gender, Law, and Society in Connecticut, 1639–1789;* and Lisa Wilson, *Life after Death: Widows in Pennsylvania, 1750–1850.* Dayton points out, though, that widows tended to lend money close to home, i.e., in the same county.

42. Mary Cooper, *The Diary of Mary Cooper: Life on a Long Island Farm, 1768–1773,* 16, 18, 30, 31, 33.

43. 2 Kings 4: 1–7.

44. Samuel Moodey, "The Debtors Monitor Directory & Comforter: Or The Way to get & keep out of Debt; In Three Sermons" (Boston, 1715), New-York Historical Society.

45. "Debtor and Creditor: or A Discourse On the following Words, Have Patience with me, and I will pay thee all" (Boston, 1762), New-York Historical Society. The quotation in the title is from Matthew 18:26.

46. Wyndham Beawes, *Lex Mercatoria Rediviva, or, The Merchant's Directory. Being a Compleat Guide to all Men in Business* (London, 1754), New-York Historical Society.

47. Letter to *New-York Weekly Journal* from "Paterculus," July 15, 1734.

48. John Sanders to Samuel Stork and Alexander Champion, June 3, 1751, John Sanders Letter Book, 1749–79, New-York Historical Society.

49. John Sanders to James Bonbonous, July 11, 1761, October 29, 1763, and May 11, 1764, John Sanders Letter Book.

50. John Sanders to John Wendell, October 28, 1766, and May 29, 1768, John Sanders Letter Book.

51. For example, see John Sanders to Champion and Hayley, December 10, 1755 (wrong items sent and other requested items not sent), and September 11, 1766 (number of items sent was fewer than requested and less than on the invoice), John Sanders Letter Book. See also merchant Gerard B. Beekman's repeated requests for payment of money owed him, in letters to his debtors and to his friends who lived in the same colonies as his non-New York debtors, whom he used as agents for collecting debts. White, ed., *Beekman Mercantile Papers,* vol. 1.

52. Note that creditors had only two opportunities a year (in March and October) to commence lawsuits against their debtors in the Dutchess County Court of Common Pleas. The period between due dates and lawsuit commencement dates was calculated based on a study of the 140 original bonds and notes from the period 1754–55 that are still extant among court records in the Ancient Documents collection. Those instruments came due an average of only six months after the date of the obligation; they were apparently intended to be short-term loans.

53. William Livingston to Elizabeth Beaven, June 6, 1755, William Livingston Papers, Letter Book. Note also Livingston's refusal to delay legal action against a Jewish debtor, one "Mr. Torres," who perhaps was not considered a full member of the business community. Livingston doubted Torres's financial reliability, noting that "it being lately become very fashionable for indebted Jews to make off." William Livingston to Robert Freeland, June 22, 1761, William Livingston Papers, Letter Book.

54. The financial position of widows is discussed in chap. 6.

55. *New-York Mercury,* February 25, 1754 (Rutgers); *New-York Weekly Journal,* September 8, 1735 (Winkler and LeMountess); and ibid., March 17, 1735 (Lattouch and Lucas). When a creditor planned to move out of the colony, he would place a similar ad to collect his debts before departing.

56. Ibid., January 23, 1749 (shoemaker); July 9, 1750 (Becker); February 4, 1751 (Zenger).

57. James D. Folts, Jr., *"Duely and Constantly Kept": A History of the New York Supreme Court, 1691–1847 and An Inventory of Its Records (Albany, Utica, and Geneva Offices), 1797–1847.*

58. Min Com Coun 2:256, March 17, 1704. It has been estimated that in early eighteenth-century England, at any given time, approximately one of every 260 men was in prison for debt; by the end of the century only one out of 1,000 was incarcerated. Overall during the century, between 3 and 8% of all adult males spent time in debtor's prison at some point in their lives. The percentage was even higher in urban areas, especially among artisans and shopkeepers. Paul Hess Haagen, "Imprisonment for Debt in England and Wales," 55–78. The rate of imprisonment would be expected to be lower in colonial America—if for no other reason than the relative shortage of labor—but debtors were still imprisoned in significant numbers.

59. *New-York Weekly Journal,* August 18, 1735 (Zenger); William Livingston to Thomas and James Hayward, April 20, 1754, and June 7, 1755, William

Livingston Letter Book (Lattouch, Lane, and Goelet); NY Col Ms 38:193 (Coe); NY Col Ms 56:104 (Provoost); *New-York Weekly Journal,* April 22, 1734, and August 5, 1734 (Trusdell); Hendrick Oudenarde, *Seven Letters to the Honourable Daniel Horsmanden, Esq; Concerning the unnecessary and cruel Imprisonment of Hendrick Oudenarde, Late Merchant in the City of New-York;* NY Col Ms 83:121 (Gale); NY Col Ms 93:149 (McCulleum); and NY Col Ms 54:46 and 60:18 (Sydenham). McCulleum's original petition is no longer extant, though it is described in Edmund B. O'Callaghan's *Calendar of Historical Manuscripts in the Office of the Secretary of State, Albany, N.Y.* Probably none of these New Yorkers spent as much time in prison as one Englishman who spent the last thirty-eight years of his life in a London prison because he was unable to pay his debt of £170. Haagen, "Imprisonment for Debt in England and Wales," 9.

60. "The Ill Policy and Inhumanity of Imprisoning Insolvent Debtors, Fairly Stated and Discussed, by an Impartial Hand" (1754). New York Public Library (and Evans Reprint 7215).

61. See Col Laws NY 1:6–71, at 14 and 62 (1665), and 1:159–60, at 160; 1:345–46 (1695), 1:438–39 (1700), 1:680–81 (1709), 1:866–67 (1715), 1:610–11 (1708), 1:887 (1716), 2:34 (1720), 2:298 (1726), 2:818 (1732), 3:37–38 (1739), and 3:759–60 (1750), 2:669–75, 3:312–18 (1743), 3:694–700 (1748), 3:822–28 (1750), 3:866–72 (1751), 3:924–30 (1753), 3:1019–25 (1754), 4:10–16 (1755), 4:19–21 (1756), and 4:103–4 (1756), 2:753–56 (1732), and 3:1099. See also Revised Statutes (1829) part III, chaps. 5, 6, 8. Note that the original statutes themselves used the pronouns "he, she, or they." For comparative discussion of debtor-relief laws in different colonies, see Coleman, *Debtors and Creditors.*

Chapter 3

1. See, in particular, Morton J. Horwitz, *The Transformation of American Law 1780–1860;* William E. Nelson, *Americanization of the Common Law: The Impact of Legal Change on Massachusetts Society, 1760–1830;* Roscoe Pound, *The Formative Era of American Law* (Boston, 1938); and Grant Gilmore, *The Ages of American Law* (New Haven, 1977). Note that the legal discussion in this chapter is placed primarily in relation to the work of legal historians rather than with regard to the theoretical scholarship of political scientists, anthropologists, and sociologists.

2. See Horwitz, *Transformation of American Law,* chaps. 4 and 6, and Nelson, *Americanization of the Common Law,* chaps. 1 and 4.

3. Bruce H. Mann, *Neighbors and Strangers: Law and Community in Early Connecticut.*

4. See Horwitz, *Transformation of American Law,* chaps. 6 and 7.

5. Ibid., 110–11. See also Nelson, *Americanization of the Common Law,* chap. 4.

6. Joel Munsell, *The Annals of Albany,* 10 vols. (Albany, N.Y., 1850–59) 8: 280–82, 8: 286–90, 293–94; 9: 16–17; SC Min 1723–27, 22, 162, 170, 172, 221, 226–27. See also *Ecclesiastical Records of the State of New York,* 2292–93.

7. *Proprietors of the Charles River Bridge v. Proprietors of the Warren Bridge,* 11 Peters 420 (1837). Legal historians have generally accepted that *Charles River Bridge* represented a major shift in the economic theory applied by courts. See, for example, the monograph by Stanley I. Kutler, *Privilege and Creative Destruction: The Charles River Bridge Case* (New York, 1971); and the survey of American legal history by Kermit L. Hall, *The Magic Mirror: Law in American History,* 117–18.

8. Compare, for example, *Lynch v. Roberts* with *Ebbitts v. Franks. Thomas Lynch v. Thomas Roberts, Jr., and Geesie Roberts* (1721), case described in MC Min, 1720–23, beginning p. 191; *Daniel Ebbitts v. Moses Benjamin Franks* (1755), MC Min, 1753–57, pp. 484, 486, 490, 548, 555; and, for the writ of habeas corpus and the *procedendo,* see SC Min, 1754–57, pp. 183, 191, 205. See also another case against the same seller: *Richard Hale v. Moses Benjamin Franks* (1755), MC Min, 1753–57, pp. 458, 461, 464, 478, 485, 490, 543, 548, 553; and SC Min, 1754–57, pp. 183, 214.

9. Doc Hist, 3: 465–79, 1159–77.

10. Mann, *Neighbors and Strangers.* See also Philip Arthur Richardson's application of sociological and economic theories to seventeenth-century Massachusetts in his Ph.D. dissertation, "Commercial Growth and the Development of Private Law in Early Massachusetts: A Study of the Relationships between Economic and Legal Development." Richardson identifies the shift away from local arbitration and administrative decision making to formal legal proceedings, the increased codification of laws, and the growth in regulations governing—and promoting—commercial activity as markers of increased rationalization of Massachusetts's legal system between 1630 and 1686.

11. See Max Weber's comments in Max Weber, *Max Weber on Law in Economy and Society,* on the market (especially pp. 100–105, 191–97), on juries (esp. pp. 79–80, 229, and 317–21), and on legal rationalization (esp. pp. 266–68, 349–56).

12. Horwitz, *Transformation of American Law,* chaps. 1, 3, 5; Nelson, *Americanization of the Common Law,* chaps. 1, 2, 9.

13. These data are based on study of the minute books of the courts of colonial New York. Minute books are the clerk's handwritten records of the daily business of the court, listing motions, orders, and trials chronologically (not organized by case) but providing few details about the parties to lawsuits or about the underlying circumstances of cases that did not go to trial. The manuscript minutes for the Mayor's Court of New York City, covering every year from 1690 to 1760 (7,677 cases), are kept in the basement of the Courthouse of the New York Supreme Court in New York City. Minutes have survived from the Dutchess County Court of Common Pleas beginning in 1721 (2,989 cases) and are available in the Dutchess County Clerk's Office in Poughkeepsie, N.Y. There were no law reporters in New York during the colonial period to publish judicial opinions; printed law reports begin in New York only in 1800. Few other colonial court documents (such as declarations, bonds, and judgments) from New York City have survived, but some supportive documents from Dutchess

County are extant in a collection known as the Ancient Documents [Anc Doc], which are kept in the Dutchess County Clerk's Office.

14. The population of New York City rose from 4,937 in 1698 to 13,040 in 1756. Doc Hist 1: 467–74.

15. Richard Lempert, "More Tales of Two Courts: Exploring Changes in the 'Dispute Settlement Function' of Trial Courts."

16. MC Min. The rate of jury trial rose slightly in the short term (around the turn of the century) partly because there was a need to define the rules governing new relationships between people from different communities and partly because the new relationships resulted in societal tension that resulted in actionable offenses.

Some additional cases went to special panels that determined the amount of damages in default cases. Those "juries of inquisition" did not determine fault or guilt. They typically merely examined plaintiff-creditors' books and papers and confirmed the amounts plaintiffs alleged to be due so that the court could enter judgment. Defendants who had defaulted in the court proceedings did not, it appears, usually even participate in these inquisitions. The proportion of cases in which inquisitions were ordered by the Mayor's Court judges increased from 1694–95 (4%) to 1754–55 (13%), but in only a fraction of those cases do the minutes indicate that an inquisition was actually held.

17. The population of Dutchess County rose from 1,083 in 1723 to 14,148 in 1756. Doc Hist 1: 467–74.

18. Richard B. Morris, *Studies in the History of American Law, with Special Reference to the Seventeenth and Eighteenth Centuries.*

19. The manuscript minutes of proceedings in the Supreme Court are available in the Hall of Records in New York City for the years 1691–1714, 1723–39, and 1750–60. The population of the colony of New York increased from 18,067 in 1698 to 96,765 in 1756. Doc Hist 467–74.

20. The minutes of Dutchess County Justice of the Peace Roswell Hopkins (beginning 1763) are available in the New York State Archives, Albany, N.Y. Proceedings before JPs were resolved by jury trial only when one of the parties requested it, and the cost was born by that party desiring trial. Col Laws NY 1: 226–31 (1691).

21. William E. Nelson asserts that legal devices to control or avoid jury verdicts were extremely rare in the colonial period and were commonly used only in the nineteenth century. Nelson, *Americanization of the Common Law,* 20–30. In colonial New York, however, jury-control devices were not uncommon. For a description of jury-control devices and appeals to higher courts, see Deborah A. Rosen, "The Supreme Court of Judicature of Colonial New York: Civil Practice in Transition, 1691–1760."

22. Morton Horwitz acknowledged the use of penal bonds to further the interests of merchants in the eighteenth century. However, he went further and concluded that therefore the entire legal system was antagonistic to the interests

of commercial classes. If the legal system had truly been procommercial, Horwitz seems to have been saying, merchants would have trusted the system to deal with the details of commercial disputes. Instead, merchants chose to keep the details from the court, bringing into the courtroom only agreements that left juries and judges no room for investigation and interpretation and no room for discretion in enforcement. At a time when, Horwitz says, contracts were deemed to be justified and enforceable only to the extent that the exchange was inherently just and fair—contrasting with the nineteenth century view that a contract was enforceable if it represented the converging wills of the contracting parties, whether or not the agreement was objectively fair and just—bonds were a particularly important device used by merchants to prevent juries from examining too closely the fairness of the exchange. Horwitz also maintained that the bond system really was not ideal for merchants because it had the effect of retarding the development of a law of executory contracts (contracts based on mutual promises), a necessary component of a strongly procommercial substantive law of contracts. Horwitz, *Transformation of American Law,* 167–70.

Horwitz is right that bonds were used to avoid juries, but hostility to juries is not the same as hostility to courts, and just because merchants found a way to manipulate legal process does not mean that they found the courts inherently anticommercial. Unlike the nineteenth century, when the economic elite achieved their ends by changing the substance of the law, in the eighteenth century merchants achieved their goals by shaping the legal process. In fact, as shown later in this chapter, merchants found that the legal system served their interests quite well.

23. See figures A.2 to A.7. The clerk of the Dutchess County Court of Common Pleas did not systematically record judgments for want of a plea, so the rate of default is difficult to determine for that court. In his study of Connecticut law, Bruce Mann similarly attributed the increase in the proportion of cases resolved by default to the increased use of legal instruments that, he noted, increased certainty and predictability. Mann, *Neighbors and Strangers.*

24. See figures A.8 and A.9. For a more detailed discussion of cases ending in default, arbitration, and out-of-court settlement, see Deborah A. Rosen, "Courts and Commerce in Colonial New York."

25. William Smith, Jr., "A Supream Court Register," Manuscript Division, New York Public Library, New York. See figure A.10.

26. See Marc Galanter, "Reading the Landscape of Disputes: What We Know and Don't Know (and Think We Know) about Our Allegedly Contentious and Litigious Society"; Lempert, "More Tales of Two Courts"; and J. Joseph Burns, "Civil Courts and the Development of Commercial Relations: The Case of North Sumatra."

27. See Vilhelm Aubert, "Competition and Dissensus: Two Types of Conflict and Conflict Resolution"; David Thomas Konig, *Law and Society in Puritan Massachusetts: Essex County, 1629–1692,* xii–xv, 188–89; Peter Charles Hoffer, "Honor and the Roots of American Litigiousness"; and Hoffer, *Law and People in Colonial America.*

28. RCCCP Min. William Offutt's calculations of the percentage of debt-related actions in four rural Delaware Valley counties were similar: 82% of his cases were debt related. William Mc Enery Offutt, Jr., *Of "Good Laws" and "Good Men": Law and Society in the Delaware Valley, 1680–1710,* 93.

29. Clinton W. Francis, "Practice, Strategy, and Institution: Debt Collection in the English Common-Law Courts, 1740–1840."

30. On the importance of honor, see Hoffer, "Honor and the Roots of American Litigiousness."

31. *Thomas Byersly v. Thomas George and Lydia George* (1714), MC Min, 1710–15, pp. 432, 433, 434, 438, 439, 441.

32. Ordinarily, the Mayor's Court minutes do not specify the occupations of jurors, but the occupations of most of them can be determined from other sources. In the 1710s, 67% of the jurors could be identified as craftsmen, 18% were merchants or shopkeepers, and the rest were ship captains, mariners, tavern keepers, gentlemen, or farmers; in the 1750s, 70% of the jurors were craftsmen, only 8% were merchants or shopkeepers, and the rest included not only mariners, tavern keepers, and farmers but also a minister, a schoolmaster, and two laborers. The two trials from the 1740s in which the occupations of jury members are specified in the minutes confirm the statistical impression. A jury of 1746 included the following twelve men: two printers, two joiners, a blacksmith, a tinman, a baker, a shopkeeper, a mason, a turner, a wigmaker, and a cordwainer. A jury of 1747 included a baker, two hatters, two shopkeepers, a chandler, a brazier, a mariner, a mason, a tailor, a butcher, and a joiner, MC Min. The two cases referred to are *Andrew Cordner v. John Aspinwall,* description of case and list of jurors in MC Min, 1742–49, p. 443; and *Jonathan Ogden v. Henry Worster,* MC Min, 1742–49, p. 521.

In the rural counties, most jurors were farmers or part-time farmers. Documents from the late 1730s, 1740s, and early 1750s reveal the occupations of members of six jury pools in the Dutchess County Court of Common Pleas. Out of the 285 names on the lists, 241 (85%) were yeomen and 36 (13%) were craftsmen or craftsmen-yeomen. Among the potential jurors were only 1 merchant, 2 doctors, 3 mariners or ship captains, and 1 laborer. (No occupation was listed for just one man among the 285.) The jury venires studied were from the following cases: *Johannis VanBenthusen v. William Smith* (1753), *Peter Shapprong v. John Cornell* (1750), *Godfried Gieselbreght v. Isaiah Ross* (1747), *Devey v. McGregory* (1747), *William Hamersly v. Lewis Hunt* (1746), and *Isaac Titsort v. Lawrence Hoff* (1738). See Anc Doc 477, 533, 501, 523, and 191. Twenty-four men were included in two of the six jury pool lists while 4 men were included in three of the lists. Therefore, although there were 285 names on the jury pool lists, there were only 225 different men in the pools studied.

33. On the mentality of craftsmen in the seventeenth and eighteenth centuries, see Gary B. Nash, "Artisans and Politics," in Ian M. G. Quimby, ed., *The Craftsman in Early America,* 62–88; and Nash, *The Urban Crucible: Social Change, Political Consciousness, and the Origins of the American Revolution,* esp. 148, 156–57,

161–65, 175–76, 197, and 346–50. See also E. P. Thompson, "The Moral Economy of the English Crowd in the Eighteenth Century," *Past and Present* 50 (1971): 76–136; and C. B. MacPherson, *The Political Theory of Possessive Individualism: Hobbes to Locke* (Oxford, 1962).

34. Note that the attorney did not keep all the fees paid; he had to pay some of the money collected from his client to the judge, the clerk, the cryer, the sheriff, the jurors, and the witnesses.

35. See Jackson Turner Main, *The Social Structure of Revolutionary America,* 68–114; Nash, *Urban Crucible,* 12–13, 64; United States Department of Labor, Bureau of Labor Statistics, Bulletin 499, *History of Wages in the United States from Colonial Times to 1928* (Washington, D.C., 1929); Samuel McKee, Jr., *Labor in Colonial New York, 1664–1776;* and Marcus Rediker, *Between the Devil and the Deep Blue Sea: Merchant Seamen, Pirates, and the Anglo-American Maritime World, 1700–1750* (New York, 1987), 304–5.

36. Memo from James Duane to John Chambers, April 20, 1761, John Chambers Papers, New York State Archives, Albany N.Y.

37. See Francis, "Practice, Strategy, and Institution," 821–24.

38. These findings contrast with the conclusions of some historians of European criminal law. Philip Uninsky found a high degree of conciliatory behavior between economic equals, which he attributes to the fact that "[n]either party [has] a greater intrinsic ability to maneuver the system in his or her favor, nor [can] either side expect preferential treatment from the court." Philip B. Uninsky, "Violence, Honor and Litigation: *Injures et Voies de Fait* in Late 18th-Century Rouen," unpublished paper (a version of which was presented at the Annual Meeting of the American Society for Legal History, 1988), 32. Bruce Lenman and Geoffrey Parker found in their study of criminal law in early modern Europe that "criminal suits involving social equals of some standing tended to be settled by monetary compensation; suits between persons of different status were normally pursued to the bitter end." Bruce Lenman and Geoffrey Parker, "The State, the Community and the Criminal Law in Early Modern Europe," in V. A. C. Gatrell, Bruce Lenman, and Geoffrey Parker, eds., *Crime and the Law: The Social History of Crime in Western Europe since 1500* (London, 1980), 11–48. The quotation is on p. 27.

39. Another manifestation of the formalization of law is suggested by surviving documents: it appears that the number of private petitions to the governors declined. Since other documents relating to the governors' business in the late colonial period are extant, it seems unlikely that the decline in the number of petitions is attributable to a higher rate of survival of earlier than of later petitions. A more likely explanation is that, because discretionary justice was not good for business, redress through petitions was being increasingly discouraged and justice through the law courts was being promoted as the only fair and proper official form of dispute resolution. The available sources are inadequate, however, to demonstrate with assurance this decline in petitionary justice. Such a decline would, though, be consistent with the other legal changes described here because

the development of a rational, procommercial legal system required clear separation of the powers of government and the elimination of discretionary justice that was based not on fixed, abstract rules but on the decision maker's assessment of equitable and political factors in each individual case. Such a form of justice (e.g., in the form of petitions to the governor) was not sufficiently predictable for a smooth-working market economy. Commercial people had to be confident that their contracts would be enforced in accordance with their original terms, without concern for other, personal, factors. They thus favored formal courtroom justice over looser, less predictable, informal princely discretion. See Max Weber's analysis of rational and irrational legal systems and formal versus informal justice, in *Max Weber on Law in Economy and Society,* esp. pp. 57–64, 224–55, and 349–56.

Chapter 4

1. Allan Kulikoff provides an excellent analysis of the complexities and definitional problems of writing about the transition to capitalism in America. See the introduction and chap. 1 of his book *The Agrarian Origins of American Capitalism,* and his article "The Transition to Capitalism in Rural America." See also Michael Merrill, "Putting 'Capitalism' in Its Place: A Review of the Recent Literature"; Rona Stephanie Weiss, "The Market and Massachusetts Farmers, 1750–1850: Comment"; and Michael A. Bernstein and Sean Wilentz, "Marketing, Commerce, and Capitalism in Rural Massachusetts."

2. Christopher Clark, *Roots of Rural Capitalism: Western Massachusetts, 1780–1860,* 33, 67–69, 224–27. The quotation is on p. 33.

3. Thomas S. Wermuth, " 'To Market, To Market': Yeoman Farmers, Merchant Capitalists and the Development of Capitalism in the Hudson River Valley, 1760–1820," 28. See also Michael A. Bellesiles, *Revolutionary Outlaws: Ethan Allen and the Struggle for Independence on the Early American Frontier* (Charlottesville, Va., 1993).

4. Winifred Barr Rothenberg, *From Market-Places to a Market Economy: The Transformation of Rural Massachusetts, 1750–1850.*

5. Ibid., 54.

6. On these factors, see ibid., 125–26 and 136–43; and Clark, *Roots of Rural Capitalism,* 64–71.

7. Probate inventory of Sarah Arnold (1768).

8. Francis Filkin, *Account Book of a Country Store Keeper in the Eighteenth Century at Poughkeepsie,* 87, 95, 41.

9. *Abstracts of Wills on File in the Surrogate's Office, City of New York, 1665–1800,* in *Collections of the New-York Historical Society for the Years 1892–1908,* 3:199 (Elsworth); 8:68 (Hoffman); 8:155 (Ludlow); 11:191 (Magra); 6:192 (leather dresser Smith); 5:11 (Rutgers); 4:67 (Noble); 6:370 (cartman Smith); 5:261 (Dwight); 11:197 (Cuyler); 7:414 (J. Reade); 4:299 (Watts); and 8:243 (L. Reade).

10. Letter to *New-York Weekly Journal* from "John Farmer," May 20, 1734. See also the front page letter of May 2, 1737, similarly advocating the issuance of bills of credit.

11. Letter to *New-York Weekly Journal* from "Paterculus," July 8, 1734.

12. Col Laws NY 2:980.

13. Rothenberg, *From Market-Places to a Market Economy*, 122–25. Christopher Clark, too, lists charging interest as an indicator of a commercial, or distanced, relationship. Clark, *Roots of Rural Capitalism*, 34–38.

14. Col Laws NY 1:909–10, 1:1004, and 2:980–81.

15. Cathy Diane Matson, "Fair Trade, Free Trade: Economic Ideas and Opportunities in Eighteenth-Century New York City Commerce," 276–78.

16. Filkin, *Account Book*, 72–73.

17. Clark, *Roots of Rural Capitalism*, 34–38 (description of long-distance and local exchange ethics), 44–50 (analysis of the temporary breach of local exchange ethic leading to Shays's Rebellion), and 122–28 (continuing force of local exchange ethic into the early nineteenth century).

18. Rothenberg, *From Market-Places to a Market Economy*, 118–19; Clark, *Roots of Rural Capitalism*, 34–38. David Konig, William E. Nelson, and Bruce Mann all found that intratown litigation was very low in early New England because most debts were "neighborly loans." Litigation was necessary primarily between people of different neighborhoods. The three legal historians describe a shift "from communalism to litigation" (to borrow Konig's chapter title). David Thomas Konig, *Law and Society in Puritan Massachusetts: Essex County, 1629–1692*, 79–88; William E. Nelson, *Dispute and Conflict Resolution in Plymouth County, Massachusetts, 1725–1825;* and Bruce H. Mann, *Neighbors and Strangers: Law and Community in Early Connecticut.*

19. Donald J. Black, *The Behavior of Law.* See particularly his discussion of stratification, differentiation, and relative distance in chaps. 2 and 3. Stratification and quantity of law are consistently directly related. Differentiation, or specialization of function, varies curvilinearly with law over the long term, but during the early years of a society (e.g., the colonial period in New York) the relationship would be closer to a direct one; the amount of law would increase as differentiation increased.

20. Generally, the legal system was not directly affected by military events, although the *economic* ramifications of war and peace had an impact on litigation rates at times. In particular, the highest litigation rates for the period coincided with the depression of the years between King George's War and the French and Indian War. The sudden end of wartime profits from privateering and provisioning English and American soldiers may have led to increased debt and may thus have contributed to the dramatic rise of debt litigation. Another factor may have been the inflation resulting from shortages of money during the interwar period. As creditors saw the sums owed to them losing value, they had reason to try to collect the debts as quickly as possible. Finally, of course, in peacetime people are freer to spend money on consumer goods, thus increasing their debt levels and their susceptibility to lawsuit.

21. For an especially useful description of urban colonial merchant communities, see Thomas M. Doerflinger, *A Vigorous Spirit of Enterprise: Merchants and Economic Development in Revolutionary Philadelphia.*

22. Figures have been given for these particular years because they were census years. Census information is available for the following years: 1698, 1703, 1712, 1723, 1731, 1737, 1743, 1749, and 1756. Doc Hist 1:467–74.

23. These data are drawn from the MC Min, the DCCCP Min, and the SC Min. For more detail on the increasing volume and rate of litigation, see figures A.11–A.14.

24. RCCCP Min.

25. Nelson, *Dispute and Conflict Resolution;* Konig, *Law and Society;* A. G. Roeber, *Faithful Magistrates and Republican Lawyers: Creators of Virginia Legal Culture, 1680–1810,* 128; Richard L. Bushman, *From Puritan to Yankee: Character and the Social Order in Connecticut, 1690–1765,* 128–29, 136, 297; Mann, *Neighbors and Strangers;* and Peter Charles Hoffer, "Honor and the Roots of American Litigiousness."

26. Hendrick Schenk Account Book, Ledger B, New York Public Library, New York; and DCCCP Min.

27. Some people appeared as both plaintiffs and defendants during that period.

28. The increased participation of poorer taxpayers as litigants is shown in figure A.15.

29. Bruce Martin Wilkenfeld, "The Social and Economic Structure of the City of New York, 1695–1796," 28, 87; *The Burghers of New Amsterdam and the Freemen of New York 1675–1866,* in *Collections of the New-York Historical Society for the year 1885,* vol. 18 (New York, 1886). To become a freeman in New York City, one had to register and pay a fee. One had to be a freeman in order to conduct business or vote in the city.

30. William McEnery Offutt, Jr., *Of "Good Laws" and "Good Men": Law and Society in the Delaware Valley, 1680–1710.* Note that as in the Dutchess County Court of Common Pleas, debt-related cases were a very high proportion (82%) of all cases in the Delaware Valley county courts. Ibid., 93.

31. Offutt estimates that in the Delaware Valley farmers were only about half the "legal population," people who participated in the legal system as litigants, criminal defendants, witnesses, jurors, or officeholders. He does not estimate farmers' proportion of the whole population. Men were 93% of Offutt's litigants. Ibid., 69–70.

32. Not enough is known about the two regions to be able to determine the extent to which these factors might have been true. The work of James Lemon and Paul Clemons indicates that Chester County and Burlington County were affluent, but only a few probate inventories survive from colonial Dutchess County, so comparable figures are not calculable for that county. James T. Lemon, *The Best Poor Man's Country: A Geographical Study of Early Southeastern Pennsylvania,* quotation on xiii; Paul G. E. Clemens, "Afterword: Material Culture and the Rural Economy: Burlington County, New Jersey, 1760–1820,"

in Peter O. Wacker and Paul G. E. Clemens, *Land Use in Early New Jersey: A Historical Geography* (New Brunswick, N.J., 1995), 265–96, at 283.

33. Population figures by ethnicity are from Joyce D. Goodfriend, *Before the Melting Pot: Society and Culture in Colonial New York City, 1664–1730.*

Chapter 5

1. For an excellent survey of men's economic roles, see Edwin J. Perkins, *The Economy of Colonial America,* chaps. 3–5, and the sources cited in his bibliographical essays.

2. These data are based on the MC Min. The percentages for the 1700s and 1740s cover every case brought during those decades, but, because of the large number of cases in the 1790s, the data for that decade are based on a study of just two years (1794–95) rather than on a count of all cases in every year of the decade.

3. DCCCP Min; OCCCP Min; and WCCCP Min. Between 1721 and 1760 there were 2,989 cases in Dutchess County, 2,757 in Westchester County, and 890 in Orange County.

4. Roswell Hopkins Records, (handwritten transcription, 1895) New York State Archives, Albany, N.Y. There were female plaintiffs in just 8 cases and female defendants in 3 cases among the total of 314 cases heard by Hopkins in the two-year period. Two of the female plaintiffs appeared with their husbands and one appeared as an executor of an estate.

5. SC Min.

6. Cornelia Hughes Dayton, *Women before the Bar: Gender, Law, and Society in Connecticut, 1639–1789,* 84–85, 99.

7. Ibid., 89, 96, 100.

8. Anc Doc 3111.

9. Joseph Murray, "Precedent Book," 152, Columbia University Law Library, Special Collections, New York.

10. MC Min.

11. Of those 13 female plaintiffs, 5 (38%) were single or widowed (2 single, 3 widowed) and 8 (62%) were married women suing with their husbands. Of the 10 female defendants, 6 (60%) were single or widowed (3 single, 3 widowed), and 4 (40%) were married.

12. The nature of the slander is known in 7 of the 10 cases in which women were accused of slandering someone. The slander by the female defendant involved sexual misconduct in 3 cases (in which all the slandered victims were other women) and illegal or dishonest conduct in 4 cases.

13. On women and slander in other colonies, see Dayton, *Women before the Bar,* chap. 6; and Mary Beth Norton, "Gender and Defamation in Seventeenth-Century Maryland."

14. Sally Engle Merry, *Getting Justice and Getting Even: Legal Consciousness among Working-Class Americans* (Chicago, 1990).

15. See Carole Pateman, *The Sexual Contract* (New York, 1989); and Susan Moller Okin, *Women in Western Political Thought* (Princeton, N.J., 1979), chaps. 9–11.

16. In connection with his study of litigation in seventeenth-century England, Clinton W. Francis has said that an all-or-nothing approach was part of judges' "controlled-delegation strategy," which they developed in order to serve their financial interest in dealing with as many cases as possible in the shortest time. Clinton W. Francis, "The Structure of Judicial Administration and the Development of Contract Law in Seventeenth-Century England."

17. On women's economic roles in seventeenth- and eighteenth-century northern colonies, see Laurel Thatcher Ulrich, *Good Wives: Image and Reality in the Lives of Women of Northern New England, 1650–1750;* Alice Morse Earle, *Home Life in Colonial Days;* and Alice Clark, *Working Life of Women in the Seventeenth Century.*

18. Ulrich's description of women's roles and the female economy in colonial and late eighteenth-century New England include *Good Wives;* " 'A Friendly Neighbor': Social Dimensions of Daily Work in Northern Colonial New England"; "Housewife and Gadder: Themes of Self-Sufficiency and Community in Eighteenth-Century New England," in Norton and Groneman, eds., *"To Toil the Livelong Day": America's Women at Work, 1780–1980;* "Martha Ballard and Her Girls: Women's Work in Eighteenth-Century Maine," in Innes, ed., *Work and Labor in Early America;* and *A Midwife's Tale: The Life of Martha Ballard, Based on Her Diary, 1785–1812.* William Chester Jordan notes that married and widowed women in preindustrial Europe frequently made small, informal, domestic loans, often to other women in their social network. That domestic credit corresponds to the nature of the exchanges in the American "female economy" described by Ulrich. Jordan, *Women and Credit in Pre-Industrial and Developing Societies* (Philadelphia, 1993).

19. Frances Filkin, *Account Book of a Country Store Keeper in the 18th Century at Poughkeepsie,* 89, 23, 69.

20. Ibid., 51, 79.

21. Ibid., 93, 10, 111.

22. Ulrich, *Midwife's Tale,* 77–81. On textile production in colonial America, see also Adrienne Dora Hood, "Organization and Extent of Textile Manufacture in Eighteenth-Century Rural Pennsylvania: A Case Study of Chester County," Ph.D. dissertation, University of California at San Diego, 1988.

23. Joan M. Jensen, *Loosening the Bonds: Mid-Atlantic Farm Women, 1750–1850,* 37.

24. Ibid., chaps. 5, 6. See also Jensen, "Butter Making and Economic Development in Mid-Atlantic America from 1750 to 1850."

25. Filkin, *Account Book,* 10, 17, 40.

26. Ibid., 72–73.

27. For examples of such wills, see *Abstracts of Wills,* 8:141 (Allen); 5:55

(Myer); 6:78 (Beekman); 7:95 (Bonnett); 7:270 (Cosine); 7:272 (Jackson); 4:444 (Merrit); 6:294 (Brown); 6:352 (Arnaut); 3:202 (Williams); 6:376 (Cosine); 5:410 (Jennings); 6:118 (Davis); 6:216 (Foster); and 7:239 (Carpenter). The last will was written and signed in 1749 but not probated until 1769, by which time the son would have been an adult, so the widow would not have managed the land at all.

28. Kenneth Scott, *Data from Quarter Sessions,* 1735 and August 6, 1712.

29. Mary Beth Norton, "Eighteenth-Century American Women in Peace and War: The Case of the Loyalists."

30. *New-York Gazette or the Weekly Post-Boy,* December 31, 1767, and May 8, 1766, and the *New-York Mercury,* February 25, 1765; and Rita Susswein Gottesman, *The Arts and Crafts in New York, 1726–1776: Advertisements and News Items from New York City Newspapers,* in *Collections of the New York Historical Society for the Year 1936,* vol. 69 (New York, 1938), 258–59, 249, 254.

31. *New-York Gazette or the Weekly Post-Boy,* February 18, 1762, in *Arts and Crafts,* 258.

32. Julie A. Matthaei, *An Economic History of Women in America: Women's Work, the Sexual Division of Labor, and the Development of Capitalism,* 62–65; Thomas Dublin, "Rural Putting-Out Work in Early Nineteenth-Century New England: Women and the Transition to Capitalism in the Countryside," *New England Quarterly* 64 (1991): 531–73.

33. *New York Journal and Weekly Register,* May 4, 1786, quoted in Matthaei, *Economic History of Women,* 62.

34. *New-York Gazette, Revived in the Weekly Post-Boy,* April 1, 1751 (Boyd); ibid., May 21, 1759 (Callander); and *New-York Journal or the General Advertiser,* June 17, 1773 (Campbell). *Arts and Crafts,* 325–26, 282, 285.

35. *New-York Gazette or the Weekly Post-Boy,* June 13, 1765, in *Arts and Crafts,* 308; *New-York Weekly Journal,* June 26, 1738. The life of a (married) widwife in Maine is described in detail in Ulrich, *Midwife's Tale.*

36. NY Col Ms 42:138, 53:158.

37. *New-York Gazette or the Weekly Post-Boy,* February 29, 1768, *Arts and Crafts,* 288 (Sells); Mayor's Court Papers, 1714 (Salnave); *New-York Gazette or the Weekly Post-Boy,* August 26, 1771 (Hay); *New-York Gazette,* July 10, 1769, *Arts and Crafts,* 332 (Morcomb); *New York Journal,* April 11, 1737, cited in Elisabeth Dexter, *Colonial Women of Affairs* (Boston, 1931), 44 (Brasher); and *New York Journal,* March 29, 1736, quoted in Dexter, *Colonial Women,* 71 (Edwards).

38. Isacca Newton Phelps Stokes, ed., *The Iconography of Manhattan Island, 1498–1909,* includes references to tavern keepers Scurlock (1740), Post (1718), Jourdaine (1717, 1736), and Stockton (1751). *New-York Gazette or the Weekly Post-Boy* mentions tavern keepers Vernon (July 6, 1765) and Brett (November 28, 1748) (as cited in Elisabeth Dexter, *Colonial Women of Affairs,* 11). The *New York Genealogical and Biographical Record* lists tavern keepers Van Gusen (1757) and Harris (1745). *Burghers and Freeman* mentions tavern keeper Broughton in 1706.

39. *New-York Gazette or the Weekly Post-Boy,* March 29, 1773, (Hay); *New-York Mercury,* May 20, 1765 (Bosworth); *New-York Journal or General Advertiser,* October 13, 1768 (Edwards); *New-York Gazette or the Weekly Post-Boy,* January 14, 1771 (Gibbon), *New-York Mercury,* October 8, 1753 (Gray), May 6, 1765 (Carroll), and April 27, 1767 (Jones), *New-York Gazette and the Weekly Mercury,* April 17, 1769 (Ferguson), and September 6, 1773 (Cole), and *New-York Gazette or the Weekly Post-Boy,* December 13–21, 1731 (Gazley), in *Arts and Crafts,* 279, 277, 278, 311, 275, 276, 277–78, 278, 279–80, and 275.

40. Carole Shammas, "The Female Social Structure of Philadelphia in 1775," *Pennsylvania Magazine of History and Biography,* 76.

41. *Zachariah Hutchins v. Margaret Norton* (1715) and *Henry Pontenay v. Margaret Norton,* MC Min 1715–18. Hester Kortright and Tryntie Remsen were two of the bakers and bolters given brand marks for flour casks in Quarter Sessions records in 1751. Scott, *Data from Quarter Sessions.* Catherine Zenger announced her intention to continue John Peter Zenger's newspaper in 1747. *New-York Weekly Journal,* September 14, 1747.

42. Jean P. Jordan, "Women Merchants in Colonial New York"; Patricia A. Cleary, " 'She Merchants' of Colonial America: Women and Commerce on the Eve of the Revolution"; Cleary, " 'She Will Be In the Shop': Women's Sphere of Trade in Eighteenth-Century Philadelphia and New York"; and Dexter, *Colonial Women.* See also Cynthia A. Kerner, "From Entrepreneurs to Ornaments: The Livingston Women, 1679–1790," *Hudson Valley Regional Review* 4 (1987): 38–55; and Lisa Wilson Waciega, "A 'Man of Business': The Widow of Means in Southeastern Pennsylvania, 1750–1850." David Narrett found that widows of Dutch ancestry were more likely than those of English background to engage in trade in colonial New York. David E. Narrett, *Inheritance and Family Life in Colonial New York City.*

43. Shammas, "Female Social Structure," 75–76.

44. Joan Hoff Wilson, "The Illusion of Change: Women and the American Revolution." The quotation is on p. 78.

45. Edwin J. Perkins, "The Entrepreneurial Spirit in Colonial America: The Foundations of Modern Business History"; Amy Louise Erickson, *Women and Property in Early Modern England* (New York, 1993), 235.

46. Matthaei, *Economic History,* 70–71.

47. *Burghers and Freemen.*

48. Norton, "Eighteenth-Century American Women in Peace and War."

49. Philip L. White, ed., *The Beekman Mercantile Papers, 1746–1799* (New York, 1956).

Chapter 6

1. Cornelia Hughes Dayton, *Women before the Bar: Gender, Law, and Society in Connecticut, 1639–1789,* introduction and chap. 2.

2. On the legal rights of women in colonial New York, see Marylynn

Salmon, *Women and the Law of Property in Early America;* Linda Briggs Biemer, *Women and Property in Colonial New York: The Transition from Dutch to English Law, 1643–1727;* Joan R. Gunderson and Gwen Victor Gampel, "Married Women's Legal Status in Eighteenth-Century New York and Virginia"; and Marylynn Salmon, "Equality or Submersion? Feme Covert Status in Early Pennsylvania."

3. William Blackstone, *Commentaries on the Laws of England* (Oxford, 1765), 1:106–8.

4. In fact, Marylynn Salmon's study of women's property rights between 1750 and 1830 shows that if there was any change in New York between the colonial period and the early nineteenth century, it was marginally to women's advantage: the courts became slightly more protective of women's property rights, not less so. Salmon, *Women and the Law of Property,* 28–30.

5. On married women's limited contractual and property rights, see *Jackson v. Vanderheyden,* 17 Johns. Rep. 167–69, *Reports of Cases Adjudged and Determined in the Supreme Court of Judicature and Court for the Trial of Impeachments and Correction of Errors of The State of New York* [hereafter *Reports of Cases*], 6:325–26 (1819); *Whitbeck v. Cook et ux,* 15 Johns 483–92, *Reports of Cases,* 5:1167–69 (1818); *Rumsey v. Leek* 5 Wend. 20–22, *Reports of Cases,* 10:757–58 (1830); *Martin v. Dwelly et al.,* 6 Wend. 9–22, *Reports of Cases* 10:1001–8 (1830); *Hyde v. Stone,* 9 Cowen 230–32, *Reports of Cases,* 9:624–25 (1828); *Minard v. Mead,* 7 Wend. 68–70, *Reports of Cases,* 11:57–58 (1831); *Mott v. Comstock,* 8 Wend. 544–45, *Reports of Cases,* 11:463 (1832). The quotation in the text is from *Jackson v. Vanderheyden.*

6. NY Col Ms 42:138, 53:158. Rose's indictment on charges of "entertaining negro slaves" in 1693 suggests one possible source of income: she may have kept a tavern. NYCGQS Min, May 2 and August 1, 1693. Alternatively, she may have depended on family charity for the years during which she was waiting to collect her money.

Examples of widowed women petitioning instead of bringing a trespass, or trespass and ejectment, action include Elizabeth Joriss, who in 1690 petitioned the governor to recover for her land wrongfully held from her by Robert Burgess; Elizabeth Banker, who in 1691 appealed to the governor to end the interference by Thomas Clarke in her attempt to build on a lot in New York City; and Hester Glen, who in 1693 petitioned the governor to confirm her right to land being claimed by Richard Owen. Examples of women petitioning instead of bringing a replevin action include Dorothy Worsoncroft, who petitioned the governor in 1691 to order Peter Chock to give her certain papers belonging to her; Bathshua Wessells, who complained to the governor in 1695 that her brother John Pells detained her cattle; and Rebeccah Randall, who petitioned the governor in 1699 to order the collector Ducie Hungerford to restore certain goods of hers taken by him. NY Col Ms 36:142 (Joriss), 37:243 (Bancker), 39:108 (Glen), 37:57 (Worsoncroft), 40:81 and 40:84 (Wessells), 43:61 (Randall).

7. For a more extensive discussion of women and petitionary justice, see

Deborah A. Rosen, "Mitigating Inequality: Women and Justice in Early New York," in Larry D. Eldridge, ed., *Women and Freedom in Early America* (New York, 1997).

8. Richard B. Morris, *Studies in the History of American Law, with Special Reference to the Seventeenth and Eighteenth Centuries,* chap. 3; Mary R. Beard, *Woman as Force in History: A Study in Traditions and Realities.*

9. Morris, *Studies in the History of American Law,* 200.

10. Linda K. Kerber, *Women of the Republic: Intellect and Ideology in Revolutionary America,* chap. 5.

11. It should also be noted that, by comparing colonial practice to formal common law rules rather than to English practice, Morris exaggerated the difference between mother country and colonies. Amy Louise Erickson has found that in early modern England common law rules were commonly mitigated in practice not only by equity courts but also by manorial courts (which often advocated partibility in inheritance among siblings) and ecclesiastical courts (which supported a form of community property within marriage). Erickson herself concludes that practice deviated more from theory in England than in America and that overall women fared worse under the law in the American colonies than in England. Amy Louise Erickson, *Women and Property in Early Modern England* (New York, 1993), esp. 6 and 233–34.

12. Lisa Wilson, *Life after Death: Widows in Pennsylvania, 1750–1850;* Patricia A. Cleary, " 'She Merchants' of Colonial America: Women and Commerce on the Eve of the Revolution."

13. Salmon, *Women and the Law of Property,* xiii.

14. Ibid., xii.

15. Note that women were also unable to contractualize their relationships with their main financial supporters, their husbands, because of the assumption that family relationships had to be protected from intrusions by law. Thus while men had the opportunity to protect their interests by buttressing their economic relationships with contracts, they were at the same time shielded from the possible consequences of other members of the family having contractual rights. Men did not have to put their relationships with their familial dependents into contractual form, nor could they be obligated to others by the independent promises of their dependents. Men retained their power and authority in their families most significantly because their wives were not empowered to make contracts of their own. Consequently men benefited both from the availability of contractualized relationships with business partners and from the unavailability of contractualized relationships with their wives, who were dependent on them.

16. NY Col Laws 1:9–10, 1:114–15. On inheritance and widow's property rights in early America, see Salmon, *Women and the Law of Property,* chap. 7; Carole Shammas, Marylynn Salmon, and Michel Dahlin, *Inheritance in America from Colonial Times to the Present;* David E. Narrett, *Inheritance and Family Life in Colonial New York City;* and the following essays in Ronald Hoffman and Peter J.

Albert, eds., *Women in the Age of the American Revolution:* Daniel Scott Smith, "Inheritance and the Social History of Early American Women" (45–66), Gloria L. Main, "Widows in Rural Massachusetts on the Eve of the Revolution" (67–90), David E. Narrett, "Men's Wills and Women's Property Rights in Colonial New York" (91–133), Carole Shammas, "Early American Women and Control over Capital" (134–54), and Lois Green Carr, "Inheritance in the Colonial Chesapeake" (155–208). On women and property ownership in England in the period from 1580 to 1720, see esp. Erickson, *Women and Property.*

17. Toby Ditz, *Property and Kinship: Inheritance in Early Connecticut, 1750–1820,* chaps. 4, 5.

18. See, for example, the probate records of John Price, Conrad Ten Eyck, John Ten Eyck, Alexander Wyley, John West, and John Ball. "Abstracts of Wills on File in the Surrogate's Office, City of New York, 1665–1800," 11:13 (Price); 5:25 (C. Ten Eyck); 5:329 (J. Ten Eyck); 6:443 (Wyley); 1:235 (West); *Genealogical Data from New York Administration Bonds, 1753–1799,* at p. 10 (Ball). The remarriage rate of older widows was probably lower than that of younger widows. Both Lisa Wilson and Alexander Keyssar have noted that widows did not remarry as often as is usually thought. See Wilson, *Life after Death;* and Alexander Keyssar, "Widowhood in Eighteenth-Century Massachusetts: A Problem in the History of the Family."

19. Carole Shammas, "The Female Social Structure of Philadelphia in 1775."

20. For examples, see *Abstracts of Wills,* 6:376 (Cosine); 7:43 (Hicks); 6:192 (Smith); 8:19 (Harris); 7:337 (Gomez); and 5:81 (Green).

21. Lisa Wilson Waciega, "A 'Man of Business': The Widow of Means in Southeastern Pennsylvania, 1750–1850," 48–49.

22. Although common law rules protected the widow's dower portion from her husband's debts, any legacy she might take by her husband's will would be reduced by his debts. Salmon, *Women and the Law of Property,* 143–44.

23. Probate inventories of John Dewsbury (1698), Jane Dewsbury (1703), William Pinckney, Jr. (1747), Sarah Pinckney (1747), Christopher Youngs (1727), and Elizabeth Youngs (1748).

24. Probate inventories of William Teller (1701), Mary Teller (1702), William Cox (1689), and Alice Cox (1694). Many of the nineteenth-century Philadelphia widows described by Lisa Wilson also gained wealth in the years after their husbands died. Wilson, *Life after Death,* 122–31. Toby Ditz has also pointed out that as large inherited estates consisted less of land and more of negotiable instruments in the late eighteenth century, wealthy widows often could have greater independent control over assets than they had previously enjoyed. Ditz, *Property and Kinship.*

25. Shammas, "Early American Women and Control over Capital," pp. 143–47.

26. Christine H. Tompsett, "A Note on the Economic Status of Widows in Colonial New York," 322–23 and 329.

27. By the end of the nineteenth century, probate inventories showed

women owning 34.6% of wealth, and in 1979 they owned 52.8% of wealth. As Carole Shammas concludes, "When women received the legal right during the nineteenth century to possess property that they had inherited, it greatly diminished the percentage of total wealth owned by men." Women were 9.5% of probated decedents in Bucks County in 1685–1755, 16.5% in 1791–1801, 37.8% in 1891–93, and 47.4% in 1979. They were 6.7% of probated decedents in 1774 Massachusetts and 10.6% in 1774 Virginia and Maryland. Shammas, "Early American Women and Control over Capital," quotation on 154; Alice Hanson Jones, *American Colonial Wealth: Documents and Methods.*

28. Dutchess County Tax Lists, Dutchess County Clerk's Office, Poughkeepsie, N.Y.

29. Shammas, Salmon, and Dahlin, *Inheritance in America,* chap. 2. Gloria Main has observed that that phenomenon is due not to changing social attitudes but to the older age of the widows—men were more reluctant to appoint older widows executors. Main, "Widows in Rural Massachusetts." Cornelia Hughes Dayton observes that given the large proportion of female litigators who appeared in court to settle their deceased husbands' estates, the decline in female executors and administrators resulted in some decline in female litigators. Dayton, *Women before the Bar,* 91–93.

30. Tompsett, "Economic Status of Widows"; Narrett, "Men's Wills and Women's Property Rights"; Shammas, "Early American Women and Control over Capital."

31. Erickson, *Women and Property,* 201.

32. NYC Tax Lists. The only woman listed with a man was Mary Colex, who was listed with an unnamed "Free Negro." Otherwise, whenever there was an adult man living in a house, only his name appeared on the tax lists.

33. Tompsett, "Economic Status of Widows"; Elaine Forman Crane, "Dependence in the Era of Independence: The Role of Women in a Republican Society," in Greene, *The American Revolution: Its Character and Limits.*

34. Shammas, "Female Social Structure," 74.

35. For advertisements seeking charity for poor widows and others, see esp. the *New-York Weekly Journal,* January 19, 1741, and see also the *Journal* for January 5 and 12, 1741, and for February 16, 1741.

36. The arrest of the prostitutes was described in the *New-York Mercury* on July 23, 1753. The 22 were committed to the workhouse, and 5 of them received 15-lash whippings "before a vast Number of Spectators" with orders to leave town within 48 hours.

37. NYCCGQS Min, vol. 1722–42, p. 246.

38. NY Col Ms 63:13, 63:16 (Mary Barnet). In 1711 Elizabeth Collins petitioned the governor for permission to beg for the support of her family. In 1771 Elizabeth Pugsley obtained an order forcing her husband to support the family. NY Col Ms 54:171 (Collins); CC Min, 1770–76, pp. 28, 40, 48, 51, 60, 63, 66–67 (Pugsley).

39. In most cases, their petitions were successful. We cannot determine how

many single women had to go to the justices of the peace or the courts for child support because not all such cases were recorded in the minute books. Among surviving Dutchess County documents, however, are recognizances or orders in bastardy in approximately 45 cases between 1752 and 1770, so bastardy was hardly an unusual situation. (See Anc Doc.) The adult (over age 16) population of Dutchess County was about 6,300 in 1756 and about 10,500 in 1771 (Doc Hist 1:473, 474). Typically the justice of the peace ordered the father to make weekly payments of 2 or 3 shillings toward the support of the child. See, for example, Recognizance in Bastardy, Order in Bastardy, Deposition of Mary Fuller, and Indemnification Bond, Anc Doc 3650, 3653, and 3849; DCCGS Min 1750–57, pp. 55, 60 and 1758–65, p. 20.

40. For example, in 1719 the widow Anna Maria Cochin was brought before two justices of the peace at Livingston Manor in Albany County to explain what had happened to her "bastard child." She said that "Great Poverty had Reduced her on the Sixth Day of September to Comitt fornication with Joseph the Negro man of Mr Livingston who gott her with Child he being half Drunk Promiseing her a pair of Shoes." The baby, she asserted, had died accidentally. Cochin was not convicted on the murder charge, but she was found guilty of having two other bastard children, sentenced to 31 lashes, and banished from the county. NY Col Ms 61:146; ACCGS Min 1717–23, February 4, 1719, and June 3, 1719. Court records mention four additional cases: Christina Meyer, an unmarried servant in New York City (1718), Elizabeth Rainer of Suffolk County, also a single woman (1677), Angle Hendricks (1669), and an unnamed slave woman in Suffolk County (1678). NY Col Ms 61:77 (Meyer); 26:56 (Rainer); 22:63–75 (Hendricks); and 27:86, 27:61, and 27:86 (the slave woman). Three other cases of apparent infanticide were reported in the newspapers in 1739, 1746, and 1749. *New-York Weekly Journal,* April 28, 1746, July 3, 1749, September 18, 1749, August 8, 1737, and August 29, 1737.

41. See the following appeals of servants, slaves, and wives for protection against abuse: NYCGQS Min (servant Margaret Anderson); NY Col Ms 33:28 (the servant daughter of Elie Coppin); NY Col Ms 31:148 (servant Alice Fisher); NY Col Ms 32:56 (servant Elizabeth Stratton); NY Col Ms 44:147, 47:18, 19 (slave named Mando); NY Col Ms 43:26 (slave Mary Drew); NY Col Ms 56:96 (slave Sarah Robinson); NY Col Ms 43:83, 43:84 (abused wife Ann Everendon); NY Col Ms 54:46, 60:18 (abused wife Elizabeth Sydenham). For more detail regarding these petitions, see Rosen, "Mitigating Inequality."

42. Studies of working-class and poor people in the eighteenth century include Robert E. Cray, Jr., *Paupers and Poor Relief in New York City and Its Rural Environs, 1700–1830;* Billy G. Smith, *The "Lower Sort": Philadelphia's Laboring People, 1750–1800;* and Gary B. Nash, *The Urban Crucible: Social Change, Political Consciousness, and the Origins of the American Revolution.*

43. Cornelia Hughes Dayton agrees that women's limited financial resources contributed to their low litigation rate. She also mentions another factor affecting

women's litigation rates: women's lower literacy and numeracy. She notes that colonial women's lesser writing and ciphering skills were a barrier to their participating in trade and credit relationships and therefore lessened the likelihood of their ending up in court. Dayton, *Women before the Bar,* 102–3.

44. Dayton explains that notions of gentility and divergent expectations of men's and women's sexual behavior were imported from England as part of the Anglicization of American culture. Dayton, *Women before the Bar,* 63–68, 102–3, and 225–30. The other significant aspect of Anglicization relating to law was the importation of a more technical and professional legal system with more "orderly" pleading. Ibid., 44–49.

45. *New-York Weekly Journal,* August 19, 1734.

46. Ibid., September 30, 1734.

47. Carol Karlsen points out that in colonial New England, women who were assertive or who questioned the authority of (i.e., failed to defer to) ministers, magistrates, masters, or husbands could be branded witches. Carol F. Karlsen, *The Devil in the Shape of a Woman: Witchcraft in Colonial New England* (New York, 1987). See esp. chap. 4.

48. Ibid.

49. Other scholars have shown how the expectation of domesticity increasingly shaped women's lives in the late eighteenth century and in the nineteenth century. See, for example, Nancy F. Cott, *The Bonds of Womanhood: "Woman's Sphere" in New England, 1780–1835;* and Barbara Welter, "The Cult of True Womanhood, 1820–1860."

50. Those who argued that women's position declined between the seventeenth century and the early nineteenth century include Morris, *Studies in the History of American Law;* Elisabeth Anthony Dexter, *Colonial Women of Affairs;* Gerda Lerner, "The Lady and the Mill Girl: Changes in the Status of Women in the Age of Jackson"; Mary R. Beard, *Woman as Force in History: A Study in Traditions and Realities;* and Ann D. Gordon and Mari Jo Buhle, "Sex and Class in Colonial and Nineteenth-Century America," in Berenice Carroll, ed., *Liberating Women's History* (Urbana, Ill., 1976), 278–300. That view has been challenged by Mary Beth Norton and Carol Ruth Berkin, "Women and American History"; and Norton, "The Myth of the Golden Age"; Marylynn Salmon, "The Legal Status of Women in Early America: A Reappraisal"; and Salmon, *Women and the Law of Property.*

51. Carol Ruth Berkin, "A Modest Proposal, or How to Escape Old Paradigms in Colonial Women's History," unpublished talk given at the Columbia University Seminar on Early American History and Culture, New York City, April 13, 1993. Berkin made similar remarks at the Gipson Institute, Lehigh University, Bethlehem, Pennsylvania, November 17, 1995.

52. For example, see Mary P. Ryan, *Womanhood in America from Colonial Times to the Present;* and Lerner, "The Lady and the Mill Girl." See also Morris, *Studies in the History of American Law.*

53. Norton and Berkin, "Women and American History"; Norton, "The Myth of the Golden Age"; and Norton, *Liberty's Daughters: The Revolutionary Experience of American Women, 1750–1800.*

54. Norton and Berkin, "Women and American History"; and Norton, "The Myth of the Golden Age."

55. On women's lack of citizenship rights, see Linda K. Kerber, "The Paradox of Women's Citizenship in the Early Republic: The Case of *Martin vs. Massachusetts,* 1805."

56. Jeanne Boydston, *Home and Work: Housework, Wages, and the Ideology of Labor in the Early Republic,* chap. 1, quotation on p. 20.

57. Cott, *Bonds of Womanhood.*

58. Much of the legal scholarship on this subject has relied heavily on the psychological studies of Carol Gilligan in *In a Different Voice: Psychological Theory and Women's Development.* See also Mary Field Belenky, Blythe McVickar Clinchy, Nancy Rule Goldberger, and Jill Mattuck Tarule, *Women's Ways of Knowing: The Development of Self, Voice, and Mind* (New York, 1986). Legal and economic scholars are cited in later notes.

59. On the female approach to justice, see Lucinda M. Finley, "Breaking Women's Silence in Law: The Dilemma of the Gendered Nature of Legal Reasoning"; Eve Hill, "Alternative Dispute Resolution in a Feminist Voice"; Suzanna Sherry, "Civic Virtue and the Feminine Voice in Constitutional Adjudication"; Carrie Menkel-Meadow, "Portia in a Different Voice: Speculations on a Women's Lawyering Process"; Ann C. Scales, "The Emergence of Feminist Jurisprudence: An Essay"; Rand Jack and Dana Crowley Jack, *Moral Vision and Professional Decisions: The Changing Values of Women and Men Lawyers* (New York, 1989); and Joan Hoff, *Law, Gender, and Injustice: A Legal History of U.S. Women.*

60. Nancy Grey Osterud, "Gender and the Transition to Capitalism in Rural America," quotations on 24 and 25. See also Osterud, *Bonds of Community: The Lives of Farm Women in Nineteenth-Century New York.*

Chapter 7

1. Jour Gen Ass, December 14, 1765, p. 806.

2. The three quoted statements are included in Samuel Eliot Morison, ed., *Sources and Documents Illustrating the American Revolution, 1764–1788, and the Formation of the Federal Constitution* (New York, 1923; repr. ed., 1979), 33, 121, 159.

3. See Nancy F. Cott, *The Bonds of Womanhood: 'Woman's Sphere' in New England, 1780–1835.*

4. Mary P. Ryan, *Womanhood in America, from Colonial Times to the Present,* 69; Glenna Matthews, *The Rise of Public Woman: Woman's Power and Woman's Place in the United States, 1630–1970,* 32.

5. See, for example, Lawrence Stone, *The Family, Sex and Marriage in England, 1500–1800* (London, 1977); Randolph Trumbach, *The Rise of the Egalitarian Family: Aristocratic Kinship and Domestic Relations in Eighteenth-Century England*

(London, 1978); Michael Mitterauer and Reinhard Sieder, *The European Family: Patriarchy to Partnership from the Middle Ages to the Present,* trans. Karla Oosterveen and Manfred Horzinger (Oxford, 1982); and Edward Shorter, *The Making of the Modern Family* (New York, 1975).

6. Amy Louise Erickson, *Women and Property in Early Modern England* (New York, 1993), 7. Other scholars, too, have questioned the portrayal of family history as a story of steady progress toward gender equality. For example, Suzanne Lebsock, writing about Virginia, and Barbara Harris, writing about England, have observed that there is no evidence that companionate marriage increased women's power. Suzanne Lebsock, *The Free Women of Petersburg: Status and Culture in a Southern Town, 1784–1860,* 53; Barbara Harris, "Marriage Sixteenth-Century Style: Elizabeth Stafford and the Third Duke of Norfolk," *Journal of Social History* 15 (1982): 371–82, at 371–72.

7. See Linda K. Kerber, "The Paradox of Women's Citizenship in the Early Republic: The Case of *Martin vs. Massachusetts,* 1805."

8. Toby L. Ditz, *Property and Kinship: Inheritance in Early Connecticut, 1750–1820,* 135–36.

9. Barbara Welter, "The Cult of True Womanhood: 1820–1860."

Selected Bibliography

Manuscript Sources

Adriance Memorial Library, Poughkeepsie, New York
    Livingston Family Correspondence

Columbia University Law Library, New York
    John Chambers Commonplace Book
    Joseph Murray Precedent Book

Dutchess County Clerk's Office, Poughkeepsie, New York
    Ancient Documents, Dutchess County Court of Common Pleas
    Minute Books, Dutchess County Court of Common Pleas, 1721–60
    Tax Lists, Dutchess County, 1717–60

Hall of Records, New York
    Minute Books, Court of Chancery, 1711–19, 1720–48, 1770–76
    Minute Books, New York Court of General Quarter Sessions, 1694–1731
    Minute Books, Supreme Court of Judicature, 1691–1714, 1723–39, 1750–60
    Parchment Rolls, Supreme Court of Judicature
    Pleadings, Supreme Court of Judicature
    Pleadings, Mayor's Court of New York City

Museum of the City of New York, New York
    DeLancey Family Papers
    Livingston Family Papers

New-York Historical Society, New York
    James Alexander Papers
    James Alexander Supreme Court Register
    Hendrick Denker Account Book
    DePeyster Family Papers
    Charles DeWitt Diary and Account Book
    James Duane Papers
    James Duane Legal Papers
    Daniel Horsmanden Papers
    Morgan Lewis Papers
    Livingston Family Papers

Robert R. Livingston Collection
Minute Book, Mayor's Court of the Borough Town of Westchester
Charles Nicoll Ledger Book
John Sanders Letter Book
Henry Smith Ledger Book
John Van Cortlandt Precedent Book

New York Public Library, New York
William Alexander Papers
William Livingston Cost Book
William Livingston Papers
Hendrick Schenk Account Book, Ledger B
William Smith Papers
William Smith Supreme Court Register

New York State Library and Archives, Albany, New York
John Chambers Papers
Roswell Hopkins Records
William Livingston, Lawyers Book of Precedents
New York Colonial Manuscripts
Van Schaick Papers

New York State Supreme Court Courthouse, New York
Minute Books, Mayor's Court of New York City, 1690–1760

Orange County Clerk's Office, Goshen, New York
Minute Books, Orange County Court of Common Pleas, 1727–60

Richmond County Clerk's Office, Staten Island, New York
Minute Books, Richmond County Court of Common Pleas, 1711–45

Westchester County Records Center and Archives, Elmsford, New York
Minute Books, Westchester County Court of Common Pleas, 1710–1760

Manuscript Sources on Microfilm

New York City Tax Lists (Originals in the New York State Library)
New York Gazette
New York Mercury
New-York Weekly Journal
Probate Inventories from Colonial New York (Originals in New-York Historical Society and New York State Library)
Redmond-Livingston Manuscripts (Original in Franklin D. Roosevelt Library, Hyde Park, New York)
William Livingston Papers (Original in Massachusetts Historical Society, Boston, Massachusetts)

Printed Primary Sources: Official Documents and Records

Abstracts of Wills on File in the Surrogate's Office, City of New York, 1665–1800. In *Collections of the New-York Historical Society for the Years 1892 to 1908.* Compiled by William S. Pelletrean. 17 vols. New York, 1893–1909.

The Annals of Albany. Edited by Joel Munsell. 10 vols. Albany, N.Y., 1850–59.

Book of the Supervisors of Dutchess County, New York, 1718–1722. Poughkeepsie, N.Y., 1908.

The Burghers of New Amsterdam and the Freemen of New York, 1675–1866. In *Collections of the New-York Historical Society for the Year 1885.* New York, 1886.

Calendar of Historical Manuscripts in the Office of the Secretary of State, Albany, N.Y. Edited by Edmund B. O'Callaghan. 2 vols. Albany, N.Y., 1866.

The Colonial Laws of New York from the Year 1664 to the Revolution. 5 vols. Albany, N.Y., 1849–51.

Colonial Records of the New York Chamber of Commerce, 1768–1784. Edited by John Austin Stevens, Jr. New York, 1867; reprint, New York, 1971.

The Documentary History of the State of New York. Edited by Edmund B. O'Callaghan. 4 vols. Albany, N.Y., 1849–51.

Documents Relating to the Administration of Leisler. In *Collections of the New-York Historical Society for the Year 1868.* New York, 1868.

Documents Relative to the Colonial History of the State of New-York. Edited by Edmund B. O'Callahgan and Berthold Fernow. 15 vols. Albany, N.Y., 1853–87.

Ecclesiastical Records: State of New York. Compiled by Hugh Hastings and Edward T. Corwin. 7 vols. Albany, N.Y., 1901–16.

Eighteenth Century Documents of the Nine Partners Patent, Dutchess County, New York. In vol. 10 of *Collections of the Dutchess County Historical Society,* edited by William McDermott. Baltimore, 1979.

Eighteenth Century Records of the Portion of Dutchess County, New York that was included in Rombout Precinct and the Original Town of Fishkill. In vol. 6 of *Collections of the Dutchess County Historical Society,* edited by Helen Wilkinson Reynolds. Poughkeepsie, N.Y., 1938.

Facsimile of the Laws and Acts of the General Assembly for Their Majesties Province of New-York. New York, 1694.

Genealogical Data from New York Administration Bonds, 1753–1799. In vol. 10 of *Collections of the New York Genealogical and Biographical Society,* abstracted by Kenneth Scott. New York, 1969.

Journal of the Legislative Council of the Colony of New-York, 1691–1775. 2 vols. Albany, N.Y., 1861.

Journal of the Votes and Proceedings of the General Assembly of the Colony of New York, 1691–1765. 2 vols. New York, 1764–66.

Minutes of the Common Council of the City of New York, 1675–1776. Edited by Herbert L. Osgood. 8 vols. New York, 1905.

Minutes of the Executive Council of the Province of New York. Edited by Victor Hugo Paltsits. Albany, N.Y., 1910.

Minutes of the Supreme Court of Judicature of the Province of New York, 1693–1701. In *Collections of the New-York Historical Society for the Year 1912.* New York, 1913.

New York City Court Records, 1684–1760: Genealogical Data from the Court of Quarter Sessions. Compiled by Kenneth Scott. N.d.

The New York Genealogical and Biographical Record.

The New York Genealogical and Biographical Society Collections.

Old Miscellaneous Records of Dutchess County (The Second Book of Supervisors and Assessors). Poughkeepsie, N.Y., 1909.

Registers of the Births, Marriages, and Deaths of the "Eglise Françoise à la Nouvelle York," from 1688–1804. Edited by Alfred V. Wittmeyer. New York, 1886.

Reports of Cases Adjudged and Determined in the Supreme Court of Judicature and Court for the Trial of Impeachments and Correction of Errors of The State of New York. Newark, N.Y., 1994.

Reports of Cases in the Vice Admiralty of the Province of New York and in the Court of Admiralty of the State of New York, 1715–1788. Edited by Charles Merrill Hough. New Haven, 1925.

Supreme Court of Judicature of the Province of New York, 1691–1704. Edited by Paul M. Hamlin and Charles E. Baker. Vol. 2, "The Minutes." New York, 1952.

Printed Primary Sources: Memoirs, Letters, Essays

Alexander, James. *A Brief Narrative of the Case and Trial of John Peter Zenger, Printer of The New York Weekly Journal.* New York, 1736. Reprint edited by Stanley N. Katz. 2d ed. Cambridge, Mass., 1972.

The Beekman Mercantile Papers, 1746–1799. Edited by Philip L. White. 3 vols. New York, 1956.

Burnaby, Andrew. *Travels through the Middle Settlements in North-America in the Years 1759 and 1760 with Observations upon the State of the Colonies.* 2d ed. London, 1775; reprint Ithaca, N.Y., 1968.

Colden, Cadwallader. *The Colden Letter Books, 1760–1775.* In *Collections of the New-York Historical Society for the Years 1876 and 1877.* New York, 1877, 1878.

Cooper, Mary. *The Diary of Mary Cooper: Life on a Long Island Farm, 1768–1773.* Edited by Field Horne. Oyster Bay, N.Y., 1981.

Crèvecoeur, St. John de. *Sketches of Eighteenth Century America: More "Letters from an American Farmer."* Edited by Henri L. Bourdin, Ralph H. Gabriel, and Stanley T. Williams. New Haven, 1925.

Filkin, Francis. *Account Book of a Country Store Keeper in the 18th Century at Poughkeepsie.* Poughkeepsie, N.Y., 1911.

Hamilton, Alexander. *Gentleman's Progress: The Itinerarium of Dr. Alexander Hamilton, 1744.* Edited by Carl Bridenbaugh. Chapel Hill, 1948.

Kalm, Peter. *Peter Kalm's Travels in North America: The English Version of 1770.* Revised from the original Swedish and edited by Adolph B. Benson. New York, 1987.

Livingston, William, et al. *The Independent Reflector; or Weekly Essays on Sundry Important Subjects, More particularly adapted to the Province of New-York, by William Livingston and Others.* New York, 1752–53. Reprint edited by Milton M. Klein. Cambridge, Mass., 1963.

Miller, John. *A Description of the Province and City of New York.* London, 1696.

Oudenarde, Hendrick. *Seven Letters to the Honourable Daniel Horsmanden, Esq; Concerning the unnecessary and cruel Imprisonment of Hendrick Oudenarde, Late Merchant in the City of New-York.* New York, 1766.

Smith, William, Jr. *Historical Memoirs of William Smith.* Edited by William H. W. Sabine. 2 vols. New York, 1956.

——. *The History of the Late Province of New-York, From its Discovery, to the Appointment of Governor Colden, in 1762.* New York, 1830.

Watts, John. *Letter Book of John Watts, 1762–1765.* In *Collections of the New-York Historical Society for the Year 1928.* New York, 1928.

Secondary Sources

Abel, Richard L. "A Comparative Theory of Dispute Institutions in Society." *Law & Society Review* 8 (1973): 217–347.

——. "The Rise of Capitalism and the Transformation of Disputing: From Confrontation over Honor to Competition for Property." Review of June Starr, *Dispute and Settlement in Rural Turkey: An Ethnography of Law. University of California at Los Angeles Law Review* 27 (1979): 223–55.

Aiken, John Robert. *Utopianism and the Emergence of the Colonial Legal Profession: New York, 1664–1710, a Test Case.* New York, 1989.

Anderson, B. L. "Money and the Structure of Credit in the Eighteenth Century." *Business History* 12 (1970): 85–101.

——. "Provincial Aspects of the Financial Revolution of the Eighteenth Century." *Business History* 11 (1969): 11–22.

Appleby, Joyce. *Capitalism and a New Social Order: The Republican Vision of the 1790s.* New York, 1984.

——. *Economic Thought and Ideology in Seventeenth-Century England.* Princeton, N.J., 1978.

——. "Locke, Liberalism and the Natural Law of Money." *Past and Present* 71 (1976): 43–69.

Archdeacon, Thomas J. *New York City, 1664–1710: Conquest and Change.* Ithaca, N.Y., 1976.

Armour, David Arthur. *The Merchants of Albany, New York: 1686–1760.* New York, 1986.

Ashton, Thomas Southcliffe. *An Economic History of England: The Eighteenth Century.* New York, 1955.

Atiyah, P. S. *The Rise and Fall of Freedom of Contract.* New York, 1979.

Aubert, Vilhelm. "Competition and Dissensus: Two Types of Conflict and of Conflict Resolution." *Journal of Conflict Resolution* 7 (1963): 26–42.

Bailyn, Bernard. *The New England Merchants in the Seventeenth Century.* Cambridge, Mass., 1955.

Ball, Duane Eugene, and Walton, Gary M. "Agricultural Productivity Change in Eighteenth-Century Pennsylvania." *Journal of Economic History* 36 (1976): 102–17.

Beard, Mary R. *Woman as Force in History: A Study in Traditions and Realities.* New York, 1946; reprint, 1962.

Becker, Carl Lotus. *The History of Political Parties in the Province of New York, 1760–1776.* Madison, Wis., 1909; reprint, 1960.

Benes, Peter, ed. *The Farm.* Annual Proceedings, the Dublin Seminar for New England Folklife 1986, vol. 11. Boston, 1988.

Bernstein, Michael A., and Wilentz, Sean. "Marketing, Commerce, and Capitalism in Rural Massachusetts." *Journal of Economic History* 44 (1984): 171–73.

Bidwell, Percy Wells, and Falconer, John I. *History of Agriculture in the Northern United States, 1620–1860.* Washington, D.C., 1925; reprint, 1941.

Biemer, Linda Briggs. *Women and Property in Colonial New York: The Transition from Dutch to English Law, 1643–1727.* Ann Arbor, Mich., 1983.

Billias, George Athan, ed. *Law and Authority in Colonial America.* Barre, Mass., 1965.

Black, Donald J. *The Behavior of Law.* New York, 1976.

Bodle, Wayne. "Themes and Directions in Middle Colonies Historiography, 1980–1994." *William and Mary Quarterly,* 3d ser., 51 (1994): 355–88.

Bonomi, Patricia U. *A Factious People: Politics and Society in Colonial New York.* New York, 1971.

Bowler, Clara Ann. "Carted Whores and White Shrouded Apologies: Slander in the County Courts of Seventeenth-Century Virginia." *Virginia Magazine of History and Biography* 85 (1977): 411–26.

Boydston, Jeanne. *Home and Work: Housework, Wages, and the Ideology of Labor in the Early Republic.* New York, 1990.

Breen, T. H. " 'Baubles of Britain': The American and Consumer Revolutions of the Eighteenth Century." *Past and Present* 119 (1988): 73–104.

———. "Narrative of Commercial Life: Consumption, Ideology, and Community on the Eve of the American Revolution." *William and Mary Quarterly,* 3d ser., 50 (1993): 471–501.

Brewer, John, and Porter, Roy, eds. *Consumption and the World of Goods.* New York, 1993.

Brewer, John, and Styles, John, eds. *An Ungovernable People: The English and Their Law in the Seventeenth and Eighteenth Centuries.* New Brunswick, N.J., 1980.

Bridenbaugh, Carl. *The Colonial Craftsman.* New York, 1950.

Brock, Leslie V. *The Currency of the American Colonies, 1700–1764, A Study in Colonial Finance and Imperial Relations.* New York, 1975.

Brooks, Christopher W. "Interpersonal Conflict and Social Tension: Civil Litigation in England, 1640–1830." In *The First Modern Society: Essays in English History in Honour of Lawrence Stone,* edited by A. L. Beier, David Cannadine, and James M. Rosenheim, pp. 357–99. Cambridge, 1989.

——. "Litigants and Attorneys in the King's Bench and Common Pleas, 1560–1640." In *Legal Records and the Historian: Papers Presented to the Cambridge Legal History Conference,* edited by John H. Baker, pp. 41–59. London, 1978.

Bruchey, Stuart, comp. and ed. *The Colonial Merchant: Sources and Readings.* New York, 1966.

——. "Economy and Society in an Earlier America." *Journal of Economic History* 47 (1987): 299–319.

——. *Enterprise: The Dynamic Economy of a Free People.* Cambridge, Mass., 1990.

——. *The Roots of American Economic Growth, 1607–1861: An Essay in Social Causation.* New York, 1965.

——. "The Sources of the Economic Development of the United States," *International Social Science Journal* 44 (1992): 531–48.

Bruegel, Martin. "The Rise of a Market Society in the Rural Hudson Valley, 1780–1860." Ph.D. dissertation, Cornell University, 1994.

Budd, Martin L. "Law in Colonial New York: The Legal System of 1691." *Harvard Law Review* 80 (1967): 1757–72.

Burns, J. Joseph. "Civil Courts and the Development of Commercial Relations: The Case of North Sumatra." *Law & Society Review* 15 (1980–81): 347–68.

Bushman, Richard L. "Family Security in the Transition from Farm to City, 1750–1850." *Journal of Family History* 6 (1981): 238–56.

——. *From Puritan to Yankee: Character and the Social Order in Connecticut, 1690–1765.* Cambridge, Mass., 1967.

——. "Opening the American Countryside." In *The Transformation of Early American History: Society, Authority, and Ideology,* edited by James A. Henretta, Michael Kammen, and Stanley N. Katz, pp. 239–56. New York, 1991.

——. *The Refinement of America: Persons, Houses, Cities.* New York, 1992.

Cain, Maureen, and Kulcsár, Kálmán. *Disputes and the Law.* Budapest, 1983.

Carr, Lois Green. "Diversificiation in the Colonial Chesapeake: Somerset County, Maryland, in Comparative Perspective." In *Colonial Chesapeake Society,* edited by Lois Green Carr, Philip D. Morgan, and Jean B. Russo, pp. 342–88. Chapel Hill, 1988.

Carr, Lois Green, and Walsh, Lorena S. "Changing Lifestyles and Consumer Behavior in the Colonial Chesapeake." In *Of Consuming Interests: The Style of Life in the Eighteenth Century,* edited by Cary Carson, Ronald Hoffman and Peter J. Albert, pp. 59–166. Charlottesville, Va., 1994.

——. "Inventories and the Analysis of Wealth and Consumption Patterns in St. Mary's County, Maryland, 1658–1777." *Historical Methods* 13 (1980): 81–104.

Carson, Cary, Hoffman, Ronald, and Albert, Peter J., eds. *Of Consuming Interests: The Style of Life in the Eighteenth Century.* Charlottesville, Va., 1994.

Church, Thomas, Jr., et al. *Justice Delayed: The Pace of Litigation in Urban Trial Courts.* Williamsburg, Va., 1978.

Clark, Alice. *Working Life of Women in the Seventeenth Century.* New York, 1919.

Clark, Charles E., and Shulman, Harry. *A Study of Law Administration in Connecticut: A Report of an Investigation of the Activities of Certain Trial Courts of the State.* New Haven, 1937.

Clark, Christopher. *The Roots of Rural Capitalism: Western Massachusetts, 1780–1860.* Ithaca, N.Y., 1990.

Clark, Christopher, Vickers, Daniel, Aron, Stephen, Osterud, Nancy Grey, and Merrill, Michael. "The Transition to Capitalism in America: A Panel Discussion," *History Teacher* 27 (1994): 263–88.

Cleary, Patricia A. " 'She Merchants' of Colonial America: Women and Commerce on the Eve of the Revolution." Ph.D. dissertation, Northwestern University, 1989.

———. " 'She Will Be in the Shop': Women's Sphere of Trade in Eighteenth-Century Philadelphia and New York." *Pennsylvania Magazine of History and Biography* 119 (1995): 181–202.

Cohen, Jay. "The History of Imprisonment for Debt and Its Relation to the Development of Discharge in Bankruptcy." *Journal of Legal History* 3 (1982): 153–74.

Cole, Arthur Harrison. *Wholesale Commodity Prices in the United States, 1700–1861.* Cambridge, Mass., 1938.

Coleman, Peter J. *Debtors and Creditors in America: Insolvency, Imprisonment for Debt, and Bankruptcy, 1607–1900.* Madison, Wis., 1974.

Cott, Nancy F. *The Bonds of Womanhood: 'Woman's Sphere' in New England, 1780–1835.* New Haven, 1977.

Cranch, William. "Promissory Notes Before and After Lord Holt." 1804. Reprinted in *Select Essays in Anglo-American Legal History,* compiled and edited by a committee of the Association of American Law Schools, 3: 72–97. Boston, 1907.

Crane, Elaine Forman. "Dependence in the Era of Independence: The Role of Women in a Republican Society." In *The American Revolution: Its Character and Limits,* edited by Jack P. Greene, pp. 253–75. New York, 1987.

Cray, Robert E., Jr. *Paupers and Poor Relief in New York City and Its Rural Environs, 1700–1830.* Philadelphia, 1988.

Crowley, Jacob E. *This Sheba, Self: The Conceptualization of Economic Life in Eighteenth-Century America.* Baltimore, 1974.

Dayton, Cornelia Hughes. "Turning Points and the Relevance of Colonial Legal History." *William and Mary Quarterly,* 3d ser., 50 (1993): 7–17.

———. *Women before the Bar: Gender, Law, and Society in Connecticut, 1639–1789.* Chapel Hill, 1995.

Dexter, Elisabeth Anthony. *Colonial Women of Affairs.* 1924; rev. ed., Boston, 1931.

Dillon, Dorothy Rita. *The New York Triumvirate: A Study of the Legal and Political Careers of William Livingston, John Morin Scott, and William Smith, Jr.* New York, 1949.

Ditz, Toby L. *Property and Kinship: Inheritance in Early Connecticut, 1750–1820.* Princeton, N.J., 1986.

Doerflinger, Thomas M. "Farmers and Dry Goods in the Philadelphia Market Area, 1750–1800." In *The Economy of Early America: The Revolutionary Period, 1763–1790,* edited by Ronald Hoffman et al., pp. 166–95. Charlottesville, Va., 1988.

———. *A Vigorous Spirit of Enterprise: Merchants and Economic Development in Revolutionary Philadelphia.* Chapel Hill, 1986.

Dructor, Robert Michael. "The New York Commercial Community: The Revolutionary Experience." Ph.D. dissertation, University of Pittsburgh, 1975.

Earle, Alice Morse. *Home Life in Colonial Days.* New York, 1898.

Egnal, Marc. "The Economic Development of the Thirteen Continental Colonies, 1720 to 1775." *William and Mary Quarterly,* 3d ser., 32 (1975): 191–222.

Engerman, Stanley L., and Gallman, Robert E., eds. *The Cambridge Economic History of the United States,* vol. 1. New York, 1996.

Fineman, Martha Albertson, and Thomadsen, Nancy Sweet, eds. *At the Boundaries of Law: Feminism and Legal Theory.* New York, 1991.

Finley, Lucinda M. "Breaking Women's Silence in Law: The Dilemma of the Gendered Nature of Legal Reasoning." *Notre Dame Law Review* 64 (1989): 886–910.

Flaherty, David H., ed. *Essays in the History of Early American Law.* Chapel Hill, 1969.

Flick, Alexander C., ed. *History of the State of New York.* 10 vols. New York, 1933–37.

Folts, James D., Jr. *"Duely and Constantly Kept": A History of the New York Supreme Court, 1691–1847 and An Inventory of Its Records (Albany, Utica, and Geneva Offices), 1797–1847.* Albany, N.Y., 1991.

Francis, Clinton W. "Practice, Strategy, and Institution: Debt Collection in the English Common-Law Courts, 1740–1840." *Northwestern University Law Review* 80 (1986): 807–955.

———. "The Structure of Judicial Administration and the Development of Contract Law in Seventeenth-Century England." *Columbia Law Review* 83 (1983): 35–137.

Friedman, Lawrence M. *A History of American Law.* 2d ed. New York, 1985.

———. "Trial Courts and Their Work in the Modern World." In *Zur Soziologie des Gerichtsverfahrens* (Sociology of the judicial process), *Jahrbuch für Rechts-*

soziologie und Rechtstheorie, edited by Lawrence M. Friedman and Manfred Rehbinder, 4: 25–38. Wiesbaden, Germany, 1976.

Friedman, Lawrence M., and Percival, Robert V. "A Tale of Two Courts: Litigation in Alameda and San Benito Counties." *Law & Society Review* 10 (1976): 267–301.

Galanter, Marc. "The Modernization of Law." In *Modernization: The Dynamics of Growth,* edited by Myron Weiner, pp. 153–65. New York, 1966.

——. "Reading the Landscape of Disputes: What We Know and Don't Know (and Think We Know) about Our Allegedly Contentious and Litigious Society." *University of California at Los Angeles Law Review* 31 (1983): 4–71.

Garrison, J. Ritchie. *Landscape and Material Life in Franklin County, Massachusetts, 1770–1860.* Knoxville, 1991.

Gilligan, Carol. *In a Different Voice: Psychological Theory and Women's Development.* Cambridge, Mass., 1982.

Goebel, Julius, Jr. "The Courts and the Law in Colonial New York." In *Essays in the History of Early American Law,* edited by David H. Flaherty, pp. 245–77. Chapel Hill, 1969.

Goebel, Julius, Jr., and Naughton, T. Raymond. *Law Enforcement in Colonial New York: A Study in Criminal Procedure (1664–1776).* 1944. Reprint, Montclair, N.J., 1970.

Goodfriend, Joyce D. *Before the Melting Pot: Society and Culture in Colonial New York City, 1664–1730.* Princeton, N.J., 1992.

Grant, Charles S. *Democracy in the Connecticut Frontier Town of Kent.* New York, 1961.

Greenberg, Douglas. *Crime and Law Enforcement in the Colony of New York, 1691–1776.* Ithaca, N.Y., 1976.

——. "The Effectiveness of Law Enforcement in Eighteenth-Century New York." *American Journal of Legal History* 19 (1975): 173–207.

Greene, Evarts B., and Harrington, Virginia D. *American Population before the Federal Census of 1790.* New York, 1932.

Greene, Jack P., *Pursuits of Happiness: The Social Development of Early Modern British Colonies and the Formation of American Culture.* Chapel Hill, 1988.

Greene, Jack P., and Pole, J. R., eds. *Colonial British America: Essays in the New History of the Early Modern Era.* Baltimore, 1984.

Gunderson, Joan R., and Gampel, Gwen Victor. "Married Women's Legal Status in Eighteenth-Century New York and Virginia." *William and Mary Quarterly,* 3d ser., 39 (1982): 114–34.

Gwyn, Julian, "Private Credit in Colonial New York: The Warren Portfolio, 1731–95." *New York History* 54 (1973): 269–93.

Haagen, Paul Hess. "Imprisonment for Debt in England and Wales." Ph.D. dissertation, Princeton University, 1986.

Hahn, Steven. *The Roots of Southern Populism: Yeoman Farmers and the Transformation of the Georgia Upcountry, 1850–1890.* New York, 1983.

Hahn, Steven, and Prude, Jonathan, eds. *The Countryside in the Age of Capitalist Transformation: Essays in the Social History of Rural America.* Chapel Hill, 1985.

Hall, Kermit L. *The Magic Mirror: Law in American History.* New York, 1989.

Hamlin, Paul M., and Baker, Charles E. Introduction to *Supreme Court of Judicature of the Province of New York, 1691–1704.* Vol. 1. New York, 1952.

Hancock, David. *Citizens of the World: London Merchants and the Integration of the British Atlantic Community, 1735–1785.* New York, 1995.

Hansen, Marcus L. "The Minor Stocks in the American Population of 1790." In American Council of Learned Societies Report of Committee on Linguistic and National Stocks in the Population of the United States, in *Annual Report of the American Historical Association for the Year 1931.* Vol. 1, Proceedings. Washington, D.C., 1932.

Harrington, Virginia D. *The New York Merchant on the Eve of the Revolution.* New York, 1935.

Hartmann, Heidi I. "The Family as the Locus of Gender, Class, and Political Struggle: The Example of Housework." *Signs* 6 (1981): 366–94.

Hartog, Hendrik. *Public Property and Private Power: The Corporation of the City of New York in American Law, 1730–1870.* Chapel Hill, 1983.

Hasbrouck, Frank. *The History of Dutchess County, New York.* Poughkeepsie, N.Y., 1909.

Haskell, Thomas L. "Litigation and Social Status in Seventeenth-Century New Haven." *Journal of Legal Studies* 7 (1978): 219–41.

Henretta, James A. *The Evolution of American Society, 1700–1815: An Interdisciplinary Analysis.* Lexington, Mass., 1973.

——. "Families and Farms: *Mentalité* in Pre-Industrial America." *William and Mary Quarterly,* 3d ser., 35 (1978): 3–32.

——. *The Origins of American Capitalism: Collected Essays.* Boston, 1991.

——. "The Transition to Capitalism in America." In *The Transformation of Early American History: Society, Authority, and Ideology,* edited by James A. Henretta, Michael Kammen, and Stanley N. Katz, pp. 218–238. New York, 1991.

Hershkowitz, Leo, and Klein, Milton M., eds. *Courts and Law in Early New York: Selected Essays.* Port Washington, N.Y., 1978.

Heyrman, Christine Leigh. *Commerce and Culture: The Maritime Communities of Colonial Massachusetts, 1690–1750.* New York, 1984.

Higgenbotham, A. Leon, Jr. *In the Matter of Color: Race and the American Legal Process—The Colonial Period.* New York, 1978.

Hill, Eve. "Alternative Dispute Resolution in a Feminist Voice." *Ohio State Journal on Dispute Resolution* 5 (1990): 337–79.

Hoff, Joan. *Law, Gender, and Injustice: A Legal History of U.S. Women.* New York, 1991.

Hoffer, Peter Charles. "Honor and the Roots of American Litigiousness." *American Journal of Legal History* 33 (1989): 295–319.

——. *Law and People in Colonial America.* Baltimore, 1992.

Hoffman, Ronald, and Albert, Peter J., eds. *Women in the Age of the American Revolution*. Charlottesville, Va., 1989.

Hoffman, Ronald, McCusker, John J., Menard, Russell R., and Albert, Peter J. *The Economy of Early America: The Revolutionary Period, 1763–1790*. Charlottesville, Va., 1988.

Holden, James Milnes. *The History of Negotiable Instruments in English Law*. London, 1955.

Holderness, B. A. "Credit in a Rural Community, 1660–1800: Some Neglected Aspects of Probate Inventories." *Midland History* 3 (1975–76): 94–115.

——. "Credit in English Rural Society before the Nineteenth Century, with Special Reference to the Period 1650–1720." *Agricultural History Review* 24 (1976): 97–109.

——. *Preindustrial England: Economy and Society, 1500–1750*. London, 1976.

Holdsworth, William Searle. *A History of English Law*. 12 vols. London, 1922–38.

Horwitz, Morton J. *The Transformation of American Law, 1780–1860*. Cambridge, Mass., 1977.

Innes, Stephen, *Creating the Commonwealth: The Economic Culture of Puritan New England*. New York, 1995.

Jensen, Joan M. "Butter Making and Economic Development in Mid-Atlantic America from 1750 to 1850." *Signs* 13 (1988): 813–29.

——. *Loosening the Bonds: Mid-Atlantic Farm Women, 1750–1850*. New Haven, 1986.

Johnson, Herbert Alan. *Essays on New York Colonial Legal History*. Westport, Conn., 1981.

——. *The Law Merchant and Negotiable Instruments in Colonial New York, 1664 to 1730*. Chicago, 1963.

Jones, Alice Hanson. *American Colonial Wealth: Documents and Methods*, 2d ed. 3 vols. New York, 1978.

——. "Wealth Estimates for the American Middle Colonies, 1774." *Economic Development and Cultural Change* 18 (1970): 1–172.

——. *Wealth of a Nation to Be: The American Colonies on the Eve of the American Revolution*. New York, 1980.

Jones, Douglas Lamar. "The Strolling Poor: Transiency in Eighteenth Century Massachusetts." *Journal of Social History* 8 (1975): 28–54.

Jones, William C. "An Inquiry into the Adjudication of Mercantile Disputes in Great Britain and the United States." *University of Chicago Law Review* 25 (1958): 445–64.

Jordan, Jean P. "Women Merchants in Colonial New York." *New York History* 58 (1977): 412–39.

Kagan, Robert A. "The Routinization of Debt Collection: An Essay on Social Change and Conflict in the Courts." *Law & Society Review* 18 (1984): 323–71.

Kalven, Harry, and Zeisel, Hans. *The American Jury*. Chicago, 1971.

Kammen, Michael. *Colonial New York: A History.* New York, 1975.

Katz, Stanley Nider. "Between Scylla and Charybdis: James DeLancey and Anglo-American Politics in Early Eighteenth-Century New York." In *Anglo-American Political Relations, 1675–1775,* edited by A. G. Olson and R. M. Brown, pp. 92–108. New Brunswick, N.J., 1970.

———. *Newcastle's New York: Anglo-American Politics, 1732–1753.* Cambridge, Mass., 1968.

Kerber, Linda K. "The Paradox of Women's Citizenship in the Early Republic: The Case of *Martin vs. Massachusetts,* 1805." *American Historical Review* 97 (1992): 349–78.

———. *Women of the Republic: Intellect and Ideology in Revolutionary America.* Chapel Hill, 1980.

Keyssar, Alexander. "Widowhood in Eighteenth-Century Massachusetts: A Problem in the History of the Family." *Perspectives in American History* 8 (1974): 83–119.

Kim, Sung Bok. *Landlord and Tenant in Colonial New York: Manorial Society, 1664–1775.* Chapel Hill, 1978.

Klein, Milton M. "New York in the American Colonies: A New Look." New York History 53 (1972): 132–56.

———. *The Politics of Diversity: Essays in the History of Colonial New York.* Port Washington, N.Y., 1974.

Konig, David Thomas. *Law and Society in Puritan Massachusetts: Essex County, 1629–1692.* Chapel Hill, 1979.

Kross, Jessica. *The Evolution of an America Town: Newtown, New York, 1642–1775.* Philadelphia, 1983.

Kulikoff, Allan. *The Agrarian Origins of American Capitalism.* Charlottesville, Va., 1992.

———. "Households and Markets: Toward a New Synthesis of American Agrarian History." *William and Mary Quarterly,* 3d ser., 50 (1993): 342–55.

———. "The Transition to Capitalism in Rural America." *William and Mary Quarterly,* 3d ser., 46 (1989): 120–44.

Kupperman, Karen Ordahl. *Providence Island, 1630–1641: The Other Puritan Colony.* New York, 1993.

Larkin, Jack. "The Merriams of Brookfield: Printing in the Economy and Culture of Rural Massachusetts in the Early Nineteenth Century." *Proceedings of the American Antiquarian Society* 96 (1986): 39–73.

Lebsock, Suzanne. *The Free Women of Petersburg: Status and Culture in a Southern Town, 1784–1860.* New York, 1984.

Lemon, James T. *The Best Poor Man's Country: A Geographical Study of Early Southeastern Pennsylvania.* Baltimore, 1972.

———. "Household Consumption in Eighteenth-Century America and Its Relationship to Production and Trade: The Situation among Farmers in Southeastern Pennsylvania." *Agricultural History* 41 (1967): 59–70.

Lemon, James T., and Nash, Gary B. "The Distribution of Wealth in Eighteenth-Century America: A Century of Change in Chester County, Pennsylvania, 1693–1802." *Journal of Social History* 2 (1968): 1–24.

Lempert, Richard. "More Tales of Two Courts: Exploring Changes in the 'Dispute Settlement Function' of Trial Courts." *Law & Society Review* 13 (1978): 91–138.

Lerner, Gerda, "The Lady and the Mill Girl: Changes in the Status of Women in the Age of Jackson." *MidContinent American Studies Journal* 10 (1969): 5–15.

Lewis, James Hoffman. "Farmers, Craftsmen and Merchants: Changing Economic Organization in Massachusetts, 1730 to 1775." Ph.D. dissertation, Northwestern University, 1984.

Lynd, Staughton. *Anti-Federalism in Dutchess County, New York: A Study of Democracy and Class Conflict in the Revolutionary Era.* Chicago, 1962.

Main, Gloria L. "The Distribution of Consumer Goods in Colonial New England: A Subregional Approach." In *Early American Probate Inventories,* edited by Peter Benes, pp. 153–68. Boston, 1989.

——. "Probate Records as a Source for Early American History." *William and Mary Quarterly,* 3d ser., 32 (1975): 89–99.

——. "The Standard of Living in Colonial Massachusetts." *Journal of Economic History* 43 (1983): 101–8.

——. "The Standard of Living in Southern New England, 1640–1773." *William and Mary Quarterly,* 3d ser., 45 (1988): 124–34.

Main, Gloria L., and Main, Jackson T. "Economic Growth and the Standard of Living in Southern New England, 1640–1774." *Journal of Economic History* 48 (1988): 27–46.

Main, Jackson Turner. *The Social Structure of Revolutionary America.* Princeton, N.J., 1965.

——. *Society and Economy in Colonial Connecticut.* Princeton, N.J., 1985.

Mann, Bruce H. *Neighbors and Strangers: Law and Community in Early Connecticut.* Chapel Hill, 1987.

Mark, Irving. *Agrarian Conflicts in Colonial New York, 1711–1775.* New York, 1940.

Mark, Irving, and Handlin, Oscar. "Land Cases in Colonial New York, 1765–1767: The King vs. William Prendergast." *New York University Law Review* 19 (1942): 165–94.

Martin, John Frederick. *Profits in the Wilderness: Entrepreneurship and the Founding of New England Towns in the Seventeenth Century.* Chapel Hill, 1991.

Martin, Margaret E. *Merchants and Trade of the Connecticut River Valley, 1750–1820.* Northampton, Mass., 1939.

Matson, Cathy Diane. "Fair Trade, Free Trade: Economic Ideas and Opportunities in Eighteenth-Century New York City Commerce." Ph.D. dissertation, Columbia University, 1985.

Matthaei, Julie A. *An Economic History of Women in America: Women's Work,* the Sexual Division of Labor, and the Development of Capitalism. New York, 1982.

Matthews, Glenna. *The Rise of Public Woman: Woman's Power and Woman's Place in the United States, 1630–1970*. New York, 1992.

McAnear, Beverly. "Politics in Provincial New York, 1689–1761." Ph.D. dissertation, Stanford University, 1935.

McCusker, John J. "The Current Value of English Exports, 1697 to 1800." *William and Mary Quarterly*, 3d ser., 28 (1971): 607–28.

McCusker, John J., and Menard, Russell R. *The Economy of British America, 1607–1789*. Chapel Hill, 1985.

McKee, Samuel, Jr. *Labor in Colonial New York, 1664–1776*. New York, 1935.

McKendrick, Neil, Brewer, John, and Plumb, J. H. *The Birth of a Consumer Society: The Commercialization of Eighteenth-Century England*. Bloomington, Ind., 1982.

Menkel-Meadow, Carrie. "Portia in a Different Voice: Speculations on a Women's Lawyering Process." *Berkeley Women's Law Journal* 1 (1985): 39–63.

Merrill, Michael. "Cash Is Good to Eat: Self-Sufficiency and Exchange in the Rural Economy of the United States." *Radical History Review* 4 (1977): 42–72.

———. "Putting 'Capitalism' in Its Place: A Review of Recent Literature." *William and Mary Quarterly*, 3d ser., 52 (1995): 315–26.

———. "Self-Sufficiency and Exchange in Early America: Theory, Structure, Ideology." Ph.D. dissertation, Columbia University, 1986.

Michel, Jack. " 'In a Manner and Fashion Suitable to Their Degree: A Preliminary Investigation of the Material Culture of Early Pennsylvania." *Working Papers from the Regional Economic History Research Center* 5 (1981): 1–83.

Mitchell, Robert D. *Commercialism and Frontier: Perspectives on the Early Shenandoah Valley*. Charlottesville, Va., 1977.

Moglen, Eben. "Commercial Arbitration in the Eighteenth Century: Searching for the Transformation of American Law." *Yale Law Journal* 93 (1983): 135–52.

Morris, Richard B. *Government and Labor in Early America*. New York, 1946.

———. Introduction to *Select Cases of The Mayor's Court of New York City, 1674–1784*, edited by Richard B. Morris, pp. 1–62. Washington, D.C., 1935.

———. *Studies in the History of American Law, with Special Reference to the Seventeenth and Eighteenth Centuries*. New York, 1930.

Murrin, John. "Anglicizing an American Colony: The Transformation of Provincial Massachusetts." Ph.D. dissertation, Yale University, 1966.

———. "Magistrates, Sinners, and a Precarious Liberty: Trial by Jury in Seventeenth-Century New England." In *Saints and Revolutionaries: Essays on Early American History*, edited by David D. Hall, John Murrin, and Thad W. Tate, pp. 152–206. New York, 1984.

———. "Review Essay." *History and Theory* 11 (1972): 226–75.

Mutch, Robert E. "The Cutting Edge: Colonial America and the Debate about Transition to Capitalism." *Theory and Society* 9 (1980): 847–63.

——. "Yeoman and Merchant in Pre-Industrial America: Eighteenth Century Massachusetts as a Case Study." *Societas* 7 (1977): 279–302.

Nader, Laura, and Todd, Harry F., Jr., eds. *The Disputing Process—Law in Ten Societies.* New York, 1978.

Narrett, David E. *Inheritance and Family Life in Colonial New York City.* Ithaca, N.Y., 1992.

Nash, Gary B. "The Transformation of Urban Politics, 1700–1765." *Journal of American History* 60 (1973–74): 605–32.

——. *The Urban Crucible: Social Change, Political Consciousness, and the Origins of the American Revolution.* Cambridge, Mass., 1979.

——. "Urban Wealth and Poverty in Pre-Revolutionary America." *Journal of Interdisciplinary History* 6 (1976): 545–84.

Nelson, William E. *Americanization of the Common Law: The Impact of Legal Change on Massachusetts Society, 1760–1830.* Cambridge, Mass., 1975.

——. *Dispute and Conflict Resolution in Plymouth County, Massachusetts, 1725–1825.* Chapel Hill, 1981.

Nettles, Curtis Putnam. *The Money Supply of the American Colonies before 1720.* Madison, Wis., 1934.

Nobles, Gregory. "Capitalism in the Countryside: The Transformation of Rural Society in the United States." *Radical History Review* 41 (1988): 163–76.

——. "The Rise of Merchants in Rural Market Towns: A Case Study of Eighteenth-Century Northampton, Massachusetts." *Journal of Social History* 24 (1990): 5–23.

Norton, Mary Beth. "Eighteenth-Century Women in Peace and War: The Case of the Loyalists." *William and Mary Quarterly,* 3d ser., 33 (1976): 386–409.

——. *Founding Mothers and Fathers: Gendered Power and the Forming of American Society.* New York, 1996.

——. "Gender and Defamation in Seventeenth-Century Maryland." *William and Mary Quarterly,* 3d ser., 44 (1987): 3–39.

——. *Liberty's Daughters: The Revolutionary Experience of American Women, 1750–1800.* Boston, 1980.

——. "The Myth of the Golden Age." In *Women of America: A History,* edited by Carol Ruth Berkin and Mary Beth Norton, pp. 37–47. Boston, 1979.

Norton, Mary Beth, and Berkin, Carol Ruth. "Women and American History." In *Women of America: A History,* edited by Carol Berkin and Mary Beth Norton, pp. 3–15. Boston, 1979.

Offutt, William McEnery, Jr. *Of "Good Laws" and "Good Men": Law and Society in the Delaware Valley, 1680–1710.* Urbana, Ill., 1995.

Osterud, Nancy Grey. *Bonds of Community: The Lives of Farm Women in Nineteenth-Century New York.* Ithaca, N.Y., 1991.

——. "Gender and the Transition to Capitalism in Rural America." *Agricultural History* 67 (1993): 14–29.

Perkins, Edwin J. *American Public Finance and Financial Services, 1700–1815.* Columbus, 1994.

——. "Conflicting Views on Fiat Currency: Britain and Its North American Colonies in the Eighteenth Century." *Business History* 33 (1991): 8–30.

——. *The Economy of Colonial America.* 2d ed. New York, 1988.

——. "The Entrepreneurial Spirit in Colonial America: The Foundations of Modern Business History." *Business History Review* 63 (1989): 160–86.

Peyer, Jean B. "Jamaica, Long Island, 1656–1776: A Study of the Roots of American Urbanism." Ph.D. dissertation, City University of New York, 1974.

Plummer, Wilbur C. "Consumer Credit in Colonial Philadelphia." *Pennsylvania Magazine of History and Biography* 66 (1942): 385–409.

Pruitt, Bettye Hobbs. "Agriculture and Society in the Towns of Massachusetts, 1771: A Statistical Analysis." Ph.D. dissertation, Boston University, 1981.

——. "Self-Sufficiency and the Agricultural Economy of Eighteenth-Century Massachusetts." *William and Mary Quarterly,* 3d ser., 41 (1984): 333–64.

Quimby, Ian M. G., ed. *The Craftsman in Early America.* New York, 1984.

Randell, Edwin T. "Imprisonment for Debt in America: Fact and Fiction, 1672–1832." *Mississippi Valley Historical Review* 39 (1952): 89–102.

Richardson, Philip Arthur. "Commercial Growth and the Development of Private Law in Early Massachusetts: A Study of the Relationships between Economic and Legal Development." Ph.D. dissertation, University of Pennsylvania, 1977.

Ritchie, Robert C. *The Duke's Province: A Study of New York Politics and Society, 1664–1691.* Chapel Hill, 1977.

Roeber, A. G. *Faithful Magistrates and Republican Lawyers: Creators of Virginia Legal Culture, 1680–1810.* Chapel Hill, 1981.

Rosen, Deborah A. "Courts and Commerce in Colonial New York." *American Journal of Legal History* 36 (1992): 139–63.

——. "The Supreme Court of Judicature of Colonial New York: Civil Practice in Transition, 1691–1760." *Law and History Review* 5 (1987): 213–47.

Rothenberg, Winifred Barr. *From Market-Places to a Market Economy: The Transformation of Rural Massachusetts, 1750–1850.* Chicago, 1992.

Rubin, G. R., and Sugarman, David, eds. *Law, Economy and Society, 1750–1914: Essays in the History of English Law.* Abingdon, England, 1984.

Russo, Jean B. "Self-Sufficiency and Local Exchange: Free Craftsmen in the Rural Chesapeake Economy." In *Colonial Chesapeake Society,* edited by Lois Green Carr, Philip D. Morgan, and Jean B. Russo, pp. 389–432. Chapel Hill, 1988.

Ryan, Mary P. *Womanhood in America, from Colonial Times to the Present.* 3d ed. New York, 1983.

Salmon, Marylynn. "Equality or Submersion? Feme Covert Status in Early Pennsylvania." In *Women of America, A History,* edited by Carol Ruth Berkin and Mary Beth Norton, pp. 92–111. Boston, 1979.

——. "The Legal Status of Women in Early America: A Reappraisal." *Law and History Review* 1 (1983): 129–51.

——. *Women and the Law of Property in Early America.* Chapel Hill, 1986.

Scales, Ann C. "The Emergence of Feminist Jurisprudence: An Essay." *Yale Law Journal* 95 (1986): 1373–403.

Schlebecker, John T. "Agricultural Markets and Marketing in the North, 1774–1777." *Agricultural History* 50 (1976): 21–36.

Schumacher, Max George. *The Northern Farmer and His Markets during the Late Colonial Period.* New York, 1975.

Schweitzer, Mary M. *Custom and Contract: Household, Government, and the Economy in Colonial Pennsylvania.* New York, 1987.

Sellingsloh, Ellen A. "A More Equal Proportion: Public Finance and the Social Order in Rumbout Precinct and the Town of Fishkill, N.Y., 1737–1800." Ph.D. dissertation, State University of New York at Albany, 1984.

Shammas, Carole. "Consumer Behavior in Colonial America." *Social Science History* 6 (1982): 67–86.

——. "Early American Women and Control over Capital." In *Women in the Age of the American Revolution,* edited by Ronald Hoffman and Peter Albert, pp. 134–54. Charlottesville, Va., 1989.

——. "The Female Social Structure of Philadelphia in 1775." *Pennsylvania Magazine of History and Biography* 107 (1983): 69–83.

——. "How Self-Sufficient Was Early America?" *Journal of Interdisciplinary History* 13 (1982): 247–72.

——. *The Pre-Industrial Consumer in England and America.* New York, 1990.

Shammas, Carole, Salmon, Marylynn, and Dahlin, Michel. *Inheritance in America from Colonial Times to the Present.* New Brunswick, N.J., 1987.

Sheridan, Eugene R. *Lewis Morris, 1671–1746: A Study in Early American Politics.* Syracuse, N.Y., 1981.

Sherry, Suzanna. "Civic Virtue and the Feminine Voice in Constitutional Adjudication." *Virginia Law Review* 72 (1986): 543–616.

Smith, Billy G. *The "Lower Sort": Philadelphia's Laboring People, 1750–1800.* Ithaca, N.Y., 1990.

Smith, James H. *History of Duchess County, New York.* Syracuse, N.Y., 1882.

Smith, Joseph H., and Hershkowitz, Leo. "Courts of Equity in the Province of New York: The Cosby Controversy, 1732–1736." *American Journal of Legal History* 16 (1972): 1–50.

Spencer, Charles Worthen. "Sectional Aspects of New York Provincial Politics." *Political Science Quarterly* 30 (1915): 397–424.

Stoker, Herman M. *Wholesale Prices for 213 Years, 1720 to 1932. Part II: Wholesale Prices at New York City, 1720 to 1800.* Ithaca, N.Y., 1932.

Stokes, Isaac Newton Phelps, ed. *The Iconography of Manhattan Island, 1498–1909.* 6 vols. New York, 1915–28.

Sugarman, David, and Rubin, G. R. "Towards a New History of Law and

Material Society in England, 1750–1914." In *Law, Economy and Society, 1750–1914: Essays in the History of English Law,* edited by G. R. Rubin and David Sugarman, pp. 1–124. Abingdon, England, 1984.

Sweeney, Kevin M. "Furniture and the Domestic Environment in Wethersfield, Connecticut, 1639–1800." In *Material Life in America, 1600–1860,* edited by Robert Blair St. George, pp. 261–90. Boston, 1988.

Toharia, José Juan. "Economic Development and Litigation: The Case of Spain." In *Zur Soziologie des Gerichtsverfahrens* (Sociology of the judicial process), *Jahrbuch für Rechtssoziologie und Rechtstheorie,* 4: 39–82. Wiesbaden, Germany, 1976.

Tompsett, Christine H. "A Note on the Economic Status of Widows in Colonial New York." *New York History* 55 (1974): 319–32.

Ulrich, Laurel Thatcher. " 'A Friendly Neighbor': Social Dimensions of Daily Work in Northern Colonial New England." *Feminist Studies* 6 (1980): 392–405.

——. *Good Wives: Image and Reality in the Lives of Women in Northern New England, 1650–1750.* New York, 1982.

——. "Housewife and Gadder: Themes of Self-Sufficiency and Community in Eighteenth-Century New England." In *"To Toil the Livelong Day": America's Women at Work, 1780–1980,* edited by Mary Beth Norton and Carol Groneman, pp. 21–34. Ithaca, N.Y., 1987.

——. "Martha Ballard and Her Girls: Women's Work in Eighteenth-Century Maine." In *Work and Labor in Early America,* edited by Stephen Innes, pp. 70–105. Chapel Hill, 1988.

——. *A Midwife's Tale: The Life of Martha Ballard, Based on Her Diary, 1785–1812.* New York, 1990.

Varga, Nicholas. "New York Government and Politics during the Mid-Eighteenth Century." Ph.D. dissertation, Fordham University, 1960.

Vickers, Daniel. "Competency and Competition: Economic Culture in Early America." *William and Mary Quarterly,* 3d ser., 47 (1990): 3–29.

——. *Farmers and Fishermen: Two Centuries of Work in Essex County, Massachusetts, 1630–1850.* Chapel Hill, 1994.

Waciega, Lisa Wilson. "A 'Man of Business': The Widow of Means in Southeastern Pennsylvania, 1750–1850." *William and Mary Quarterly,* 3d ser., 44 (1987): 40–64.

Walsh, Lorena S. "Urban Amenities and Rural Sufficiency: Living Standards and Consumer Behavior in the Colonial Chesapeake, 1643–1777." *Journal of Economic History* 43 (1983): 109–17.

Ward, Barbara McLean. "The Craftsman in a Changing Society: Boston Goldsmiths, 1690–1730." Ph.D. dissertation, Boston University, 1983.

Ward, Gerald W. R. "Silver and Society in Salem, Massachusetts, 1630–1820: A Case Study of the Consumer and the Craft." Ph.D. dissertation, Boston University, 1984.

Weber, Max. *Max Weber on Law in Economy and Society.* Edited by Max Rheinstein. Translated from Weber's *Wirtschaft und Gesellschaft,* 2d ed., 1925, by
Edward Shils and Max Rheinstein. Cambridge, Mass., 1954.

Weiss, Rona Stephanie. "The Development of the Market Economy in Colonial
Massachusetts." Ph.D. dissertation, University of Massachusetts, 1981.

———. "The Market and Massachusetts Farmers, 1750–1850: Comment." *Journal
of Economic History* 43 (1983): 475–78.

Welter, Barbara. "The Cult of True Womanhood, 1820–1860." *American Quarterly* 18 (1966): 151–75.

Wermuth, Thomas S. " 'To Market, To Market': Yeoman Farmers, Merchant
Capitalists and the Development of Capitalism in the Hudson River Valley,
1760–1820." *Essays in Economic and Business History* 9 (1991): 20–34.

———. " 'To Market, To Market': Yeoman Farmers, Merchant Capitalists, and the
Transition to Capitalism in the Hudson River Valley, Ulster County, 1760–
1840." Ph.D. dissertation, State University of New York at Binghamton,
1991.

———. "Were Early Americans Capitalists? An Overview of the Development of
Capitalist Values and Beliefs in Early America." *Mid-America* 74 (1992): 85–
97.

Wilkenfeld, Bruce Martin. "The Social and Economic Structure of the City of
New York, 1695–1796." Ph.D. dissertation, Columbia University, 1973.

Williams, Raymond. *The Country and the City.* New York, 1973.

Wilson, Joan Hoff. "The Illusion of Change: Women and the American Revolution." In *Our American Sisters: Women in American Life and Thought,* edited by
Jean E. Friedman, William G. Shade, and Mary Jane Capozzoli, pp. 76–95.
4th ed. Lexington, Mass., 1987.

Wilson, Lisa. *Life after Death: Widows in Pennsylvania, 1750–1850.* Philadelphia,
1992.

Wolf, Stephanie Grauman. *Urban Village: Population, Community, and Family
Structure in Germantown, Pennsylvania, 1683–1800.* Princeton, N.J., 1976.

Woloch, Nancy. *Women and the American Experience.* 2d ed. New York, 1994.

Wright, Langdon Goddard. "Local Government in Colonial New York, 1640–
1710." Ph.D. dissertation, Cornell University, 1974.

Index

Historical Perspectives on Business Enterprise Series
Mansel G. Blackford and K. Austin Kerr, Editors

The scope of the series includes scholarly interest in the history of the firm, the history of government-business relations, and the relationships between business and culture, both in the United States and abroad, as well as in comparative perspective.

BFGoodrich: Transition and Transformation, 1870–1995
  Mansel G. Blackford and K. Austin Kerr

Regulated Enterprise: Natural Gas Pipelines and Northeastern Markets, 1938–1954
  Christopher James Castaneda

Managing Industrial Decline: Entrepreneurship in the British Coal Industry between
  the Wars
  Michael Dintenfass

Werner von Siemens: Inventor and International Entrepreneur
  Wilfried Feldenkirchen

Siemens, 1918–1945
  Wilfried Feldenkirchen

Henry E. Huntington and the Creation of Southern California
  William B. Friedricks

Making Iron and Steel: Independent Mills in Pittsburgh, 1820–1920
  John N. Ingham

Eagle-Picher Industries: Strategies for Survival in the Industrial Marketplace, 1840–1980
  Douglas Knerr

Wolf Creek Station: Kansas Gas and Electric Company in the Nuclear Era
  Craig Miner

A Mental Revolution: Scientific Management since Taylor
  Edited by Daniel Nelson

American Public Finance and Financial Services, 1700–1815
  Edwin J. Perkins

A History of Accountancy in the United States: The Cultural Significance of Accounting
  Gary John Previts and Barbara Dubis Merino

The Passenger Train in the Motor Age: California's Rail and Bus Industries, 1910–1941
  Gregory Lee Thompson

Rebuilding Cleveland: The Cleveland Foundation and Its Evolving Urban Strategy
  Diana Tittle

Daniel Willard and Progressive Management on the Baltimore & Ohio Railroad
  David M. Vrooman